Home Book of
PICTURE
FRAMING

0 11557 02793 8

Home Book of
PICTURE
FRAMING

2nd Edition

*Professional secrets of mounting, matting, framing,
and displaying artwork, photographs, posters,
fabrics, collectibles, carvings, and more*

KENN OBERRECHT

STACKPOLE
BOOKS

Copyright © 1988, 1998 by Kenn Oberrecht

Published by
STACKPOLE BOOKS
5067 Ritter Road
Mechanicsburg, PA 17055

Printed in the United States of America

10 9 8 7 6 5

Cover design by Wendy Reynolds

Library of Congress Cataloging-in-Publication Data

Oberrecht, Kenn.
    Home book of picture framing : professional secrets of
mounting, matting, framing, and displaying artwork,
photographs, posters, fabrics, collectibles, carvings, and
more / Kenn Oberrecht. —2nd ed.
        p.   cm.
    Includes index.
    ISBN 0-8117-2793-9
    1. Picture frames and framing.   I. Title.
N8550.O24   1998
749'.7—dc21   97-50142
                                                    CIP

For my old friend Sam Fadala

CONTENTS

SAFETY TIPS ON MOUNTING, MATTING, AND FRAMING

Common sense can go a long way toward keeping you out of harm's way. Remember to handle tools and materials carefully and cautiously. Whether you're a beginner or veteran craftsman, you would do well to read the following tips now and review them from time to time.

1. Store matting, framing, and woodworking tools out of the reach of children, and keep children out of your work area unless you're teaching them how to frame pictures. The first framing lesson for any youngster should be one on safety.

2. When you finish using any framing tools and materials, put them away. Keep your work area free of clutter.

3. When sawing, drilling, cutting, and performing other operations, whenever possible, secure work pieces to a solid surface with clamps or a vise. This tactic not only allows you to use tools safely but also reduces the chances of errors while increasing accuracy.

4. Keep saw and knife blades, bits, and other cutting and drilling instruments clean and sharp. Any residue buildup will dull tools, and dull cutting and boring tools are dangerous. Moreover, dull bits and blades put unnecessary strain on power-tool motors.

5. Blades used in mat cutters, utility knives, and other matting and framing tools require special handling. When they're dulled and need replacing, don't discard them as you would other trash. Keep used blades in a covered jar or can. When the container is full, discard it.

6. Before operating new tools for matting, mounting, framing, and woodworking, read the instructions that come with them. Review the instructions periodically to make sure you don't develop any bad habits. Before setting to work with any new tool, practice with it on scrap material until you develop a comfortable feel for the tool.

7. When working with power tools and hammers, always wear some sort of goggles or safety glasses. Select protective eyewear that's comfortable, and you will be more inclined to use it when you should.

8. Some noisy power tools can permanently damage your hearing. When using such tools, wear approved ear protectors, available at most hardware stores and gun shops.

9. When working with abrasives, sanders, and other tools that create dust, wear a dust mask. If you suffer from any kind of respiratory ailment, consult a physician about the type of mask you should wear for maximum protection.

10. When handling glass, be careful to avoid the sharp edges and corners that can cause serious injuries. Whenever possible, wear heavy leather work gloves or use rags folded into several layers for grasping the glass near the edges.

11. When working with solvents, adhesives, and chemicals that can cause damage to your skin, always wear rubber or chemical-proof plastic gloves.

12. Lacquers, thinners, cleaners, solvents, and adhesives that produce toxic, flammable, or explosive fumes should be used only in a well-ventilated area, away from sources of heat or open flame. Do not use power tools around any flammable or explosive substances, as fumes

might be ignited by electrical arc when the tool is switched on.

13. Read labels on all materials used in the framing process. Pay special attention to bold CAUTION and WARNING notices. When in doubt about the safe handling of any material, phone or write the manufacturer for instructions.

14. Make sure power tools are switched off before you plug them in. Always disconnect power-tool plugs before changing bits or blades or making adjustments. At the end of any work session, unplug all power tools.

15. Power tools must be properly grounded. If a tool is equipped with a three-conductor cord and three-prong plug, make sure the outlet is a proper, grounding-type receptacle. And use only the appropriate and approved extension cords with such tools.

16. Before operating any power tool, make sure power cords and extension cords are out of the way and will not interfere with tool operation.

17. Don't wear jewelry or loose-fitting clothing when operating any tools or machinery that might entangle it and cause personal injury. Remove watches, rings, and other special metal when operating any portable power tool that is not labeled "Double Insulated."

18. If a power tool stalls during operation, release the trigger or switch the machine off immediately. Then unplug the tool and work the jam loose in safety. Before resuming operation, correct the cause of the stall.

19. Always grip a portable power tool firmly before switching it on, as the torque of the motor could cause you to lose your grip. Whenever possible, grasp the tool with both hands.

20. Remove a table-saw blade guard only to make cuts that do not fully penetrate the wood, as in cutting grooves in frame molding. Immediately replace the guard after such cuts, and leave it in place for all other work. Some old-timers leave the guards off their saws, and some old-timers possess fewer than ten fingers.

21. When miter cutting or crosscutting with a table saw or bandsaw and miter gauge, remove the fence from the saw. Never use both the fence and the miter gauge together, as this practice can lead to serious injury and saw damage.

22. When using a stationary power saw to rip broad boards into narrow stock for frame moldings, always feed the material through the saw with push blocks to keep your fingers away from the blade.

23. Maintain all tools for long life—yours and the tools'. Keep them clean, free of corrosion, and lubricated according to the manufacturer's directions.

24. Worn or damaged power cords on electrically powered tools are dangerous and should be replaced. Likewise, damaged extension cords should be repaired or discarded.

25. Keep safety in mind at all times. No matter what kind of job you're engaged in, use common sense, and concentrate on the task at hand.

CHAPTER ONE

Framing Basics

No do-it-yourself activity will save the homeowner or apartment dweller more money than the mounting, matting, and framing of artwork, photographs, posters, documents, and collectibles. Moreover, with the proper instructions, anyone can easily master professional framing techniques.

Compared with other woodworking projects, framing requires relatively few tools, and most are fairly inexpensive and easy to use, if somewhat foreign in appearance. Mounting and matting tools are also inexpensive and easily mastered. Suitable materials are abundant and readily available in most communities. And anything that can't be found locally is available from several reliable mail-order suppliers specializing in mounting, matting, and framing products.

Nevertheless, the craft seems a mystery to most, a sense perhaps perpetuated by professional framers to some extent but more likely prompted by widespread misconception and misunderstanding. To be certain, some magazine articles and books on the subject have ill served the reading public by ignoring important considerations at best and dispensing nonsense at worst. So the craft remains shrouded in mystery, while people keep paying exorbitant prices for custom matting and framing jobs that are sometimes inferior in quality and even potentially damaging to the framed work.

It's not easy for the uninitiated to look at a beautifully matted and framed work and determine all that makes it a thing of beauty, because many of the framer's secrets are concealed between glass and dust seal. And even if the work were dismantled and analyzed, it would not be readily apparent to the casual observer why certain materials were chosen in lieu of others. There are many specific guidelines, rules to be observed, rules to be broken from time to time, matters of personal preference and taste, and countless tips and tricks that make the framing of any work both functional and pleasing to the eye.

SAVINGS POTENTIAL

I can't stress enough the practicality of do-it-yourself framing. Once you learn the basics, you can recognize substantial savings in every framing job you do. When you realize that most of the cost of a manufactured frame or custom matting-and-framing job is labor, its easier to understand why commercially made frames and custom-made mats and frames are so expensive—easier to understand but not to justify.

To provide an idea of the savings (or profits) possible, I made cost comparisons some years ago, using a standard 16 x 20-inch frame as the basis. I found a commercially made oak frame of simple 1 x 2 molding priced at $30.85. The same frame made to order by a professional framer might cost $50 or more. I could buy the identical molding at a local home-improvement center and build the same frame for $8.58. With oak 1 x 2, however, and an extra five minutes of setup and saw time, I could make the same frame for $4.88. And that was paying retail for materials. As a professional (and anyone with a business card can call himself a professional), I can save an additional 10 to 30 percent in discounts, depending on where I buy. By going to the mill and hauling my own material, I can save up to 50 percent.

But these savings pale in comparison with the savings possible with moldings and framing systems I have devised and will cover completely in later chapters. To determine my costs in making a basic 1 x 2 molding, for example, I timed myself. Working at a comfortable but steady pace, without rushing, I was able to turn out 200 feet of molding in one hour, at a total material cost of $25, or 12½ cents a foot. Comparable commercial moldings range in price from $1 to $2 a foot, or about eight to sixteen times as much.

Using the basic single-strip molding, I framed a pair of 20 x 22-inch prints for $1 each. With a double-strip molding, I framed a matted print measuring 29½ x 36½ inches for a mere $2.75. A large, limited-edition print by one of my favorite artists is housed in a massive 31 x 41-inch three-strip frame that set me back all of $4.38.

A local physician had that same print custom framed in a barn-siding-style molding that compares in size and appearance to my own and paid $135 for the job: $75 for the frame, $35 for the mounting and matting with standard mat board, and $25 for the glass. For a total cost of about $8, I archivally mounted and double matted my own print with the acid-free board I purchased at the same shop and special rice-paper hinges impregnated with starch paste and treated with fungicide. Instead of having a framer cut and supply my glass, I bought mine at a glass shop for $15.

The whole job—mounting, matting, glazing, and framing—cost me about $28. Not only did mine cost $107 less than the good doctor paid, but when the acidic mats have burned the margins of his print and yellowed the highlights, mine will still look good as new. What's more, as my properly framed print increases in value, which the sold-out edition promises, his will decrease, simply because it wasn't properly matted and framed.

So the savings continue and go well beyond the dollars saved initially. The potential, in fact, is limitless. How to save those dollars at the onset and spend a few cents to protect an invest-

ment is something the average person doesn't know about—but which you are about to learn.

Consider the average modest dwelling: a three-bedroom, two-bath house, apartment, or condominium. There's a good bit of wall space to cover in any such home and a surprising number of items to be framed: perhaps a couple of colorful prints for the kitchen; several drawings, prints, or paintings for the dining room and living room; posters and photographs for children's rooms; a few favorite prints and paintings for the master bedroom; possibly some miniatures, collectibles, and three-dimensional art for the bathrooms; and a collection of family photographs for the hallway. The average person could easily have thirty, forty, or more items to be framed.

In larger homes there are walls in family rooms, hobby rooms, rec rooms, dens, libraries, and home offices. There are more hallways, stairways, and foyer space, and if someone in the home happens to be an artist or photographer, framing can become a continuous activity.

It should be clear to you by now that you can easily earn back the price of this book and more with your first framing project. Eventually, your savings can amount to hundreds or thousands of dollars, and if you're so inclined, you can turn enough of a profit on your hobby to pay for all your tools and materials, or you can even make this enjoyable hobby a full-time profession.

TYPES OF FRAMABLES

Among the many objects suitable for framing are oil and acrylic paintings, pastels, batiks, watercolors, pencil and pen-and-ink drawings, washes, lithographs, serigraphs, engravings, etchings, diplomas, certificates, photographs, posters, needlework, three-dimensional art, and various collectibles.

Preparation of the work and the materials, tools, and techniques you use to frame it depend on the kind of work it is. Beyond that, you will be guided by convention or tradition and your own tastes and ingenuity.

Original oil and acrylic paintings are framed without mats and glass, and there's no need for a dust seal at the rear of the frame with such

Frame It Yourself and Save

Recently, my wife, Patty, and I were browsing in a gourmet shop in Florence, Oregon, when she noticed a large, framed poster and asked the woman behind the counter if it was for sale. The proprietor said she had unframed copies available and began to tell her about getting it professionally mounted and framed. When Patty told her that I'm a framer, the woman turned to me and said, "Maybe you can tell me—I think I paid too much, but didn't ask ahead of time. So I didn't complain when the framer charged me $250."

I gulped and took a second look at the poster. It was a large, 25 x 36-inch, very busy, color cartoon, depicting amusing mayhem in the kitchen of a French restaurant. It was adequately but unremarkably set behind glass without mats in a narrow box molding, finished in matte black. I made a quick assessment and told the woman that she could have framed it herself for about $50.

"I'm no framer," she said.

"You don't need to be," I said. "You could order a simple metal-section frame cut to size, buy the glass from a glass shop, and either cut a backing board to fit, or have the poster mounted at any frame shop. You could put it all together with a screwdriver. Total labor—about fifteen minutes."

I knew I could make a simple box frame similar to hers for about $2, and I could buy all the other necessary materials at discounts. But to prove my point, I told her I would pay retail for everything, do nothing extraordinary, and keep it all so simple that anyone would be able to do the job with little time and effort expended. I bought a poster and promised to report the results of my experiment.

The following week, I stopped by a local frame shop to buy some mat board. While there, I dropped the poster off with directions to vacuum mount it on foamboard. Back home, I phoned the glass shop and ordered a piece of picture glass cut to size. The next time I had errands to run in town, I picked up my mounted poster and glass. Total time spent at frame and glass shops: about ten minutes.

The poster is mainly black and white with blue as the most prominent color and red a noticeable subordinate color. I tried both blue and red frame sample corners on the poster and decided on the latter. Then I phoned Graphik Dimensions, Ltd., and ordered a red metal-section frame cut to size. When it arrived the following week, I cleaned the glass, used a screwdriver to assemble the frame with the hardware provided, put everything together, and hung the poster. Total framing time: about fifteen minutes.

The most expensive part of the job was the custom-cut frame, which cost me $21.60, including shipping and handling. Running a close second was having a professional framer vacuum-mount the poster, for which I was charged $21.40. The glass, cut to order, was $13.

Okay, so my total expenditure was $6 over my $50 estimate. I still ended up paying $194 less than the owner of the gourmet shop was charged. Allowing five minutes for the phone calls I made, my total labor was thirty minutes. That works out to $388 an hour—a bit steep, I think.

works. Batiks are usually framed the same way, as are some fabrics.

Some professionals insist that all prints be framed as their originals would be. So if the original was an oil painting, they say, the print should be framed as an oil painting would be. Of course, if that's what you want to do, fine, but it's ridiculous to insist you do it that way. In fact, these days, with the current popularity of limited editions, most prints are matted and framed behind glass, even if the originals were oil or acrylic paintings. Certainly, any print with potential collector's value should be archivally matted and framed behind glass, regardless of what medium the original was done in.

Prints made on canvas should be treated the same as the original oils and acrylics on canvas. They should be attached to stretcher frames, then framed without mats, glass, or dust seals. Unlimited-edition prints on paper can be framed the same way, but first should be mounted to rigid stock, such as foamboard or hardboard.

Watercolors, pastels, sketches, drawings, most prints, and other artwork on paper should be matted and framed behind glass for maximum protection and most pleasing presentation. Diplomas, certificates, and other documents should also be framed behind glass, either with or without mats, depending on personal preferences.

Photographs and posters are displayed in the widest variety of ways. Photos are often mounted and displayed without mats or frames. Some are framed without mats or glass; others are treated the same as artworks on paper, with mats and glass. And there are many specialty products available for mounting and displaying photos and posters.

Three-dimensional objects are often displayed in framed collectors' cases. Some can be mounted to a suitable background, which is then framed and displayed with or without glass. Shadow boxes are also popular for framing and displaying such objects.

Framables range in value from free to priceless. With all the cheap and free items available, and the ability to frame them expertly and inexpensively, there's no excuse for bare walls any-

where. If your tastes lean toward expensive originals, rare objects, and limited editions but your budget doesn't quite stack up, display cheaper works for now, and replace them as you can afford to. You'll not only get valuable practice matting and framing the inexpensive items, but when you replace them you should also be able to sell them for considerably more than you have invested in them. What's more, you may find some you simply don't want to part with, regardless of their worth.

Cheap and free framables are everywhere. To find them, just keep your eyes open and think framing.

Many greeting and note cards are ideal as framed miniatures, and those of a similar size often make attractive sets. Occasional cards can be framed in batches and used as seasonal decorations for Thanksgiving, Christmas, Easter, and other holidays.

Posters are often given away as part of a promotional campaign. Even those sold for profit are always considerably cheaper than original art. And the freebies can even end up being worth money. Some years ago, I found a poster in a record album I had bought. I kept it for years with the idea of maybe framing it someday or perhaps giving it to a nephew or niece. But one day during a housecleaning binge, I decided I really didn't like it all that much, so I tossed it onto the trash heap I later hauled to the dump.

As Murphy would have it, no more than a week or two later, I watched a TV program on collecting and learned that the very poster I had just discarded was relatively rare and worth several hundred bucks.

Calendars—either photographs or art reproductions—are another good source of framable material. The matching sizes of calendar pages make them ideal for framed sets.

I'm not ashamed to admit that two of my favorite prints, which many of our visitors have liked as well, are calendar art that I didn't pay a dime for. I didn't even buy the calendar; *Handyman* magazine sent it free some years ago. Two of the art reproductions in the calendar struck my fancy, so I mounted, matted, and framed them.

Simple note cards showing fly-fishing scenes become attractive miniatures when they are matted and framed.

They're the same pair of 20 x 22-inch prints I mentioned earlier that I framed for $1 each. So it's certainly not their monetary value that has garnered so many appreciative comments.

Garage sales and secondhand stores are also good sources for cheap framables. Look for old photographs, paintings, and prints that appeal to you but are either poorly framed or in frames that are falling apart. These are usually slow movers that you can pick up for nearly nothing. It's amazing what new mats, glass, and frames will do for these old works.

FUNCTIONS OF FRAME AND MAT

Both frames and mats perform protective and decorative functions. To avoid undermining these purposes, you must know how to select them and match them to the works being displayed.

The right frames provide rigid encasements for works of all kinds and thereby protect them and keep them from buckling, warping, and suffering from other problems. When properly sealed and glazed (set behind glass or acrylic), they also protect works from ambient radiation, airborne pollutants, and acid damage. Finally, they add eye appeal to the works they contain.

The wrong frames might not only fail to protect what they hold, but can also *cause* buckling, warping, and other problems. If they're improperly sealed and glazed, they can assist in the destruction of monetarily or sentimentally valuable works. And they can be distracting, even downright ugly.

Mats add rigidity to whatever is being framed, but they also provide important separation between the work and the glass. You can cut mats to make odd-size works fit standard-size frames. You can exaggerate mat sizes and dimensions to emphasize the size or format of what you're framing, and you can select colors that match or contrast the colors in the artworks or photographs. You can use single or multiple mats and can cut mat windows in a variety of shapes and configurations.

MODERN FRAME DESIGN

Over the centuries, frames have changed dramatically, from the ornate and gaudy frames made from the fifteenth to eighteenth centuries to more subdued but decorative frames of the nineteenth century and on to the stark simplicity of the mid-twentieth century. Many of the early frames were complex pieces of architecture that competed with the pictures they enclosed and distracted viewers. Today, we try to keep our frames simple, their designs subtle. We want them to complement what they enclose and blend with the room's decor.

Instead of the heavy, ornamental wood frames carved in deep relief that caught the fancy of our ancestors, we prefer lighter and narrower wood frames for many applications. The gaudy gilded frames of yesteryear have largely given way to slicker, sleeker metal-section frames. Instead of silver leaf and gold leaf, we use chrome, brass plate, and anodized aluminum.

Does this mean we never use highly decorative frames, wide or massive moldings, or gilding of one kind or another? Certainly not. It means we have many options to exercise, many possibilities to choose from. And it means we can suffer a lot of confusion, especially when faced with so many design concepts that seem to contradict one another.

For example, we might be told in a book or magazine that large paintings should be framed with narrow moldings, only to turn the page and find a large painting attractively framed in a wide molding, or a small work handsomely framed with a narrow molding. Having all these options doesn't mean that there is only one best choice and all others are something less. There's

no such thing as the ideal matting or framing for any picture. Many will prove suitable, and certain ones will strike you as better than others. Personal preferences and tastes play major roles in making such selections.

When it comes to designing and making your own frames and doing your own matting, the simplest and soundest advice I can offer is to do what fits the work and pleases you. But there's a chance you aren't sure about what fits any particular artwork or even about what pleases you, mainly because you haven't examined many of the options. So spend some time in art galleries and museums, looking for what pleases you. Be conscious of all the framed works around you in public buildings, offices, and other homes. Then stop by a frame shop or well-stocked home-improvement center and find out what's available. You will soon learn that you have narrowed your options considerably by simply eliminating what you don't like or what doesn't seem to fit the project at hand.

And don't worry about making the wrong choice. It's rare that you will, but when you do, you can simply pick again. That's one of the advantages of doing your own matting and framing. If you paid somebody $150 to frame a picture, you would be reluctant to have it reframed, even if you came to despise it. If you framed it yourself, however, and spent only a few dollars doing it, you wouldn't feel so bad about reframing the work when you grew tired of the original frame.

I have a number of works in this category. A pair of prints in matching mats and frames looked good enough when I framed them, but I saw them so often that I grew bored with them. New mats and frames sparked them up and relieved my boredom. I had two oil paintings in frames someone else made that I never had liked, and I reframed them with something more in accord with my tastes. Others that looked fine in apartments and other houses we lived in just don't fit their present environment. So they will be reframed and I will keep the old mats and frames for use with other works.

GETTING INTO FRAMING
You don't have to spend four years in college, two years in a trade school, or even a year in an apprenticeship to learn all you need to know about mounting, matting, and framing. With a little time well spent and a bit of practice in the craft, you'll soon be framing as well as any professional. Before you finish this book, you should be turning out frames and mats that are every bit as fine as anything found in a professional frame shop, gallery, or museum. In fact, it won't be long before you visit museums and galleries and find the flaws in the mats and frames displayed there.

Framing is an enjoyable and rewarding hobby and something that shows results much sooner than most other do-it-yourself projects do. If you're using a prefinished molding, you can mount, mat, glaze, and frame several items in an evening or on a casual Saturday afternoon. Even if you're making your own molding from scratch, you can turn out a batch of framed works over a single weekend.

Once you master the techniques, it's easy to turn a profit on your hobby by doing framing jobs for others. You can eventually expand this into a lucrative sideline or full-time business. And I can't think of a business that's easier to get into or one that requires less overhead or a smaller initial investment.

Whether you approach framing as a hobby or later as a business is something only you can decide. Either way, you will end up money ahead while learning a useful and rewarding craft.

CHAPTER TWO

Mounting and Matting Materials and Tools

Most works to be framed first should be mounted on a mount board of some type. Mounting keeps the work in place, and the mount board provides rigidity and prevents warping. Mounting is also a way to repair some works that are warped, curled, or even bent or torn. Many works are then sandwiched between mount boards and mats prior to framing.

Before learning the various mounting and matting techniques, you should become familiar with the materials and tools at your disposal. Some are highly specialized and used only or mainly in mounting and matting. Others are more common and widely used for other purposes as well.

MOUNT BOARDS, MAT BOARDS, AND BACKING MATERIALS

Among the various materials suitable for mounting artwork, diplomas, certificates, documents, photographs, and posters, the most commonly used and widely available are mat board, rag board or museum board, archival corrugated board, and foamboard. Certainly, framers use a good many other materials, but the operative word here is *suitable*. Hardboard, for example, is suitable for some applications, but it is dense and heavy and adds significant weight to any framing project. It is also acidic and therefore inappropriate for conservation mounting. Some framers like the rigidity hardboard provides and use it for special jobs, such as mounting some kinds of needlework. If you find it suits your purposes, use only tempered hardboard, and seal all surfaces with shellac.

Although corrugated container board—the brown paper product that so-called cardboard boxes are made of—is widely used, I can't recommend it. I never use it in any phase of mounting, matting, or framing, because it is so highly acidic and potentially damaging.

Standard mat board, a wood-pulp product; neutralized mat board, which is acid-free; and rag board, which contains no wood, commonly come in two-ply and four-ply thicknesses in sheets of 32 x 40 inches. Two-ply board is about 1/32-inch thick, and four-ply about 1/16. The thinner board is suitable for most jobs. The thicker is sometimes used for adding rigidity to large works, but it is always at least half again as expensive as two-ply board, sometimes double in price. Also, if you plan to use a backing, two-ply should provide sufficient rigidity. Eight-ply mat board is also available for large works and special jobs where extra rigidity is important.

Standard mat board is acidic and should never be used as a mount board with any work of monetary or sentimental value. It can be used, however, as outer mat material in conservation mounting, matting, and framing. Both neutralized mat board and rag board are pH neutral and are suitable for all conservation applications, as either mount boards or mats. Crescent Cardboard Company, a major producer of rag and mat boards, offers its line of standard mat board with acid-free cores and backing papers, making them suitable for most matting applications.

Archival corrugated board consists of a corrugated core faced on two sides with paper. All materials are acid-free and buffered, making this board acceptable for conservation mounting. It comes in single-wall and double-wall configurations, with respective thicknesses of 1/8 and 1/4 inch.

Foamboard consists of a core of extruded polystyrene, sandwiched between sheets of white paper. It comes in thicknesses of 1/8, 3/16, 1/4, and 3/8 inch, with 3/16 being the most universally useful and probably the most widely used. An acid-free version, for conservation use, is only slightly more expensive than standard foamboard. Since it should not be used in any process requiring temperatures above 150°F, foamboard is not suitable for heat mounting. Nevertheless, it is one of the most useful materials available to the framer. Because of its light weight and rigidity, it is a superior backing material, and it is ideal for most mounting applications.

With 3/16-inch foamboard, I am able to mount and frame all but the largest works without the need for backing material; the foamboard serves as both mount and backing. With it I can save time and money on most jobs. Foamboard is also easier to cut than mat board and rag board and doesn't seem to dull blades as fast.

All these materials are available at most frame and art-supply shops and department stores that stock products for mounting, matting, and framing. Although some stores stock the various board products in standard frame sizes, from 8 x 10 to 20 x 24 inches, most shops more commonly stock them in 32 x 40-inch sheets that you can cut to any size you need. The larger sheets are also cheaper in the long run.

ADHESIVES AND TAPES
A number of aerosol adhesives, adhesive sheets, and dry-mounting tissues, used primarily for mounting photographs and posters, are covered fully in chapter 4. Although they are not generally recommended for mounting valuable artwork or limited-edition prints, when such items get bent, wrinkled, or torn, some can be successfully repaired by mounting with an aerosol adhesive or an adhesive sheet.

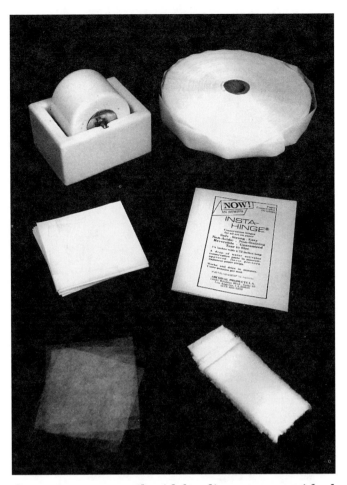

Ceramic tongue and acid-free linen tape are ideal for hinging mat and mount boards. Insta-Hinge kit provides a practical way to hinge artwork.

Most household or hobby glues, pastes, and cements contain substances that are harmful to artwork and should not be used for mounting or matting, although some are suitable for frame construction and dust-seal installation. Among the most commonly found in the home are white glue and rubber cement, neither of which is suitable for mounting or matting.

Customarily, original artwork and valuable reproductions on paper are mounted to mount boards with hinges made of rice paper or nonacidic tape. Rice-paper hinges are stuck to the back of the artwork and to the mount board with a paste of methyl cellulose, wheat starch, or rice starch.

Methyl cellulose is a powder you dissolve in water to make a paste. The paste is then applied

Scotch Removable Magic Tape is useful for temporarily holding works in place.

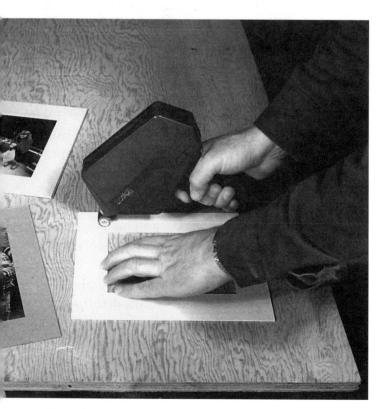

Scotch 752 ATG Adhesive Transfer Applicator in use.

to rice-paper hinges for mounting. It is easy to use, nonacidic, and reversible with water, and has an indefinite shelf life.

Although wheat-starch and rice-starch pastes are the adhesives customarily used for museum mounting, for my money they're nuisances to work with. They are indeed nonacidic but susceptible to attack by fungi, so should have a fungicide added to them. They must be mixed in water, then cooked into a paste. And leftover paste has a short shelf life. So they're impractical for the person who has only a few mounting jobs to do at any given time.

Much more practical for most of us is a product called Insta-Hinge. A kit for under $15 contains everything you need to mount up to a dozen items: paper blotters, Mylar squares, spun-nylon squares, and three 1½ x 24-inch strips of rice paper impregnated with starch paste and treated with fungicide. Insta-Hinge kits are available at well-stocked framing and art-supply outlets and by phone or mail from some mail-order sources, such as University Products (see the Source Directory at the back of this book).

Like adhesives, few general-purpose tapes are useful in mounting and matting operations. Even though some books recommend mounting watercolors and other works with masking tape, I must advise against the practice. The tape will yellow in time and is not reversible—that is, you cannot later remove the tape without pulling paper fibers from the artwork. Cellophane tape is even more harmful.

If the work you're mounting has little commercial value, you can use Scotch Magic Tape and similar so-called invisible mending tapes with good results. They aren't reversible, but they won't yellow the way other tapes do. Even if you're using tape only to temporarily hold a work in position and will remove it later, it can damage the work by removing paper fibers from it, and most leave a residue of adhesive that can harm the artwork. A nifty exception is Scotch Removable Magic Tape. I have been using this product since its introduction to temporarily hold artwork in place while I'm positioning it, and it has never lifted paper fibers or left a residue behind.

Adhesive transfer tape inside the 752 ATG.

Acid-free linen tape is widely used in the framing business and is safe for conservation mounting and matting. The tape is made of linen backed with pH-neutral, water-activated adhesive. It will not stain and is reversible with water. It comes in 1-inch and 1½-inch rolls from 20 to 300 yards long. The 1-inch tape will prove suitable for most jobs and can be used for making hinged mats and for hinging some works to mount boards. It is relatively thick, though, and can leave a visible impression if used to hinge works or documents on lightweight stock.

Acid-free paper tape is made of 24-pound buffered bond paper and backed with a water-activated adhesive. This lightweight tape is removable with water and is ideal for hinging artworks to mount boards, even those produced on lightweight stock. It is not substantial enough, however, for hinging mats to mount boards. It comes in 1-inch rolls, of 50 to 300 yards. One 50-yard roll is enough to hinge more than 200 artworks.

Tyvek tape is a strong tape suitable for hinging mats to mount boards, but is not recommended for hinging artwork. This is a polyethylene tape backed with a pressure-sensitive adhesive and release paper, so it requires no water for use. It comes in 2¼-inch rolls 50 yards long and is a good choice for hinging large mats to mount boards.

When you're using more than one mat with any single item you're framing, the mats are easier to handle if they're stuck together. You can use double-sided tape for this, but if you will be doing much matting, I can recommend a handy tool and tape for the job. The 3M Company calls the tool a Scotch 752 ATG Adhesive Transfer Applicator. I call it a tape gun, and it's the fastest in the West for laying down synthetic adhesive in a continuous line or a series of patches. I originally bought mine for laminating mats, but I've put it to dozens of other uses since, including the mounting of small photographs prior to framing.

MEASURING, MARKING, AND POSITIONING INSTRUMENTS

For measuring and marking large sheets of mat board, foamboard, and other sheet stock, I most often use a steel tape rule. Some people prefer folding rules, so the choice is yours.

For measuring artwork, I normally use an aluminum yardstick that I keep wiped clean with a rag dampened with denatured alcohol. I also have a 4-foot aluminum drywall square that I use for some measuring and marking chores, but mostly as a guide when I'm cutting sheet stock.

Here's a tip. Whatever kind of metal straightedge you use as a cutting guide, affix a strip of masking tape to the underside for its entire length. This will help keep it from slipping as you cut.

To scribe lines on the back of a mat as guides for cutting out the mat window, you can use a

Useful tools for mounting and matting: aluminum T-square or drywall square (with strip of masking tape on back), steel tape rule, aluminum yardstick, and thin-lead pencil.

corner, mark corner lines with a pencil in the appropriate cutouts, line up the straightedge, and cut the window out with a mat cutter.

The Falcon Print Positioner was available for some time before I got around to trying one. Perhaps my curiosity was tempered by my natural skepticism about new gadgets designed to do jobs I've successfully seen to with old, reliable tools. Whatever my reasons, when I consider the time I've spent at the tedious task of positioning photographs and some other works for mounting, I kick myself for ignoring this amazingly simple and foolproof aid.

With the Print Positioner, there's no need to measure and scribe layout lines on the mounting board or to put guide marks on print borders. While such chores take only a few minutes with conventional tools, the entire job is reduced to

Use Alto's Model 4501 system guide to scribe guidelines.

carpenter's marker that's adjustable up to 6 inches or a compass set for your desired width. You won't need these tools, though, if you invest in a mat-cutting guide (such as Alto's 4501 or 4505 Mat Cutting System); it also serves as a marking guide and is much faster and easier to use than any other instruments.

Those who cut mats without the aid of a mat-cutting guide might want to invest in the Boyne Mat Corner Marker or similar tools, available at framing-supply outlets. This inexpensive plastic jig is quick and easy to use. Simply determine the mat width, lay the jig at each

THE 4501 MAT CUTTING SYSTEM

THE 4505 MAT CUTTING SYSTEM

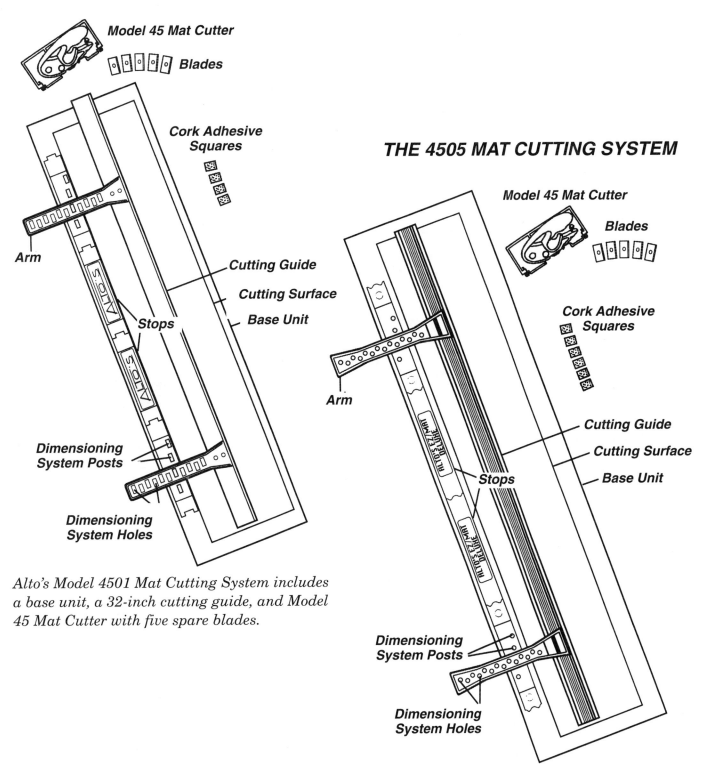

Model 45 Mat Cutter

Blades

Cork Adhesive Squares

Arm

Stops

Cutting Guide

Cutting Surface

Base Unit

Dimensioning System Posts

Dimensioning System Holes

Model 45 Mat Cutter

Blades

Cork Adhesive Squares

Arm

Stops

Cutting Guide

Cutting Surface

Base Unit

Dimensioning System Posts

Dimensioning System Holes

Alto's Model 4501 Mat Cutting System includes a base unit, a 32-inch cutting guide, and Model 45 Mat Cutter with five spare blades.

Alto's Model 4505 Mat Cutting System includes a base unit, a 36-inch cutting guide, and Model 45 Mat Cutter with five spare blades.

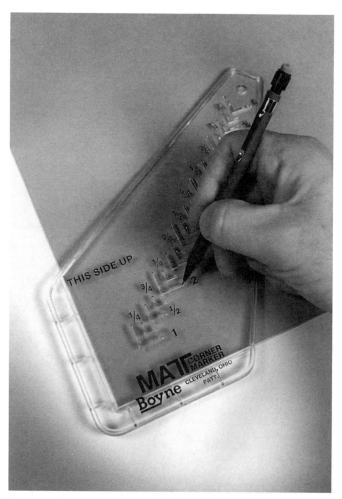

Boyne Mat Corner Marker.

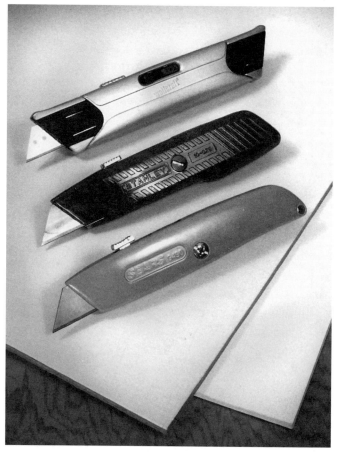

Heavy-duty utility knives from Wolfcraft (top), Stanley Tools (center), and Sears (bottom), shown atop needlepoint board and foam-core board.

seconds with the Print Positioner. And it works with any size print. For anyone who has more than a few items to mount, mat, and frame, I heartily recommend this ingenious tool. Complete directions for its use are in chapter 4.

KNIVES, CUTTERS, AND TRIMMERS

The framer's basic cutting tool is a utility knife. You will need one for cutting mat board, rag board, foamboard, and other sheet stock. The knives come in a variety of styles with different kinds of blades. Some have fairly heavy blades that are reversible and can be honed when they become dull. Others have thin snap-off blades that are discarded when dull. Still others, such as the X-Acto knives, use replaceable blades that come from the factory as sharp as a scalpel.

If you're watching your pennies, you might prefer to sharpen your utility-knife blade, but renewing an edge to razor sharpness is a time-consuming chore and one I cannot justify. I prefer to discard a dull blade and replace it with a new one, which takes only seconds and doesn't interfere with my concentration on the task at hand.

For that reason, I use X-Acto knives and have come to favor the model with a large screw-driver-type handle because of the additional leverage it offers when cutting through tough material or when the blade is beginning to dull. Replaceable blades come in a large array of styles and sizes. The ones I find best for all my mounting and matting work are the Dexter #3 and X-Acto #19. These same blades also happen to fit the Alto's Model 30 mat cutter.

If you decide on a knife with replaceable blades, don't simply toss used blades into a wastebasket or trash bag where they can do damage or cause injury. Find a small can or jar with a lid, label it *Used Blades*, and put your dull blades there. Incidentally, when your knife fails to move smoothly and effortlessly through whatever you're cutting, or if it leaves a rough edge, sharpen it or replace it. A dull blade is inefficient and dangerous.

If you will be doing much mount-board and mat cutting, you might want to invest in a heavy-duty paper cutter or trimmer that will see to most of it. Professional guillotine-style and roller-type cutters and trimmers easily handle mat board and other sheet stock. There are models that will accommodate widths up to 48 inches and even more, but their prices range from several hundred to more than a thousand dollars.

I got by without one of these cutters for a number of years, but as I began doing more and more mounting and matting, I decided it was time to invest in one. I chose a 24-inch guillotine-style cutter, however, that cost me under $100, including shipping. My guess is that it takes care of at least 75 percent of my cutting chores.

By the way, with a guillotine-style cutter, you should always cut material with the good face down on the cutter table, as the blade makes noticeable impressions on the up side.

One of the latest and niftiest cutters to come down the pike is Alto's Model 90 Cutoff Tool. In appearance, it resembles a drywall square, but it's mated with a 90-degree cutter that fits into a channel along the tool's stem. It handles standard 40-inch-wide mat and other boards, will cut material from paper-thin stock to 1/4-inch foamboard with ease, and sells for under $100.

MAT CUTTERS, GUIDES, AND STRAIGHTEDGES

Mat cutters that make a clean beveled cut with an angled, razor-sharp blade are about the handiest tools around for anyone with matting jobs to do. Several models are available, designed to be used with any straightedge thick

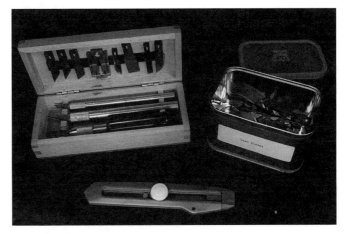

Put old blades in a jar, can, or other container you keep for such purposes.

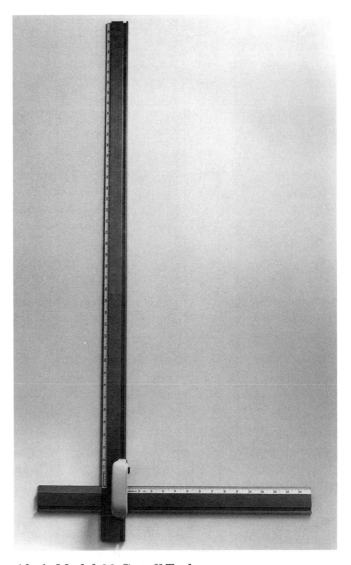

Alto's Model 90 Cutoff Tool. PHOTO COURTESY OF ALTO'S EZ MAT.

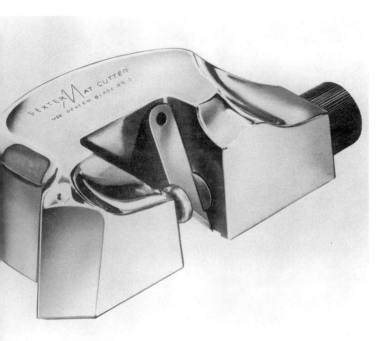

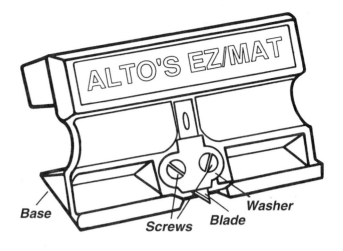

Alto's Model 30 Mat.

Dexter mat cutter.

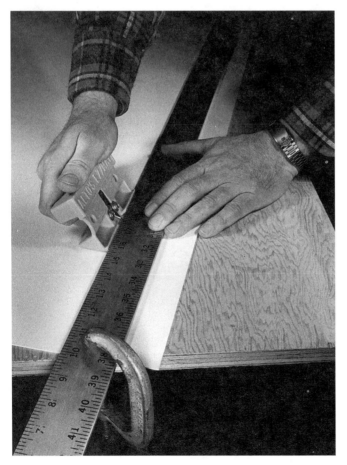

Alto's mat cutters can be used with a straight-edge.

enough to keep the cutter from riding up over the edge. The Dexter and X-Acto mat cutters are two examples.

There are also mat-cutting systems that range in price from more than $100 to well over $1,000. If you plan to work at matting and framing full time, perhaps you will want to check into one of these machines, but for now, and perhaps for always, you should get by most satisfactorily with something much less expensive.

For my money—literally—there's no better buy on the market than Alto's 4501 Mat Cutting System, which includes a hand-held mat cutter and an ingenious marking and cutting guide that adjusts from 1½ to 6⅜ inches in ⅛-inch increments. The cutter guide bar is nearly 32 inches long, thus permitting a cut of almost 30 inches in a single stroke. Moreover, the system is open at both ends, permitting cuts of any length in mats of any size. With no more than five minutes' practice, anyone can be cutting beveled mats like a pro. And the whole outfit is available for about $100.

Incidentally, a friend of mine who owns a large frame shop started some years ago with an Alto's system. As his business grew, rather than replace a tool that had served him so well, he simply added another. He and his employees must cut hundreds of mats a month, and they do

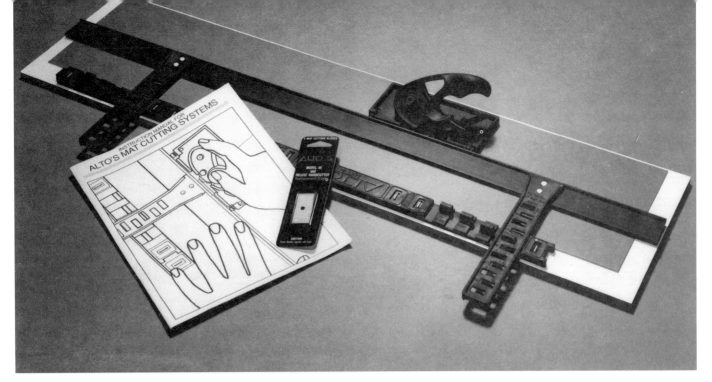

Alto's Model 4501 Mat Cutting System. PHOTO COURTESY OF ALTO'S EZ MAT.

it all with the same system I use. So I expect my Alto's system to last me a lifetime.

The Model 30 mat cutter, which came with the original Alto's EZ Mat system, is available separately for about $15. This cutter creates 30-degree bevels and is the one to use with various templates and for decorative freehand cutting.

The Model 45 mat cutter, which comes with the 4501 and 4505 systems, is also available separately for about $40. This one cuts mat windows with 45-degree bevels, and of all the mat cutters on the market, it's the easiest and most foolproof one I've tried.

For cutting and decorating mats with oval windows, you'll probably want to invest in a set of Alto's oval templates, which come with a Model 30 cutter. The set costs about $65.

For some reason, authors of framing books seem to feel obligated to describe the process of cutting beveled mats with a utility knife and mat cutter's straightedge, and I can't understand why. Making a clean, professional-looking cut armed only with these tools is no easy task. It takes a lot of practice to gain the needed skill, and no amount of skill will produce mats any better looking than those you can produce more quickly and efficiently with Alto's 4501 Mat Cutting System. What's more, a mat cutter's beveled straightedge is an expensive item of limited

Alto's Model 30 Mat Cutter is the one to use with templates and for freehand work. PHOTO COURTESY OF ALTO'S EZ MAT.

worth. In fact, for one long enough to cut large mats, you would pay nearly as much as you would for the 4501 system.

MAT-SAMPLE CORNERS AND CROPPING CORNERS

Presumably, you will be buying your sheet stock from a local frame shop, art-supply outlet, or department store where you will find color samples of mat board in the form of corner strips.

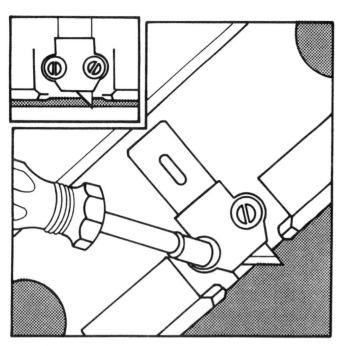

Change Alto's Model 30 blades with a screw-driver or nutdriver.

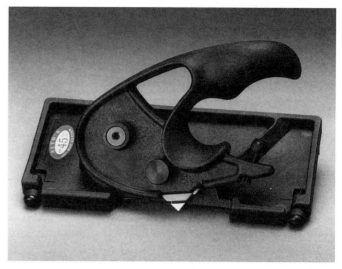

Alto's Model 45 Mat Cutter is the smoothest, eas-iest, and possibly the best cutter available today.

When you're selecting colored mats for any piece of art, it's a good idea to take the artwork with you so you can try the various mat-sample corners with it until you find the one or ones that are just right.

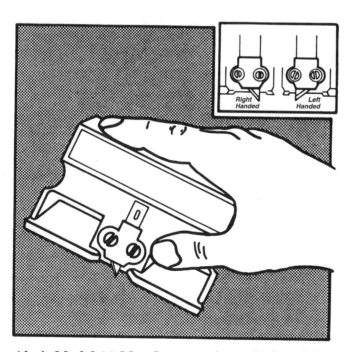

Alto's Model 30 Mat Cutter is for right-handed or left-handed use.

As you mat various items, start making your own mat-sample corners from scraps of leftover mat board. On the back of each corner, write the brand and number of the mat board or rag board: Bainbridge #731, Crescent #1082, and such. I also include the particular shade, such as Storm Blue, Bar Harbor Gray, Moss Point Green, Inca Gold, and the like.

Before you know it, you will have accumulated quite a selection of mat-sample corners that you can use at home, and the labeling will ensure that you can duplicate exactly what you have done before. This is particularly important when you work with shades of colors that are only subtly different.

Something else you will find handy, particularly for working with photographs, is a set of cropping corners that you can make from scraps. With these, you can determine the right cropping for any photograph and thereby determine the dimensions to cut the mat window or trim the photograph.

You can make cropping corners any size you wish. Obviously, if you never work with photos any larger than 8 x 10 inches, then cropping corners need be no larger than 10 x

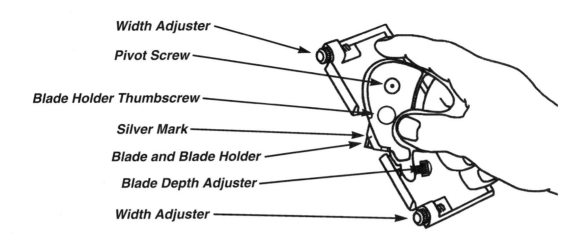

Width Adjuster
Pivot Screw
Blade Holder Thumbscrew
Silver Mark
Blade and Blade Holder
Blade Depth Adjuster
Width Adjuster

Parts of the Alto's Model 45 Mat Cutter.

10 inches along the inside edges. But if you make them larger, you will be prepared for larger prints if the need ever arises. I made mine from available scraps and ended up with a pair of 20 x 26-inch corners that are black on one side, white on the other, and have seen to all my needs so far.

OTHER USEFUL TOOLS

A number of other tools and accessories come in handy in the mounting and matting process. You will want to have on hand some of the ones I use, and you will certainly come up with a few of your own.

I prefer pencils to pens for marking guidelines on mount and mat boards. But I like a bold black pen for making notes to myself that I can read from a distance as I'm working. So I also keep a pen and pad nearby as I work.

Spring clamps are handy for keeping big sheets of foamboard, mat board, or rag board in place during cutting operations. They are also good for clamping a straightedge in place to keep it from moving during the cut.

Several large stainless-steel clips are useful for holding artwork in place on mount boards for marking layout lines. In their absence, you can cover the artwork with tissue paper and lay several books on top to keep everything in place, or you can cover each book with tissue paper.

Mat-sample corners and swatches are useful in choosing the right mats.

Cropping corners help you determine the right cropping for any photograph.

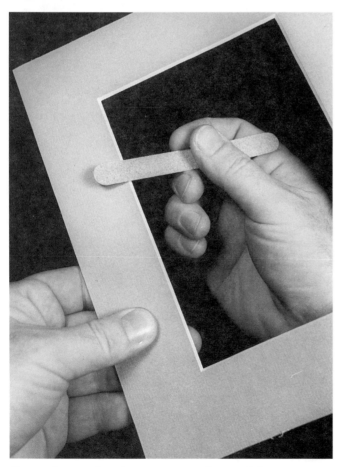

Smooth rough spots on mat edges with an emery board.

Some framers use beanbags for such purposes. When my search of toy stores, craft-supply shops, and other seemingly likely sources for beanbags proved futile, I was faced with the chore of having to make my own. When it dawned on me that dried beans come in plastic bags at supermarkets, however, I bought four one-pound bags, which I keep in my studio for use with curled posters and other unruly works.

Be sure to have a pack of double-edge razor blades on hand. When you slightly undercut a mat-window corner, you can slide one of these paper-thin blades into the cut line, carefully angle it with the bevel, and finish the cut by hand.

A fresh blade in your mat cutter will make beautiful, smooth, beveled cuts. A dull blade will make ragged cuts. So it stands to reason that you should discard dull blades to keep cuts clean. But you always end up cutting one too many mats with every blade, because you don't know a blade needs replacing until it starts bogging down during the cut and leaving little rough edges in its path. But no need to fret if you have a pack of emery boards on hand, fine grit on one side, medium on the other. Use the fine side to smooth out any rough areas in the bevel cut. And you'll find many other uses for both sides of these cheap and handy items.

To finely polish the beveled cut of a mat window and remove the tiniest of burrs and nicks, rub the cut with some sort of burnishing tool. You can buy a burnishing bone, actually made of highly polished bone. There are also plastic substitutes. Or you can use the back of a comb, but if it's a comb you also use for your hair, be sure to wipe it with a cloth dampened with denatured alcohol to remove natural oils that could stain the mat.

Erasers are essential, not only for removing any noticeable pencil lines, but also for cleaning away any other smudges, fingerprints, and the like. Keep an assortment on hand: a pencil eraser, ink eraser, art-gum eraser, kneadable eraser, and draftsman's film erasers of several densities.

A soft counter brush or dusting brush will whisk away most dust, lint, and eraser particles. And any canned-air product, such as Dust-Off, will blow away any other tiny bits of debris that

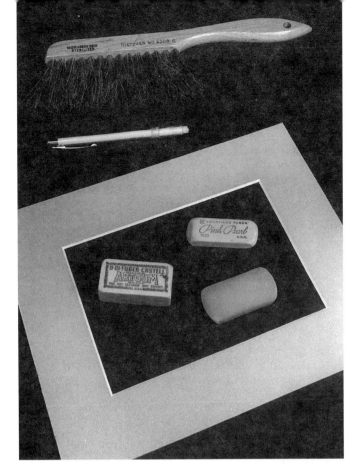

Clean mats with erasers and a soft-bristled dusting brush.

Author's 30 x 60-inch benchtop clamps into the jaws of a Workmate.

cling to the mounted and matted work. A small, hand-held vacuum cleaner is also handy in the shop for cleaning mats and mounted works before framing them.

THE MOUNTING AND MATTING BENCH

Any stable work surface that's large enough to accommodate your projects will suffice as a mounting and matting bench, but you will probably want to take a few measures to make it the most efficient work area possible.

Although tables, workbenches, and even kitchen counters and desks will do, keep in mind that you have two important requirements for your mounting and matting bench surface. First, you must be able to keep your materials clean, which means you can't work on a grimy bench used for auto repair or on a stained and dusty woodworking bench. Also, you must cut through sheet stock with sharp knives, which means you will gradually destroy your cutting surface. So you shouldn't use a workbench, table, or desk that you expect to remain intact.

A slab of plywood works well as a cutting surface that you will eventually replace. You can lay it atop a table, bench, or desk, in which case 1/2-inch thickness should suffice.

If you want something portable and storable, you might consider a bench consisting of a slab of 3/4-inch plywood that rests atop a pair of folding sawhorses or fits into a Black & Decker Workmate or other folding work center. My own takes the latter form, and I use it in my shop for various framing jobs and in my studio when I need a cleaner, more dust-free atmosphere.

I simply attached a length of 2 x 4 to the underside of a 30 x 60-inch piece of 3/4-inch plywood that I keep leaning against a wall in my workshop. When I need a bench, I lay the slab atop my Workmate, tighten the jaws on the 2 x 4, and there it is. I have been using the same slab for several years, and it's holding up quite well. When I eventually ruin the top veneer with all the cutting I do, it will cost me no more than $20 to make a new benchtop that will last me several more years. Quite a bargain, I think, and certainly one of my handiest mounting and matting tools.

CHAPTER THREE

Basic and Conservation Mounting and Matting

Mounting and matting are the first steps in framing and displaying most artworks on paper, as well as certain documents, photographs, and small to moderate-sized posters. Mount and mat boards also help keep works in good shape and protect them from damage if they are not going to be framed immediately. As soon as possible after you have acquired any item, try to get it mounted and matted, even if you don't have time to frame it.

Don't ever store lithographs, posters, and such in mailing tubes. If you buy an artwork by mail and it arrives in a mailing tube, remove it at once. The longer such items stay rolled up, the more difficult it is to remove the curl. Curled prints and posters are difficult to handle and are easily damaged. Immediate mounting and matting is the best solution here.

Even works that are shipped and stored flat can be damaged if their containers are potentially harmful. Never allow any work on paper to remain in contact with corrugated containerboard, cardboard, chipboard, newsprint, or any wood or paper product that you cannot identify as being acid-free and archivally safe.

If you don't have time to mount and mat an item immediately, sandwich it between two pieces of neutralized mat board, rag board, or acid-free foamboard that are at least slightly larger than the work. Tie the package together, or bind it with large rubber bands.

You also must be careful of how and where you store items waiting to be framed. Keep them in a clean, dry atmosphere where they will not be exposed to direct sunlight. A closet is ideal, or you can stack them under a bed. If you must lean them against a wall, make sure it's an interior wall. Unframed items leaned against an exterior wall are susceptible to damage by mold or fungi.

PRECUT MATS
Precut mats are mainly available in standard sizes from 5 x 7 inches (3 x 4 1/2-inch window) to 22 x 28 inches (15 1/2 x 19 1/2-inch window), and there's nothing wrong with using them whenever you wish, provided that you are aware of any potential shortcomings.

The chief advantage to using precut mats is that they save time, and when they're priced economically they can be quite a bargain. Most precut mats come in standard sizes, although some sources offer custom cutting.

Both Nielsen & Bainbridge and Crescent Cardboard Company offer high-quality precut mats in standard sizes that are sold through many local and national outlets. Some mail-order sources specializing in framing and matting materials offer their own precut and custom mats made from Bainbridge or Crescent boards. Many of these products are suitable for archival or conservation mounting and framing.

Precut mats sold through department stores, photography shops, and other consumer outlets may or may not be archivally safe and usually aren't labeled with any indication. Sadly, your inquiries about such matters are likely to be met with blank stares. The good news is that such mats often suffice for certain purposes, are usually economically priced, and can be made more archivally safe. I often use them for matting photographs of friends and family and other items of no significant monetary value. They're also great for matting kids' art.

Often, the precut mats are made of good quality mat board, but the mount board that comes with them is made of chipboard. If the price is low enough, you can simply discard the chipboard and cut your own mount board from less acidic stock.

Some frame-shop proprietors turn their mat-board scraps and leftovers into precut mats in standard sizes. Although these are normally a bit more expensive than department-store mats, they're usually made of better materials. What's more, the shop owner or sales clerk will probably be able to tell you whether the mats and mount boards are made of acid-free or neutralized materials.

I certainly don't want to discourage you from buying and using precut mats, but rather I want you to understand where and where not to use them and how to determine the best buys for your purposes. I keep a small quantity of them in various sizes on hand and use them regularly. When I find them available at good prices, I lay in a supply.

You'll find precut mats a great time saver, even for valuable works, provided you use those made from top-quality, acid-free boards. A number of companies specializing in such products are listed in the Source Directory at the back of this book.

REASONS FOR CONSERVATION MOUNTING AND MATTING

Museum curators and top professional framers have known for years that certain materials and techniques are essential for permanence when framing works of art on paper. Moreover, paper and parchment documents and photographs require similar care. The process is known variously as museum, archival, or conservation framing.

No doubt you have noticed that newspapers begin turning brown after a few months' storage,

PRECUT MATS STANDARD SIZES

Outside Dimensions (in inches)	Window Dimensions (in inches)
5 x 7	3 x 4 1/2
5 x 7	3 1/4 x 4 1/4
8 x 10	4 1/2 x 6 1/2
9 x 12	5 1/2 x 8 1/2
11 x 14	7 1/2 x 9 1/2
12 x 16	8 1/2 x 11 1/2
14 x 18	10 1/2 x 13 1/2
16 x 20	10 1/2 x 13 1/2
16 x 20	11 1/2 x 15 1/2
18 x 24	11 1/2 x 15 1/2
18 x 24	11 1/2 x 17 1/2
20 x 24	13 1/2 x 16 1/2
20 x 24	13 1/2 x 17 1/2
20 x 24	15 1/2 x 19 1/2
22 x 28	15 1/2 x 19 1/2

as do the pulpy pages of some magazines and books. Even many finer papers will begin to color and turn brittle in time. What causes this is acid. Wood is naturally acidic, and most paper products are made from wood pulp. Not only will the paper products themselves discolor and deteriorate, but they will also spread the damage to any paper they touch, including nonacidic papers.

Other enemies of artworks on paper include airborne pollutants, ultraviolet radiation, moisture, mold, and fungi. What protects our watercolors, pastels, lithographs, serigraphs, posters, photographs, and paper documents from the ravages of these silent marauders are the techniques and materials we use to preserve such works.

For some reason, those who write about framing for a general audience—and many custom framers—operate under the notion that only valuable works of art should be protected with archival-quality materials and conservation techniques. Those who haven't kept abreast of the field or who simply haven't done their homework insist or imply that conservation framing is difficult, expensive, and impractical for the do-it-

This pair of limited-edition Japanese woodblock prints on handmade paper cost only $5, but they deserve archival materials and conservation framing techniques.

yourselfer. When they do broach the subject, they usually botch it. So let's put to rest, here and now, the myths and misinformation they have spread.

One expert proclaimed, "Archival framing is much more costly than temporary framing . . . [and] is often best handled by a custom framer, familiar with archival techniques and proper materials." Nonsense! It's slightly more costly initially, but far cheaper in the long run, and the techniques couldn't be simpler.

Another insisted, "Museum board is, of course, more expensive than standard matboard and usually is available only in white and cream color, with a choice of possibly only a few other colors." Poppycock! Though once limited to white, off-white, and a few pastel colors, museum board or rag board is now available in many colors and has been for years. It also comes in a variety of textures and patterns. Moreover, the development of a process for neutralizing the acid in pulp-based mat board has made acid-free boards available in every color that standard mat board comes in.

Any original work is potentially valuable, as are the limited-edition prints so popular these days. What's more, to most of us, value means more than simple monetary worth. Many items we frame have sentimental value that goes well beyond any price tag.

For most of us who aren't serious art collectors, the value of any framable item is relative and personal. And sometimes it has absolutely nothing to do with how much something cost. For example, some years ago my wife and I took a trip to Japan, and while I was nosing around a small gallery, I found a pair of woodblock prints on handmade paper that I really liked. They were limited-edition prints from a small run, signed and numbered by the artist. I got the pair for the equivalent of five American dollars.

In those days, the dollar went a long way in Japan, so just by virtue of inflation and a weaker dollar abroad, these prints have increased in monetary value. And for all I know, the artist could have rocketed to fame by now, making the prints coveted collector's items. But frankly, I couldn't care less. I used archivally safe materials and accepted techniques when I framed them because I liked the prints and wanted them to last. To my way of thinking, if it's worth framing and displaying, it's worth preserving and protecting.

In the case of truly valuable or potentially valuable works, conservation framing is the only way to make sure they won't lose value because of how they were framed. If you owned such a work and wanted to sell it, any savvy buyer would examine the framing job. If it hasn't been properly done, he will pay you less, perhaps much less, or might even decide against buying.

Anything the artwork comes in contact with must be pH neutral if the work is to be preserved. That means the mount board and inner mat must be nonacidic, as must any adhesive, tape, or mounting hinges. And to qualify as museum quality, the mounting job must be reversible: that is, the artwork can be unmounted.

Rag board was once the only choice a framer had for conservation mounting and matting, and since rag board is about twice the price of standard mat board, conservation materials doubled the price of the job. But even at that, we're only talking about a few dollars for any one project.

Neutralized wood-pulp mat board offers lower prices than rag board. For comparison purposes, if your local supplier charges you $5 for a 32 x 40-inch sheet of standard mat board, you will probably pay $10 for rag board and $8 for neutralized mat board.

Let's say you have a print with an image size of 12 x 16 inches that you plan to mount and mat with neutralized mat board. Assume you have decided on mount and mat outside dimensions of 16 x 20 inches with a mat window of 11½ x 15½ inches. From a single 32 x 40-inch sheet, you can cut four 16 x 20-inch pieces, at a cost of $2 each. That means the two pieces required for a mount board and single mat will cost you a total of four bucks. Not bad, eh? But wait. When you cut the mat, you will end up with a leftover big enough to trim to 11 x 14 inches and use on another job. So, if you wanted, you could mount and triple

mat your 16 x 20-inch print for $8, with enough material left over to mount and double mat an 11 x 14-inch print free.

We're not talking big bucks here at all, folks. What's more, there are ways to save even more. And the cost of hinging materials is so low as to be nearly negligible.

Remember, I said anything that touches the artwork must be pH neutral, and what touches it are the mount board, adhesive, hinges, and inner mat. If you use only one mat, then everything must be nonacidic. In multiple matting, however, there is nothing wrong with using standard mat board for outer mats. All you need to do is seal the cut edges to keep the acidic core of the mat from contaminating the interior environment of the frame. To seal a mat, you can coat the cut edges around the periphery of the mat window with shellac applied with a small brush, or spray the whole mat with acrylic matte finish. Although the matte spray will very slightly darken the color of the mat, it's the method I always use, as it is quick, easy, and

Seal standard mats with acrylic matte spray.

cheap, and it doesn't leave a shiny finish on the mat window bevel as shellac will.

Some framing experts who should know better recommend using corrugated containerboard as backing material for mounted and matted works. I have seen precut mats sold with corrugated containerboard as backing material for mounted and matted works. I have seen precut mats sold with corrugated containerboard included as the mount board. I have found original watercolors, pastels, and drawings mounted on corrugated containerboard, and limited-edition prints shrink-wrapped against corrugated containerboard. Sure, this stuff is one of the cheapest paper products available (free, if you want to cut up old containerboard boxes), but it's also so acidic that it should never be used in any phase of framing. It will burn through mount boards within a matter of months and attack the artwork. It will even discolor resin-coated photographic papers and invade the trimmed edges of other heavily coated printing papers.

Although acid-free materials are a bit more expensive, the cost of conservation framing is relatively insignificant. For example, it cost me about $7 to mount and mat a limited-edition print to outside dimensions of 31 x 41 inches. Acidic materials would have cost about half what I paid, but I think the extra $3 was a minuscule amount to pay to protect my investment. When mounting and matting smaller works, costs are proportionately lower, so conservation materials rarely cost over a few dollars more than standard, acidic materials. Frames, glass, dust seals, and hanging hardware cost the same either way.

SELECTING MAT MATERIALS

In addition to archival considerations, you must also select mat colors and hues, as well as core colors, that fit your needs. Here, personal tastes play a more important role than in other phases of the mounting and matting process. There are hundreds of colors and shades of colors to select from—dozens of choices in white alone. Then there are many textures and patterns, with new ones showing up every year. And if you use multiple mats, the possible combinations and permutations are infinite.

Nowhere in the entire framing process do feelings and opinions run stronger than on the subject of mat selection. And nowhere are opinions more divergent.

The author of one book on the subject admitted that mat color is important but insisted that white or off-white is best. In a more daring mood, he ventured, "Occasionally black or gray works well," but warned against the use of "real colors" because they "are almost always wrong." Well, that's one person's opinion. Others are adamant about avoiding the use of any colors but black or white when matting black-and-white art and photographs.

At the other extreme, you'll find electric-colored mats that are blindingly distracting. I have seen mats covered with gaudy plaids and polka dots, and some even stuffed so that they looked more like pin cushions. One frame shop I visited not long ago was owned by an artist and on display were many works, each with multiple mats that were intricately carved—dazzling scenes and motifs, all perfectly bevel-cut. The effect was overwhelming, and to this day I remember the mats well but can't recall a single piece of art displayed in them.

There are no iron-clad rules to go by, but I can offer some suggestions and recommendations. Certain principles might help you make better decisions and selections—better for *you*, because when all is said and done, you are the one who must be happy. If you are matting and framing for others, these same principles should help you guide them toward the right selections.

Just as black mats and white mats sometimes work well with colored artworks, colored mats sometimes go with black-and-white works. If you want to use color with a pen-and-ink or pencil drawing or similar work, you will probably find a double mat will work best, in which case the inner mat should be either black or white and the outer mat colored.

Although I have satisfactorily used color when matting black and white works, by and large, I use black, white, and gray mats, usually two or more in any job. I use mat-sample corners in these shades to experiment until I find the right combination and order. It's often amazing what a difference a subtle change can make.

On pen-and-ink drawings and high-contrast black-on-white prints, I most often like a black inner mat providing a narrow border around the work, usually ⅛ or ¼ inch. Depending on the subject, I will then use white or gray for the outer mat, or perhaps a second mat of white and third or outer mat matching the inner one.

The combination of black inner mat and gray outer mat for these black-on-white works is a favorite of mine and one I use often. It is visually stunning, and it keeps me from having to spend time on the tedious task of matching whites.

There seems to be no end to the shades of white and off-white used in art and printing papers, as well as in mats. Often, white mats used with black-on-white artworks appear strangely out of sync when the white of the mat and white of the paper don't match. Gray solves that problem, and there are as many shades of gray mats as there are of off-white.

Cream-colored papers are equally problematic, and here is where colored mats are decidedly more attractive than black, white, or gray. And if the ink used in the print or drawing is not quite black—dark brown is popular these days—that's all the more reason to consider colored mats.

I recently mounted and matted a fine limited-edition print by David Hagerbaumer: a low-

This original cartoon by Jim Snook called for a black border, but a single black mat seemed too confining.

A black inner mat with white outer mat proved ideal for Snook's cartoon.

Gray, white, and black mat corners are useful in choosing the right mats for black-and-white works.

A favorite combination for many black-and-white works is a black inner mat and gray outer mat.

number reproduction of a pen-and-ink drawing of a woodcock in dark-brown ink on high-grade, cream-colored stock. I matched the ink with a Crescent mat board labeled Sable. For the second mat, I used a color Crescent calls French Gray, but which, in reality, is more a shade of buff than gray. For the outer mat, Crescent's slightly darker Pewter board was perfect. The finishing touch was a very narrow, simple frame made of black-walnut molding that matched both the ink and the Sable inner mat.

The selection of mats for colored artworks is complicated by the variety of mat colors you have to choose from, but a few guidelines should make your selections a bit easier. For starters, you might want to write or phone Crescent Cardboard Company (a major manufacturer of mat and rag board) and ask for its mat-sample sheet, which has more than 240 swatches of mat board face papers (see the Source Directory). You'll also want to write or phone Nielsen & Bainbridge to request that company's product literature. Then spend some time at galleries and art museums examining matted works to find the effects you like most. Take a notebook with you and jot reminders that you will use later in your shop or studio.

A good book for ideas on the use of colors is *Picture Framing and Wall Display* (Lane Publishing Co., 1979), which is available at bookstores and libraries.

Something that often works well for me is to determine the main color or colors in any work and then match my mat selection accordingly. With a double mat, I frequently pick two shades or hues of the one dominant color. For example, I might use a dark-blue inner mat and lighter blue outer mat, or dark brown and beige.

Certain kinds of art seem to lead me automatically to specific colors. Seascapes, for instance, often have me reaching for the blue mat-sample corners. Many scenic or landscape works call for natural earth tones, such as shades of brown or green. Bright flowers or fall colors will have me using similarly bright mats.

Contrasting colors can also be highly effective with some works. Crescent's Storm Blue and Bar Harbor Gray mat boards provide an arresting combination for waterfront scenes and other marine art. In a woodland scene, I effectively used Colonial Orange for the 1/4-inch inner mat, Fudge Brown for the 1/2-inch second mat, and Suntan (medium beige) for the outer mat. The unlikely orange was a perfect match with one of the colors in the fur of two red foxes in the print.

With a little practice and some experimentation with various artworks and mat-sample corners, you'll get the hang of mat selection. Most likely, you will soon find that certain types of art naturally lead you to specific colors and color combinations.

You also must pay attention to mat textures. Some mats are smooth, some lightly textured, and some deeply impressed, embossed, or pebbled. When you're using multiple mats, there's nothing wrong with using all smooth or all lightly textured mats. But the more noticeably textured boards seem to compete with one another or provide too much of a good thing.

If I want a highly textured appearance, I might pick a mat board that simulates natural burlap to use as an outer mat and a smooth dark-brown board to make a narrow inner mat. Or I might use a linen-textured board in cream or off-white against a narrow inner mat of smooth gold.

With these few simple guidelines in mind, you should be able to examine the work of others and determine what you like most and what will best serve your needs. Mat selection really isn't all that difficult. With a little practice and experience, you will find it to be an enjoyable part of picture framing.

BASIC MOUNTING AND MATTING

When you're framing items of little or no monetary value but some personal value, you should use archivally safe materials, but you needn't necessarily use those required for museum-quality jobs.

For example, for valuable or potentially valuable works, you should use a hinged or folder mat—that is, a mat hinged to the mount board—but you needn't hinge mats for items with no collector's value. You might want to, but it's your decision.

With hinged mats, both the mat and the mount board must be of equal thickness. Normally, you will also need to cut a piece of backing material to the outside dimensions of the hinged mat and use it to provide rigidity, especially in larger works. Works of little or no monetary value can be mounted to a piece of acid-free foamboard instead of a mount board and framed without need of additional backing.

In a museum-quality job, you must mount the artwork with rice-paper hinges and starch paste or with Insta-Hinges, which can be removed without damaging the work. If you aren't concerned about later removal and simply want to protect a work of personal or sentimental value, feel free to use acid-free linen tape or paper tape for the hinges.

Mat windows usually should be cut 1/4 inch smaller than the image size of the artwork, to overlap the image edges by 1/8 inch. With signed and numbered limited-edition prints, it is cus-tomary to leave some of the print-border area visible to show the number and artist's signature. In such cases, exposed borders usually range from 1/2 to 1 inch, which means mat windows are cut 1 to 2 inches larger than image size.

Always start every mounting and matting job with a plan sheet. And remember the old do-it-yourselfer's rule that will save you a lot of grief and a pile of money: *measure twice, cut once.*

Measure the image height and width; then measure them again, and write these dimensions on your plan sheet. Now you must decide on mat-border widths. There are various rules to apply, most of which eventually contradict one another by striking exception. The only hard-and-fast rule is this: do what pleases you.

When you're studying the work of others, compare the effects of wide and narrow mats, single and multiple mats, large and small images. Check to see if mat borders are equal or not, and determine which effect you prefer.

When hinging mats, make sure mat and mount are of equal size and thickness.

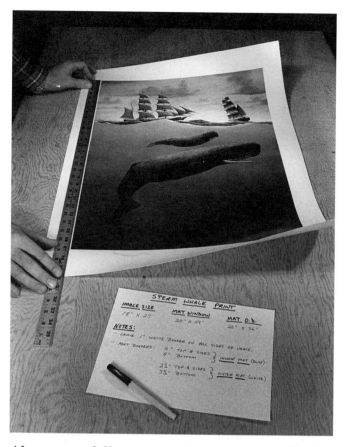

Always carefully measure the image, and double-check all dimensions.

Mat borders are usually from 1 to 4 inches wide. Commonly, bottom borders are slightly wider, though not necessarily. To my eye, equal borders look fine on diplomas, certificates, and similar documents, and narrow borders often look good on photographs and small posters.

There was a time when framers invariably put significantly wider mat borders at the bottom of any artwork they were matting. Some still do, even though the practice is now considered passé. I have never cared for overly wide bottom borders, so I usually add no more than an inch there, depending on the size of the work and its placement on the wall. Wider bottom borders look best on low-hanging pictures.

Once you've settled on appropriate border widths, add them to the mat-window dimensions to determine outside dimensions. The print in the accompanying photos has an image size of 18 x 27 inches. I wanted a 1-inch border exposed for the signature, print number, and remarque, which meant a window of 20 x 29 inches. I added 3 inches left, right, and top, and 4 inches at the bottom for mat borders, and listed 26 x 36 inches as the outside dimensions.

Use an X-Acto knife and straightedge to cut mats, mounts, and backing. Spring clamps hold straightedge in place.

At this point, the most difficult and critical part of any mounting and matting job is finished. All that's left is to cut everything out and mount the artwork.

Use an X-Acto or utility knife and straightedge to cut mats, mount board, and backing. Clamp the straightedge and board to a solid working surface with one or two spring clamps. Remember that cutting will scar the work surface, so make sure you use a piece of plywood or a benchtop specially made for such purposes.

Next, scribe window guidelines on the back of the mat board with a pencil and straightedge, a compass or marking gauge set for the border width, or a mat-cutter guide. The fastest and most foolproof way to mark guidelines and cut the mat windows is with a mat cutter and guide.

To use an Alto's mat-cutting system, for example, set the guide bar for the mat-border width. For the inner mat in the accompanying photographs, I set the guide bar at 3 inches and scribed lines inside the left, right, and top edges. I then reset the bar at 4 inches and scribed a line inside the bottom edge. I did the same on the back of the outer mat with the bar set for 2½ inches for top and side lines and 3½ inches for the bottom line.

If you haven't cut out beveled mat windows before, be sure to practice with the mat cutter on scraps of mat board or cardboard. The only tricky parts are stopping and starting the cut, and the only way to master the technique is to practice. But it doesn't take long. With an Alto's system, you can be cutting mats like a pro with five minutes' practice.

With the mat facedown on the system's cutting surface and pressed tightly against the stops, you will notice that the guide bar is actually ⅛ inch outside the path the cutter blade will travel (to the left for right-handed operation). That's where it's supposed to be. Besides, the bottom and top lines are the important ones, because they indicate, respectively, where to start and stop each cut.

Remember that the cutter blade is angled for the beveled cut, and it enters at an angle when you insert the blade into the back of the mat

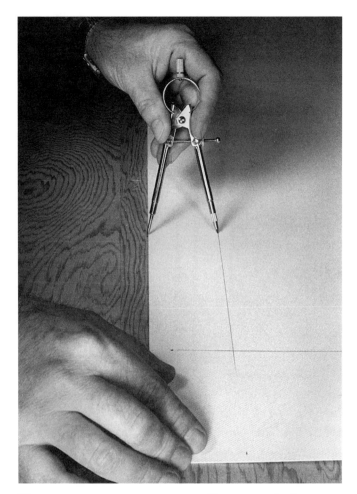

You can use a compass to scribe mat-window lines.

board. So if you're using an Alto's Model 30 or a similar cutter from another manufacturer, put the point of the blade about ⅛ inch from the guide bar and ⅛ inch below the bottom guideline. Keeping the base of the cutter parallel with the mat-board surface and using your left hand to firmly press the guide bar down against the mat board, gently push the cutter down and toward the guide bar, so the cutter edge is in firm contact with the guide bar. To make the cut, push the cutter along the guide bar in one fluid motion, stopping the blade about ⅛ inch beyond the top guideline. Rotate the mat clockwise, and continue cutting the same way until the mat window has been cut out. This method produces slight overcuts at the corners of the mat window, but they're unnoticeable when the work is displayed. It's better to overcut the corners than to

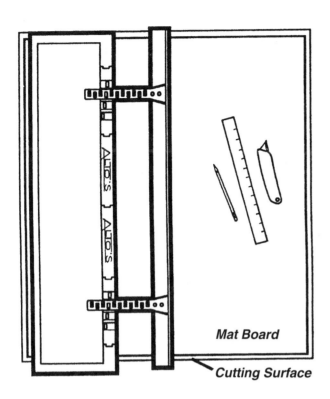

Reversing the guide bar on the base converts the Alto's Mat Cutting System into an efficient straightedge for cutting mat boards, mount boards, and backing boards to outside dimensions.

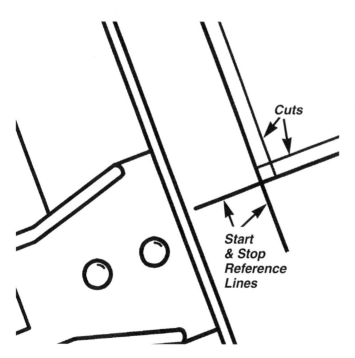

The cutter blade actually travels ¹/₈ inch inside the guidelines and guide bar.

Position the Model 45 Mat Cutter firmly against the guide bar with the point of the blade just outside the bottom (starting) horizontal guideline.

undercut them. As you gain skill and confidence, you can gradually reduce the length of the overcuts until they're almost nonexistent.

With an Alto's Model 45 cutter, which has a pivoting handle and blade, cutting out mat windows is even simpler; in fact, it's foolproof. Once you've scribed your guidelines and positioned the mat facedown on the system's cutting surface, as described above, put the Model 45 cutter on the mat with the base plate pressed against the cutting guide. Align the tip of the blade just a hair's breadth to the rear (toward you) of the bottom or starting guideline. While holding the cutter firmly against the cutting guide, push downward on the cutter's handle, allowing the blade to pivot into the mat board. While pressing down on the cutting guide with your left hand, use your right hand to slide the cutter forward in one smooth motion, stopping the cutter when the silver mark on the blade holder is aligned with the top or stopping guideline.

Southpaws fear not: the manufacturer provides complete instructions for both right-handed and left-handed operation of the Alto's systems and cutters.

If you undercut a mat-window corner, use a double-edged razor blade to complete the cut.

Carefully slide it into the beveled cut, hold it at the same angle as the bevel, and slowly cut through the mat.

Hinging the mat—or in the case of multiple mats, the inner mat—to the mount board facilitates the precise positioning of the artwork. Lay the mount board faceup and the mat facedown, butted top to top. Cut a piece of acid-free linen tape just slightly shorter than the mat width. Moisten the adhesive side of the tape with a damp sponge or ceramic tongue, press the tape along the seam between the two boards, and let it dry for several minutes.

There are several ways to position works on mount boards. You can scribe positioning lines on the mount board, or use the Falcon Print Positioner, which is covered in chapter 4.

If you want to use positioning lines, start by laying a straightedge across the artwork, along the top edge of the image area. Then make a small pencil mark at the outer edges of the left and right borders. Now lay the straightedge along the left edge of the image, and make a pencil mark at the top edge of the border. Do the same along the right edge of the image area.

Scribe a horizontal line across the mount board a distance from the top edge that's 1/8 inch less than the mat's top border width. Scribe vertical lines the same way, left and right. In the case of the print in the accompanying photographs, the inner mat borders were 3 inches, top and sides, which called for guidelines 2⅞ inches from the top and side edges of the mount board. All there is to positioning the print, then, is to lay it on the mount board and align the marks at the edges of the print borders with the lines on the mount board.

Another way to position an artwork—and here's where the value of a hinged mat becomes apparent—is to lay it on the mount board and close the mat onto it. Then carefully position the work within the mat window. Wrap a book with tissue paper (two or more books for larger works),

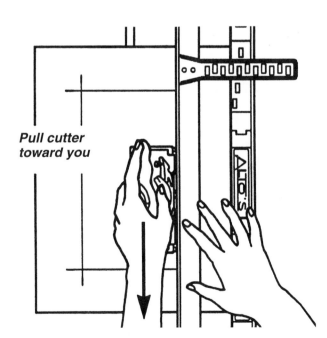

Pull cutter toward you

For left-handed use, turn the Model 4501 system around so the guide-bar arms point to the right. Then draw the cutter toward you from the top (starting) guideline to the bottom (stopping) guideline.

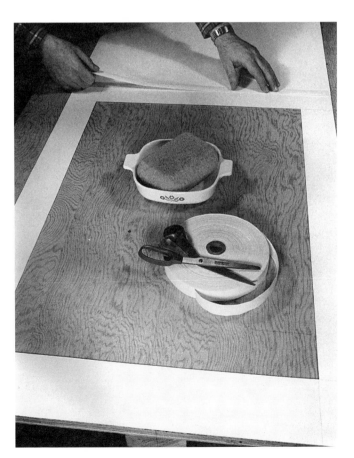

Hinge mat to mount board with acid-free linen tape.

Attaching Insta-Hinge to artwork.

and lay it atop the artwork to hold it in place. Gently lift the mat, and make small pencil marks on the mount board at the top and side edges of the artwork. Remove the artwork, and using the pencil marks as guides, scribe guidelines parallel to the top and side edges of the mount board. Lay the work back on the mount board, align its edges with the guidelines, and double-check its position with the mat in place. (Instead of tissue-covered books, you can use large, stainless-steel clips or beanbags—mentioned in chapter 2—to hold the artwork in place.)

Mounting artworks with hinges allows for natural expansion and contraction without causing the work to buckle or warp. If you use the Insta-Hinge kit, you will also be assured of protecting the work's collector's value.

The hinge material comes in strips that should be torn, not cut. Hinges about 3 inches long will work fine with most items. You can either fold and tear the material or, for best results,

Attaching hinged artwork to mount board.

moisten a small brush with water and paint a damp line across the material. Wait for about a minute until the fibers are fully moistened, and pull the hinge from the strip, leaving a frayed edge. Two hinges will suffice for most works. Large horizontal works might require three.

To attach an Insta-Hinge, first lay the artwork facedown atop one of the blotter squares in the kit. Moisten the bottom third of the hinge's dull side with a damp brush, and attach it to the back of the artwork. Brush the hinge again to moisten it, and cover the damp portion with a spun-nylon square and blotter. Put a tissue-covered book atop the hinge, and attach another hinge near the opposite top corner. Let them stand for five minutes, or until the adhesive dries.

Lay the artwork faceup on the mount board. Put the tissue-covered books on it to keep it in place, and carefully position the work. Turn back the top portion of each hinge, and moisten the glossy surface with the brush. Press the hinges to the mount board, and moisten them from the top side with the damp brush. Cover each hinge with a spun-nylon square and blotter, and put a tissue-covered book on top.

When attaching hinges to the artwork and the mount board, don't use too much water. Dampen them gradually with only enough water on the brush to make them adhere. And let them dry completely before proceeding further.

If you're using a single mat, just fold the mat over the mounted work, and it's ready for framing. If you're using multiple mats, laminate them with double-sided tape or Scotch Adhesive Transfer Tape and a tape gun.

If the work you're mounting and matting is of little or no monetary value, you might prefer to make mounting hinges with acid-free linen tape or paper tape. This is a faster and simpler process, but not acceptable for works with collector's value. Nevertheless, neither the linen nor the paper tape will harm the work, which makes them fine for mounting many items that are only of personal, sentimental, or decorative value.

Make linen-tape hinges by attaching two pieces to form a T.

With either type of tape, you'll need two 3-inch strips for each hinge. To make a hinge, moisten the top inch of the adhesive side of one strip, and press it to the center of the adhesive side of another strip to form a T.

To mount hinges to the artwork, moisten the bottom inch of the adhesive side of the pieces forming the stems of the Ts. Then attach each to the back of the work, just inside each top corner.

After positioning the work on the mount board, bend back the top of each hinge, and moisten the adhesive on the top part of each T. Then press each to the mount board, and let it stand for a minute or two until the adhesive dries. Then the work is ready for framing.

Quick-Reference Guide: Cutting a Mat in Seven Easy Steps

Using Alto's Model 4501 Mat Cutting System, you can cut any mat in a jiffy by following these seven easy steps:

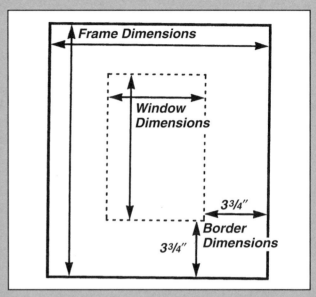

Step 1. After determining mat-window size and border widths, cut mat and mount board to frame dimensions.

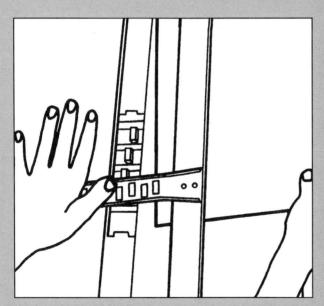

Step 2. Press down the end of the cutting-guide arm to raise it, and slide the facedown mat under and against the stops.

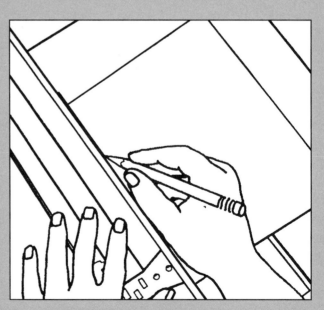

Step 3. Scribe mat-window layout lines with a pencil and guide bar.

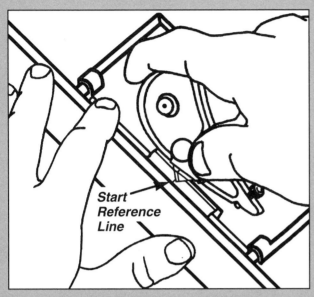

Step 4. Place the cutter against the guide bar, with the blade point just outside the bottom horizontal line.

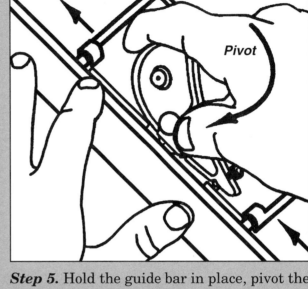

Step 5. Hold the guide bar in place, pivot the cutter blade downward and inward, and push the cutter along the guide bar.

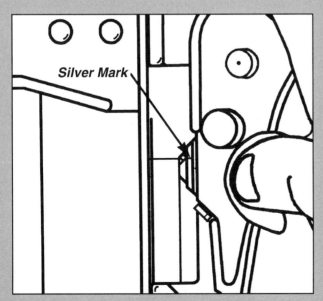

Step 6. Stop the cutter when the silver mark on the blade holder meets the top horizontal line.

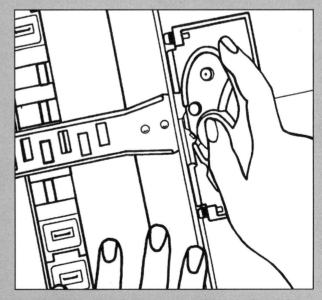

Step 7. Rotate the mat board to make subsequent cuts the same way, and adjust the guide bar if border widths vary.

CHAPTER FOUR

Mounting Photographs, Posters, and Needlework

Few areas of the framer's craft have changed as dramatically in so short a time as the mounting of photographs, posters, and similar items. Up until the mid-1970s, we either dry mounted or wet mounted them; there was no other choice.

Dry mounting, until recently the preferred method for a truly professional job, is a process that combines heat and pressure to bond a print or poster to a mount board via a special dry-mounting tissue. Although it is possible to dry mount small photographs and posters with a household iron, the best tool for the job is a dry-mounting press designed for such work. These presses are electrically operated, thermostatically controlled, and equipped with timers. But even the best presses can ruin resin-coated photographic papers and some coated posters. Additionally, the heat can adversely affect the dyes in color photographs and can ruin the various foam-cored products.

Wet mounting was the cheaper but messier and more tedious alternative. It was also the only safe way to handle the plastics and resins that would melt and bubble when subjected to too much heat. A variety of glues and pastes, either straight or diluted, were painted onto the back of a photo or poster, which was then laminated to a mount board of some sort and allowed to dry.

Dry mounting is still used on fiber-based photographs and posters at many photo labs, studios, and frame shops, especially those that were in business before the development of alternative equipment and methods. Some framers still use wet-mounting methods to repair damaged works, although vacuum mounting has generally taken over in this area as a faster and neater process.

The development and widespread use of resin-coated photographic papers in the 1970s and the growth of reprographics technology in the 1980s and 1990s were major forces behind the introduction and refinement of all the dozens of mounting products and various tools and methods we use today. There is now some kind of spray adhesive, adhesive tissue, pressure-sensitive mounting board, self-adhesive foamboard, or treated hardboard to fit every conceivable need and budget. And the modern materials are a joy to work with.

MOUNTING MATERIALS FOR PHOTOS AND POSTERS

The traditional photo-mounting board is pebbled mat board that's black on one side and white on the other. Of course, many other boards also serve the purpose. Selection depends on whether the work to be mounted is a black-and-white or color photograph and whether it will be flush mounted, border mounted, or matted. Framing and the display environment are other considerations.

If the work will have exposed borders or will be matted, apply the same principles of color selection you would to any other medium. Generally, use black, white, and shades of gray for black-and-white photographs and posters. Pick matching or contrasting colors for color photographs and posters, or go with subtler pastels, creams, and off-whites for more subdued treatment. And feel free to break these rules whenever it suits you.

As long as you won't be using heat, you can mount photographs and posters on foamboard, which I prefer for large posters, as it has less tendency to warp than mat board. Even more rigid than the paper-faced foamboards are those faced with plastic, such as Gatorfoam.

Hardboard (Masonite is one popular brand) is another excellent mounting material. I particularly like it for flush-mounted photographs that I display in floater frames that give the impression that the work is floating inside the frame. It's available in 24 x 24-inch to 48 x 96-inch sheets at lumberyards and home-improvement centers and comes in 1/8- and 1/4-inch thicknesses, either tempered or untempered. The tempered board is less affected by moisture and is the better choice for mounting jobs.

Three-dimensional mount boards, or standouts—so called because they stand out from the wall—are favored by many photographers and decorators. They can be displayed individually or in groups, as any framed objects might be, and are often bunched into montages. Some manufacturers also offer special hangers that permit floating standouts off the wall. Using standouts in various dimensions, with and without the floater hangers, allows great breadth of creativity when displaying photographs.

All the various boards can be used in conjunction with aerosol adhesives, adhesive sheets, and adhesive cards. What's more, these and other products are available as self-adhesive boards. Some come in standard sizes; others come as sheets you cut to size. Some come both ways.

The 3M Company makes Super 77 Spray Adhesive and Scotch Photo Mount and Spra-Ment aerosol adhesives. I keep all three of these on hand so I will have an adhesive that will work with any material I might use. Although I don't use these or other aerosol adhesives for conservation mounting, I often use them for mounting display photographs, snapshot collages, small posters, maps, charts, and other items. Photo Mount works well on mat board and similar surfaces, but not on leather, hardboard, or certain other materials. Spra-Ment works with most materials, including cork, fabric, and various

The nuArc vacuum-mounting frame.

plastics. And the Super 77 Spray is an aggressive, high-tack spray that works with practically any material I use. The company also manufactures positionable Mounting Adhesive in rolls and standard-sized sheets, which can be used with a squeegee for small jobs, or a press for larger items.

Coda, Inc., is a pioneer in the development of pressure-sensitive adhesives and other mounting products. The company offers a wide array of materials to fit most mounting needs. Its self-

Aerosol adhesives from 3M Company see to many mounting needs.

Coda Stand-Outs make attractive photo displays.

adhesive Cold-Mount products are available in rolls of standard widths and in various types of mount boards, such as single-weight and double-weight card stock, tempered 1/8-inch hardboard, foamboard, and Gatorfoam. It's own codaFoam consists of a foam core faced with white plastic on both sides and comes in 1/4-inch and 3/4-inch thicknesses.

Coda also offers several interesting Cold-Mount display items. Stand-Outs are three-dimensional boards, available in standard sizes, from 4 x 5 inches to 20 x 24 inches. For larger

works, its Mural Mounts come in sizes from 8 x 10 inches to 40 x 60 inches. Both are available edged in black, white, or wood grain.

Among Crescent Cardboard Company's products for picture framers are Perfect Mount self-adhesive mounting boards. They are acid-free, repositionable, and permanently bonding. Although they're not recommended for museum or conservation mounting, where reversibility is essential, they're useful for other applications, such as mounting photographs, posters, and some craft items. Perfect Mount boards are available through framing-supply outlets and come in standard sizes ranging from 5 x 7 to 40 x 60 inches.

TOOLS FOR MOUNTING PHOTOS AND POSTERS

For mounting small posters and photographs up to 16 x 20 inches, you won't need much in the way of tools. Depending on the type of adhesive you use, you might need no more than a clean cloth for pressing the work to a mount board. A print roller is a handy item with just about every kind of adhesive, so you should invest in one. You will find them at photo-supply stores and through some mail-order outlets.

You can cut mat board and trim prints with a straightedge and utility knife. If you have much of this sort of work to do, you might want to invest in a trimmer or cutter of some kind. There are dozens of makes, models, styles, and

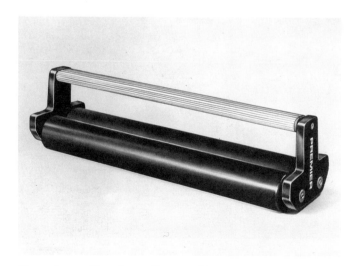

Premier roller from Doran Enterprises.

Guillotine-style cutter from Doran Enterprises.

sizes available in prices ranging from under $20 to well over $1,000.

The Falcon Print Trimmer handles photos up to 14 inches and uses ordinary razor blades. This is a simple but accurate light-duty trimmer that will cut all weights of photographic paper as well as single-weight card stock and other lightweight mount boards. Because it's so fast and handy, I use mine for trimming all small, unmounted prints.

Of the larger, heavier-duty cutters, the guillotine-type are the least expensive. Rotary trimmers are a bit more expensive, but if you ever entertain the notion of mounting and matting professionally in high volume, you should consider the advantages such tools offer. They handle material from thin tissue to mat board with equal facility. They're fast, safe, precise machines.

Dry-mount, roller, and vacuum presses range in price from a few hundred to a few thousand

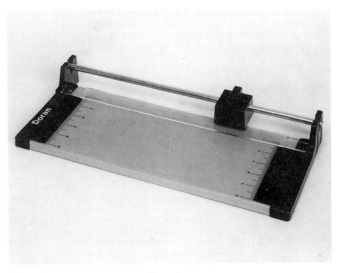

The Doran rotary-style trimmer.

Coda's hand-operated Cold-Mount press.

Falcon Print Trimmer in use.

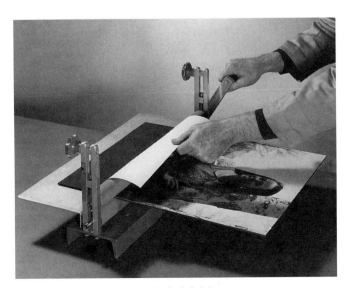

Coda's hand-operated Cold-Mount press.

dollars—an expense you can certainly forestall, perhaps indefinitely. If you never need to mount anything larger than a 16 x 20-inch print, you won't need a press. If you end up mounting many large items, though, you will have to consider a press, or you will have to have such mounting done for you.

Most of the photographs I mount are from 4 x 5 inches to 16 x 20 inches. I rarely have to mount a large poster, but when I do, I take it to a local shop where there's a press big enough to handle it, and I pay the man his fee. Certainly, I could mount such items much more cheaply with my own press, but I would have to do a lot of mounting to save enough money to justify the initial capital outlay.

I seriously doubt that I will ever need a press, but if I do, I'm sure it will be one of the hand-operated wringer or roller-type presses for use with pressure-sensitive adhesives. There are some good buys around on such presses in moderate sizes.

Using the Print Positioner, Step 1.

USING THE FALCON PRINT POSITIONER

With the Falcon Print Positioner, there's no need to measure and scribe layout lines on the mount board or to even put guide marks on the item being positioned. While such chores take only a few minutes with conventional tools and techniques, the entire job is reduced to seconds with the Print Positioner. And it works with any size photograph. It's especially nice for photographs that are border-mounted—that is, where borders of the mount board will be left exposed—and have been trimmed to size, leaving nowhere to make positioning marks.

If you're going to border mount or mat a print, determine what border widths you want, and cut the mount board to the proper outside dimensions. With the print trimmed to finished dimensions, if necessary, follow these simple steps to properly position it.

Step 1. Position the print atop the mount board in the top right corner, with top and right edges flush. Place the Positioner as shown and slide it to the left until the top left corners of the print

Using the Print Positioner, Step 2.

Using the Print Positioner, Step 3.

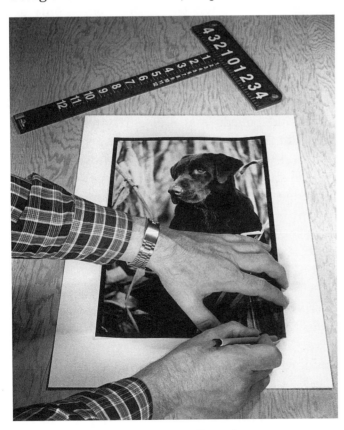

Using the Print Positioner, Step 4.

and mount board align with corresponding horizontal numbers.

Step 2. Without moving the Positioner, slide the print to the left, against the Positioner's vertical stem, then down to the bottom edge of the mount board. Check to see how the top edge of the print aligns with the large-number scale on the stem.

Step 3. Slide the print up along the Positioner stem until its top edge aligns with the small-number scale at a position corresponding with the reading noted in Step 2.

Step 4. The print is now perfectly positioned on the mount board. Using the print edges as guides, lightly scribe horizontal and vertical lines at each corner. The print is now ready for mounting.

And that's all there is to it. As if by magic, this works every time with any size print. A nifty tool, and inexpensive, too.

MODERN MOUNTING METHODS

Other than introducing you to the various materials and tools available, there's really little to tell you about mounting photographs and posters, except to offer a few tips to make the job easier. Any of the adhesive products you buy come with adequate instructions, and there are few differences in the way they work.

As you have no doubt surmised by now, I don't like to lay down rules and absolutes for you to work by, because there are always notable exceptions, and there are usually good reasons for breaking many rules that apply to arts and crafts. But I think one of my own rules might come in handy here.

Generally, don't plan to hand mount any print or poster larger than 16 x 20 inches. I have heard of one chap who can mount murals and posters up to 30 x 40 inches using only a hand roller, but he is an exception. Works larger than 16 x 20 inches are extremely difficult to handle, and for most of us they're impossible to mount by hand without problems. In fact, just handling them without ruining them is difficult.

Mount large posters to oversize boards, and trim after mounting.

If you have never mounted anything with the modern adhesives, start with small photographs, and gradually work your way up to the 11 x 14-inch and 16 x 20-inch prints. When you have larger photos or posters to mount, take them to a shop that has a roller or vacuum press big enough to accommodate your needs.

You must keep your work area clean during any mounting or matting job, but you must be meticulous about it when mounting with adhesives. Any tiny piece of lint that ends up between the work and the mount board results in a bulge or bubble in the image surface. What's more, buildup of static electricity in some plastic products acts like a magnet to dust and lint.

When you mount with aerosol adhesives, you must guard against any potential damage from overspray. Start any such job by attaching a sheet of freezer paper to your benchtop with masking tape, and replace it as necessary. After seeing to any necessary trimming and positioning, you're ready to apply adhesive.

Lay the print or poster facedown on the freezer paper. Then spray an even and complete coating of adhesive onto the back of the work. Depending on what type of adhesive you are using and the manufacturer's directions, you will either mount it immediately or let it "tack up" for a minute or so. Some porous materials require more adhesive than others, and in some cases you will need to coat both the back of the print and the surface of the mount board.

Carefully position the top corners of the print on the mount board, aligned with your guide marks, and press the top edge onto the board. Then gradually press the rest of the print onto the board, cover it with a piece of clean paper, and use a hand roller to mount it, always rolling from the center toward the edges, removing all bubbles.

There will be adhesive overspray on the freezer paper from your first print or poster. To protect the next work, lay a sheet of clean paper on the freezer paper and the next photo or poster on that. For prints up to 8 x 10 inches, you can use ordinary 8½ x 11-inch paper. For larger prints and posters, use freezer paper or cheaper tissue paper. There's no need to tape down these subsequent sheets of protective paper, as the overspray will keep them in place.

When working with adhesive-coated boards and adhesive sheets, you needn't worry about protecting your work surface, as this is a much neater process. I use the coated boards only for flush mounting and adhesive sheets for both flush mounting and border mounting, but mainly for the latter.

If I'm using adhesive boards, I prefer to mount the work first and trim it afterward. If I'm using boards made of card stock or chipboard to flush mount 8 x 10-inch prints, for example, I simply peel away the release paper to expose the adhesive, and carefully position the top edge of the print along the top edge of the mount board. Then I gradually press the print onto the board, from top to bottom, with a clean cloth. I cover the image with a sheet of paper and use a roller to bond print to board.

On most of my 8 x 10-inch prints, the borders are 3/8 inch wide, so to end up with a flush-mounted print, I simply trim 3/8 inch from each edge. With card stock, mat board, chipboard, and such, I use my guillotine cutter to trim the prints. I first use a cloth dampened with denatured alcohol to wipe the cutter table clean. Then I carefully lay each print facedown for the cutting, as this leaves a sharp, smooth cut edge on the image surface. What starts out as an 8 x 10-inch print with borders ends up as a flush-mounted print of 7¼ x 9¼ inches.

I don't like what the guillotine cutter does to foamboard, so when I'm mounting with that product, I prefer to trim it with a straightedge and utility knife, which produces a clean, smooth cut, top and bottom. In this case, I work with the print or poster faceup to make it easier to see what I'm doing.

With prints and posters larger than 16 x 20 inches, I use mount boards (usually foamboard) that are slightly larger. Then, after they're mounted, I trim the excess with a straightedge and utility knife.

When I'm mounting with hardboard, however, I do the opposite. I use boards that are slightly undersized with posters and borderless prints. When the work is mounted, I lay it face-down on the mat-cutting bench and very care-fully use the tip of my utility knife to trim away excess, letting the edge of the hardboard serve as a guide. A sharply pointed blade, such as the X-Acto #11, is best for this job.

Adhesive sheets or cards, coated on both sides, are ideal for border mounting prints and for mounting prints and posters that will be matted. Determine the border widths, and cut mount boards to the appropriate size. Mounting methods will vary only slightly from one make of adhesive sheet to another. But, typically, you can follow these steps.

Step 1. Peel back the release paper on one side of the card about a fourth of the way, and fold it against the card.

Step 2. With the print faceup, align its top edge with the top exposed edge of the adhesive card. Carefully and lightly press the print to the card.

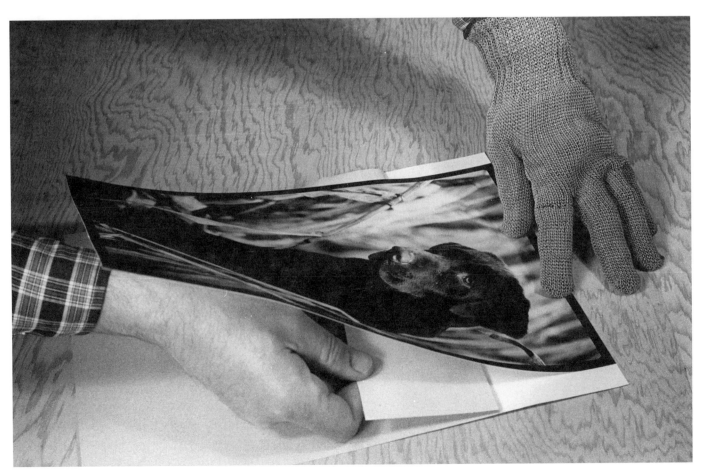

Mounting a photograph, Step 3.

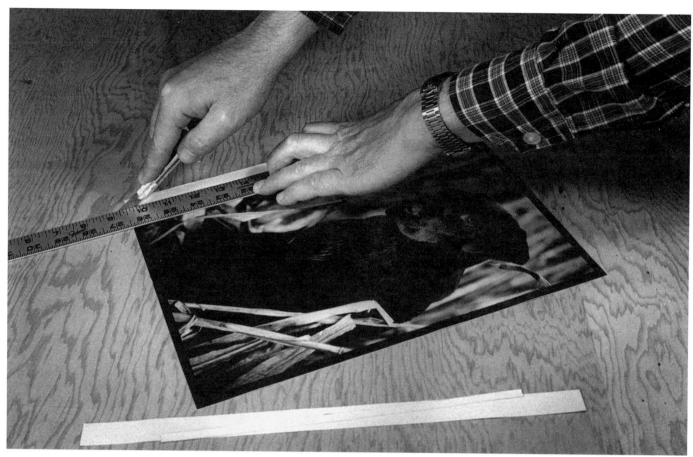

Mounting a photograph, Step 5.

Mounting a photograph, Step 10.

Step 3. Grasp the folded edge of the release paper beneath the print, and slowly pull it toward the bottom of the card, allowing the print to make contact with the adhesive as you do so.

Step 4. Press the print to the adhesive by hand with a clean cloth, or use a roller, working from the center to the edges.

Step 5. Trim the print, if required, to final size with any suitable cutter or a straightedge and utility knife. If you're going to mount with mats, trim only the excess of the oversized adhesive card.

Step 6. Position the print on the mount board, and make any necessary guide marks on the board.

Step 7. Lay the print facedown, peel back the release paper on the back of the print a fourth of the way, and fold it as in Step 1.

Step 8. With the print faceup, align its top corners with the guide marks on the mount board, and lightly press it in place.

Step 9. Slowly pull the release paper away, as you did in Step 3, allowing the print to make contact with the mount board.

Step 10. Press the print to the mount board with a clean cloth, or cover it with a sheet of paper, and use a roller to bond it to the mount board.

MOUNTING NEEDLEWORK

Many kinds of needlework—including needlepoint, cross-stitch, and various other forms of hand and machine embroidery—are suitable for framing. Among the most popular are samplers, scenic works, holiday themes, and whimsical art. Some antique works are extremely valuable and should be treated with utmost care. Even more recent or common pieces have many hours of meticulous stitching invested in them and should be treated accordingly and framed to last.

Most books on framing provide little or no information on handling needlework. Indeed, the books on needlepoint and cross-stitch I've consulted offer only scant and incomplete advice. One notable exception is *Needlework Framing*, by Vivian C. Kistler (Columbia Publishing Company, 1995). If you're a needleworker or plan to frame much needlework, you might want to order a copy of this informative volume through a local bookstore or by phone or mail from University Products, Inc. (see the Source Directory).

Cleaning and Pressing

Newly finished and properly handled needlework should require little in the way of preparation. As with any framing job, make sure your hands are clean before you handle it. Carefully inspect the piece, and snip any errant thread or yarn ends with scissors. Then gently vacuum it to remove bits of yarn and lint.

Some pieces might require more in the way of cleaning, especially older works or those you are remounting and reframing. My best advice in any such case is to avoid doing it yourself. Take the work to a dry cleaner.

Mildew can be a problem, especially in wet or humid climates, or with needlework that has been improperly mounted and framed. Dry heat kills the fungi that cause mildew, so you can use an electric blow dryer for such purposes. Then vacuum the piece and inspect it for stains. In severe cases, your best bet is to have the piece professionally dry cleaned.

Some needlework requires at least minor pressing before mounting, especially any work that has been folded or previously mounted. The usual recommendation is to lay a pressing cloth, such as a linen or terrycloth towel, on the work before pressing. I prefer terrycloth, because it's thicker and does a better job of cushioning the work. I also lay a terrycloth towel on the ironing board to further cushion the work and prevent crushing yarns or fibers. After sandwiching the piece facedown between the two towels, I use a steam iron to gently press out any wrinkles or creases in the background material. Use light pressure and a medium-hot iron. Try to avoid the actual needlework, if possible, and press only those areas of the background material that need it. Minor sags and bulges usually disappear when the piece is stretched and mounted.

Padding

Some people like to use padding behind needlework that is to be framed without glazing to give the piece a slightly puffy look. Padding also helps prevent sagging and eliminates minor bulges.

Although soft foam is available for such purposes, I don't recommend it, as it is short-lived and potentially damaging. It tends to become brittle or hardened with age and can even fuse to the mount board or, worse, to the backside of the background fabric.

A better choice is quilt batting, available at fabric shops and wherever quilting supplies are sold. Cut it to the same dimensions as the

To help align needlework, scribe centered horizontal and vertical guidelines on the backs of mount boards.

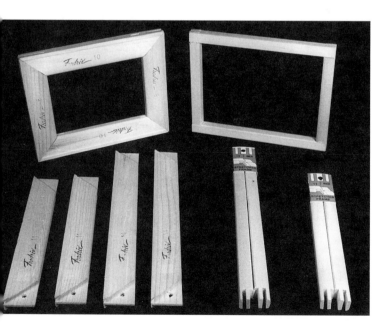

Stretcher bars are used for assembling stretcher frames, which can be used to mount needlework. Shown here are two styles of bars and frames.

mount board, and sandwich it between the background fabric and mount board during the mounting process.

Aligning

Some needlework pieces, such as counted cross-stitch, have very distinct horizontal and vertical lines that you should align with the mat's or frame's top, bottom, and sides. In others, the image might not be accurately aligned on the background fabric. In such cases, find the strongest and straightest horizontal or vertical line, and align it with the bottom or nearest side of the mat or frame.

Some free-form compositions might have no apparent horizontal or vertical lines. Position those so the lines in the weave of the background fabric match up horizontally and vertically with the top, bottom, and sides of the mat or frame.

To help align any piece of needlework, I like to have reference marks on the back of the mount board. Some framers recommend putting centered marks on the top, bottom, and side edges of the boards, but I prefer to scribe prominent vertical and horizontal guidelines, carefully centered on the back of the mount board.

NEEDLEWORK MOUNTING OPTIONS

Materials and techniques for mounting needlework are numerous. As with other kinds of artwork and photographs, you should avoid any materials and methods that are potentially harmful to the work. Before you mount and mat the work, it's best to ensure that the process will be reversible. You should also use acid-free or neutralized materials if possible. Anything acidic must be properly sealed.

You'll find many mounting materials suitable for needlework. You can mount it on stretcher frames, stretched artist's canvases, acid-free mount board, mat board, rag board, foamboard, and plastic-faced foamboards, such as Gatorfoam and codaFoam. Unsuitable materials include corrugated containerboard, chipboard, adhesive mount boards, and hardboard that hasn't been properly sealed.

Stretcher frames are made from stretcher bars or stretcher strips, usually made of select pine, poplar, or bass wood. Some bars are beaded, with mitered end laps; others are flat, with squared end laps. They're sold at art-supply outlets in pairs ranging in size from 8 to 50 inches, and you'll need two pairs for any frame. For example, for an 11 x 14-inch frame, you would buy a pair of 11-inch and a pair of 14-inch bars.

To mount needlework on a stretcher frame, you'll need a staple gun and staples; optional canvas pliers make the job easier. Most works are simply stretched around the stretcher frame and stapled along the edges of the frame. Start by centering and securing the work with one staple each in the center of the top, bottom, left, and right edges. Then stretch and staple the piece, working from each centered staple toward the corners.

Another similar method, the one to use for works to be displayed without frames, is to wrap the background fabric around the stretcher frame and staple it to the rear of the frame, instead of to the edge.

If you plan to pad the needlework and wish to use a stretcher frame, cut a piece of acid-free mat board to fit the stretcher frame, and staple it to the frame face. Then lay the padding on top and the needlework over that. Flat stretcher frames are better than the beaded type for this method. A simpler alternative is to use a stretched artist's canvas, which provides a reasonably rigid surface for the padding and needlework.

Much, if not most, needlework is mounted by wrapping it around the edges of the mount board, then securing it with one of a variety of techniques and an assortment of materials. Mount boards must exhibit a certain degree of rigidity to prevent their bowing under the tension of stretching. For that reason, the thicker, sturdier materials—such as needlepoint board, eight-ply mat board, 3/8-inch foamboard, Gatorfoam, and codaFoam—are often preferable. The type of material you select depends mainly on your personal preference and the method of mounting you choose.

After reading a fair amount on the subject of framing needlework and talking to several professional framers with experience in this area, I did some experimenting and settled on four methods and a few materials that should see to all my needs and certainly most, if not all, of yours. Following are step-by-step instructions that should take the mystery out of mounting needlework.

The Lacing Method

Of all the methods for mounting most kinds of needlework, this is probably the most widely recommended, and it seems to be the method of choice for mounting antique cross-stitch and other valuable pieces. It also happens to be one of the easiest techniques, requiring little in the way of materials. It's suitable for padded or unpadded works to be framed with or without glass. If you wish to mat the work, make sure you have enough border material to wrap around the back of the mount board while leaving sufficient face space for the mat.

You'll need an adequately sturdy piece of mount board made of eight-ply mat board, 3/8-inch foamboard, Gatorfoam, or codaFoam. You'll also need a spool of fairly heavy-duty thread, a ballpoint tapestry needle (size 20 or 22), and a supply of ballpoint ball-head pins. Cotton and linen threads are the most commonly recommended, but I like nylon, because it has just enough elasticity to make it easier to work with.

Step 1. After cutting the mount board to size with a heavy-duty utility knife and straightedge, turn it facedown on a working surface, and scribe centered horizontal and vertical guidelines on the back.

Step 2. Turn the mount board over, and lay the needlework on top, image up. Carefully position the needlework, and press a ball-head pin into the center of the top edge. Press another into the center bottom edge and two more into the centers of the left and right edges.

Step 3. Turn the pinned work facedown, and fold the top edge of the background fabric over the mount board. Starting at the top center and working from the center toward the corners,

The lacing method, Step 3.

The lacing method, Step 4.

The lacing method, Step 5.

stretch and pin the fabric about every inch or so for the entire length of that edge. Move to an adjacent edge, and pin the fabric there the same way; do likewise to pin the remaining edges.

Step 4. Thread the needle with several feet of thread. Starting at one corner, lace the thread straight across to the opposite edge of the fabric, then back to a spot about a half inch or so from the starting point. Continue lacing back and forth until two opposing sides have been secured. Then pull it just taut enough to keep the thread from sagging and tie it off. (Larger works may require several pieces of thread for lacing in one direction.)

Step 5. Rotate the piece and, starting at one corner, lace the remaining two edges of fabric together, creating a crosshatching of thread. Then remove the pins, and the piece is ready for framing.

The Edge-Pinning Method for Cross-Stitch
One of the best and simplest methods for most cross-stitch and other embroidery on Aida cloth, linen, and similar fabrics, the edge-pinning method calls for a supply of ball-head ballpoint pins (one pin per inch of edge) and twice as many stainless-steel ballpoint pins. You'll probably want a thimble, too, for pushing the straight pins into the mount board.

This method calls for some kind of foam-core board. Use either 1/4-inch or 3/8-inch foamboard or one of the plastic-faced foam-core boards.

Step 1. After cutting the mount board to size with a heavy-duty utility knife and straightedge, turn it facedown on a working surface, and scribe centered horizontal and vertical guidelines on the back.

Step 2. Turn the mount board over, and lay the needlework on top, image up. Carefully position the needlework, and press a ball-head pin into the center of the top edge. Press another into the center bottom edge and two more into the centers of the left and right edges.

Step 3. Turn the pinned work facedown, and fold the edges of the background fabric over the edge, toward each corner. Then, starting at the top edge, stretch the material and push a ball-head pin into the edge of the mount board about an inch from the center pin. Press in another about an inch from the other side of the center pin. Then continue pinning the same way until the top edge has been pinned from the center to each top corner.

Step 4. Rotate the work, and pin the edge of an adjacent side the same way. Where two pinned edges join at a corner, tuck and fold the excess background fabric into a diamond-shaped corner fold. Pin the other two edges the same way, making the corner folds at each remaining corner.

Step 5. Starting just left or right of any center-line and working toward the corners, stretch the fabric, and push stainless-steel ballpoint pins about halfway into the foam core, between the ball-head pins. After you pin one edge, use a thimble to push the straight pins all the way in, so the pin heads are flush with the fabric. Do likewise along the remaining edges.

Step 6. Once you have pinned the four edges, replace each ball-head pin, one at a time, with a straight pin, adjusting the work as necessary. When the needlework is properly positioned

The edge-pinning method, Step 4.

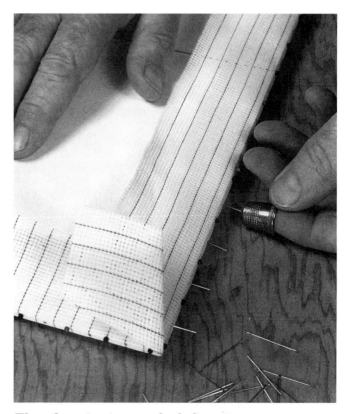

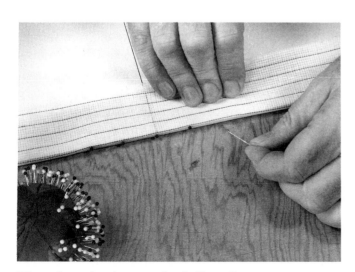

The edge-pinning method, Step 3.

The edge-pinning method, Step 5.

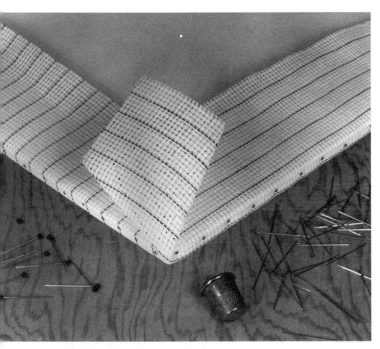

The edge-pinning method, Step 6.

and pinned to the mount board with straight pins about every half inch, the piece is ready for framing.

The Edge-Stapling Method for Needlepoint

Among the various methods for mounting needlepoint, one calls for the use of so-called

The edge-stapling method, Step 3.

needlepoint board: a thick, dense, sturdy board, particularly suited to edge stapling. For conservation mounting, you can substitute eight-ply acid-free mat board or rag board. You'll also need a supply of pushpins—about one per inch of mount-board edge. Instead of a staple gun, use an ordinary office-type stapler in the open position to drive staples straight in without crimping the staple ends.

I found the stapling process a bit tricky and troublesome. Often the stapler would move upward or downward, causing the staples to enter incompletely at an angle. I solved that problem by aligning the edge of the mount board with the edge of my work surface, providing a rigid platform for the stapler.

Step 1. After cutting the needlepoint board to size with a heavy-duty utility knife and straightedge, turn it facedown on a working surface, and scribe centered horizontal and vertical guidelines on the back.

Step 2. Turn the needlepoint board over, and lay the needlepoint on top, image up. Carefully position the needlepoint, and press a pushpin into the center of the top edge. Press another into the center bottom edge and two more into the centers of the left and right edges.

Step 3. Turn the pinned work facedown, and fold the edges of the background canvas over the edge, toward each corner. Starting at the top edge, stretch the canvas and press a pushpin into the edge of the needlepoint board about an inch from the center pin. Press in another about an inch from the other side of the center pushpin. Continue pinning in this way until the top edge has been pinned from the center to each top corner.

Step 4. Rotate the work, and pin the edge of an adjacent side the same way. Where two pinned edges join at a corner, tuck and fold the excess background canvas into a diamond-shaped corner fold. Pin the other two edges the same way, making the corner folds at each remaining corner.

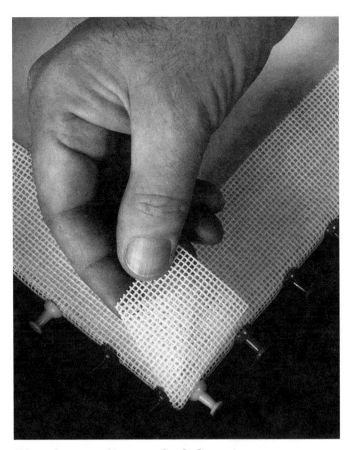

The edge-stapling method, Step 4.

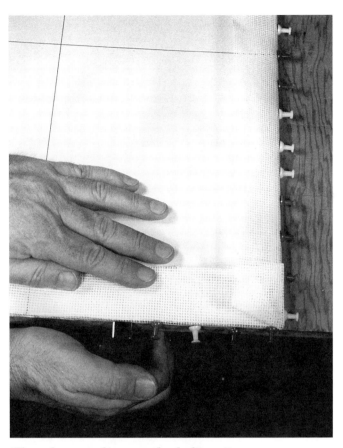

The edge-stapling method, Step 5.

Step 5. Align any edge of the needlepoint board with the edge of your workbench or work table, remove the center pushpin and the one on each side, and replace them with staples spaced approximately 1/4 inch or less apart. Continue replacing pushpins with staples, working from the center to the corners. Do likewise on the remaining three edges, and your needlepoint is ready for framing.

The Face-Stapling Method for Matted Needlework

With luck, we learn from our mistakes. Well, your luck is better than mine, because you can learn from my mistakes.

One of my earliest mounting and framing jobs was a piece of whimsical needlework my wife created, and I really botched it. That was nearly thirty years ago, and I didn't know much about framing. I knew even less about mounting needlework. I did almost everything wrong.

Edge-stapled needlepoint ready for framing.

I did know enough to measure the image size and determined that a standard-size 16 x 20-inch frame would do. I ordered a piece of non-glare glass, and cut a piece of mat board to the same dimensions. Hey, I wasn't totally stupid—not totally.

I didn't have the faintest idea how to mount the piece, so I just stretched it around the mat board and secured the edges with 2-inch-wide masking tape. The primitive mounting job at least held the piece in place, and to my youthful, untrained eye, it didn't look half-bad. In the various apartments and houses where we've lived, I've always hung it in a prominent place in a kitchen or dining room. Over the years, as I gained experience and a better-trained eye, the framed work began to grate on me. Eventually, my diplomatic wife said, "You know, I'm getting kind of tired of that old piece of needlework. Why don't we hang something else there?"

Well, you don't have to clobber me with a cast-iron skillet. I took the piece to my workshop and tore it apart, wondering if it was worth salvaging. It was easy to pull out the brads I had secured the work with, but because I hadn't bothered to use a backboard, the brads had rusted and stained the background fabric. In the absence of a dust seal, thirty years of dust invasion had made its way to the inside of the glass. No wonder it looked so dull.

You can use lighter fluid to remove masking- or other adhesive-tape residue from the edges of previously mounted needlework.

I decided to attempt cleaning the work myself, reasoning that I could always take it to a dry cleaner if I failed. To get rid of the sticky tape residue, I dampened a terrycloth towel with Ronsonol lighter fluid and carefully rubbed it away. It worked great. By the way, another product that does a good job of removing sticky stuff is called Goo Gone. It's available at hardware and department stores.

Thirty years of sunlight and artificial light had slightly darkened the exposed area of the background burlap, but that didn't bother me, because I intended to cover the margins with an attractive double mat. Likewise, the mats would also conceal the rust stains from the corroded brads.

I vacuumed the piece to remove dust and lint and pressed the edges of the work to remove the creases left by the original mounting job. It looked surprisingly good, so I set about mounting, matting, and framing it. When my wife saw the newly framed work, she couldn't believe it was the same piece, and she wanted it hung in the same place it had been occupying.

To duplicate my method for mounting and matting any piece of needlework, you'll need a piece of 3/8-inch foamboard, a supply of push-pins, and a stapler full of staples. My calculations indicated that the work had an image area of 15 x 19 inches. Allowing for 2 1/2-inch margins all around, I cut the mount board and both mats to standard outside dimensions of 20 x 24 inches. Then I cut an inner mat with 2 1/2-inch margins and an outer mat with 2 1/4-inch margins. I ordered a 20 x 24-inch piece of picture glass from the glass shop and a same-size metal-section frame from Graphik Dimensions, Ltd.

For similar jobs, here's how the mounting process goes:

Step 1. Use cropping corners and a yardstick or other measuring device to determine the image size of the work and the border widths of the mats. Keep a notebook handy to jot down all dimensions. Then cut mount board and mats to outside dimensions.

Face-stapling method, Step 1.

Step 2. Make light, centered pencil marks at the top, bottom, and side edges of the face of the mount board. Lay the needlework faceup on the mount board. Lay the inner mat on top of it, and carefully position the piece, aligning vertical and horizontal lines in the image with the sides, top, and bottom of the mat window.

Step 3. Press a pushpin into the top edge of the work—several rows of fabric inside the rough, cut edge. Press another pushpin into the bottom edge and two more into the left and right edges. Lightly stretch the work, and put a pushpin at each corner. Then lightly stretch the background fabric, and press in pushpins, about an inch apart, between the center and corner pins. Adjust and move the pins as necessary to evenly stretch the needlework.

Face-stapling method, Step 3.

Face-stapling method, Step 4.

Step 4. Lay a sheet of tissue paper on the image to protect it. Then, with the stapler in the open position, begin replacing the pushpins with staples, driven directly through the background material into the mount board. Place the staples about inch or so apart, adjusting the fabric as you proceed. Once the needlework is stretched and stapled in place, it's ready for matting, glazing, and framing.

TO GLAZE OR NOT TO GLAZE

Whether to glaze mounted needlework or frame it without glass is a matter of some conjecture. Some sources I've consulted leave the matter open, while others make recommendations one way or another without providing reasons for their suggestions. Still others ignore the topic altogether or offer contradictory advice. In a section on needlepoint projects, for example, one professional framer wrote, "When framing with a mat you may want to put a glass (glazing) on to keep the mat from damage. You can use glass as long as it does not touch the needlepoint—use a deep spacer." Later, on the same page, she wrote, "Needlepoint should not be glassed—if the customer insists, this method is great." Go figure.

My advice is simple: if you want to glaze any piece of needlework, do so; just follow the usual rules for glazing any work. You will need some space between the needlework and the inside of the glass, so either mat the work or use one of the spacer products, such as Framespace, sold for such purposes. Needlework is three-dimensional, so you will probably need two or more mats to provide adequate space. Consequently, whether you use mats or spacers, glaze with standard picture glass, not nonglare glass. Acrylic is a poor choice for glazing needlework because it attracts lint and dust.

Treat any piece of needlework you plan to frame without glass as you would any oil or acrylic painting. Use a liner or filet, or both, to separate the frame from the work for visual appeal. If the work is mounted on a stretcher frame or stretched canvas, secure it in the frame as you would any painting on canvas. Any piece mounted on a mount board can be secured with brads or glazing points.

A FEW TIPS ON FRAMING AND DISPLAYING NEEDLEWORK

Although many works mounted on sturdy mount boards require no backboards, most needlework does. Any work mounted according to the directions in the first three methods described above should have a backboard, cut to the same dimen-sions of the mount board and laid in place behind the mounted work. Brads or glazing points used to secure the work may eventually rust, staining the backboard instead of the background fabric.

In all but the driest climates, mildew is a threat to needlework, especially any framed behind glass. Proper framing, with adequate space allowed between the work and the glass, goes a long way toward preventing mildew problems, but so does careful display. Hang glazed needlework only on interior walls. Works hung on exterior walls, especially near entry doors and windows, are particularly susceptible to condensation on the inside of the glass and eventual mildew on the needlework.

For more information about framing and glazing, consult chapters 6 through 10.

CHAPTER FIVE

Advanced Matting Materials, Tools, and Techniques

Once you have mastered matting basics, it will be apparent that the possibilities for variations and creative twists are manifold. You will be limited only by your imagination and your tastes.

As I have recommended before, spend some time at galleries, examining what others are doing with mats. No doubt, some techniques will intrigue you and pique your interest, while others will scarcely catch your eye.

Although I am fairly liberal in my use of colors in matting jobs, I'm conservative with the techniques, mainly because I feel mats should complement the art, not overwhelm it or in any way distract the viewer. It would be unfair (if not downright silly) of me to insist that you follow my conservative example when making mats, or for that matter, my liberal bent in the selection of mat colors. I can't dictate tastes and preferences to you. What I can do, though, is offer suggestions, tell you why I do things a certain way, and why I don't do other things. But only you can make the ultimate decisions in any matting job—unless, of course, you're doing it for someone else who has specific requests.

Although the majority of mats I cut are simple rectangles, I do occasionally make mats with notches, cutouts, or special corner treatments. I also make oval mats, and I sometimes cover mats with various materials. So these are the topics I will cover in this chapter. They will serve you well. Master these techniques, learn from my mistakes, and you will be able to apply this knowledge to any mats you want to make, with the possible exception of intricately carved

and freehand-cut mats, which no amount of instruction will help you make. For those, you will simply have to create your own designs and practice until you achieve the effect you're after.

I don't make odd-shaped mats or mat windows because, at best, they're distracting. Some are just too ugly for words. I generally avoid square and round mats, because these formats are visually dull and almost always unnecessary. For similar reasons, I don't like mats, mat windows, or frames in the shape of equilateral hexagons and octagons.

I suppose the best advice I can offer is to think about every matting job and what you hope to accomplish with it. Consider how you might best display each work and how the mat or mats will serve those ends. And if you're occasionally overcome by whim or whimsy, ride it out. If you have a notion to do something unusual or unconventional, try it. If it doesn't work, all you will have lost is a little time and perhaps a few square feet of mat board. In the process, you might learn some important lessons.

MULTIPLE MATS

I'm a great fan of multiple mats, because they usually do the best possible job of setting off artworks or even something so personally mundane as a diploma or a certificate. A single mat can serve to confine or open an image, whichever your intention might be, and it can amplify a color or shade. Multiple mats can also provide a confining border or subtle openness, and they can combine two or more colors or shades that serve to prepare the viewer's eye for the work they contain. Or they can perform such a simple task as displaying school colors when matting a diploma, school-related certificate, or even school pictures.

Because I like what I can do with the border provided by the inner mat, I almost always use at least two mats these days, sometimes three. I rarely use more than three, and then only for special effects.

A general rule for determining exposed border width when using multiple mats is to vary the widths to avoid the visually boring stairstep effect. So if the exposed border of the innermost of three mats will be 1/4 inch, make sure the exposed border of the middle mat is wider or narrower: 1/8, 1/2, or 3/4 inch. Of course, the outer or third mat should be the widest of the three.

As with any rule, though, there are notable exceptions. Few things in art or nature are symmetrical, but when you do discover symmetry, you might wish to emphasize it by using interior mats with equal-sized borders. I have seen this done with symmetrical designs, and the effect works.

Whether the borders of the outermost mat should be equal on all sides or wider at the bottom is mainly a matter of choice. Sometimes the only way to find out is to cut the mats and see how you like the effect.

Most of the time, you will be able to pick the right colors or shades of mat board by checking the work with mat corners. And if you plan carefully and sketch the more complicated jobs, you will rarely go wrong. But when you do come onto that difficult work and don't like the results, all you have to do is try something else until you find the combination that suits you and the artwork.

I earlier warned against using more than one heavily textured mat in any job. Sometimes, because of availability or color, you might have to use a lightly textured mat with one more heavily textured. In such cases, or when I'm using a textured mat with smooth-surfaced mats, I try to put the textured mat or the most highly textured mat on the outside. Not only is the outer mat most visible and therefore the most suitable position to show off texture, but textured mats hide overcuts better than smooth mats do.

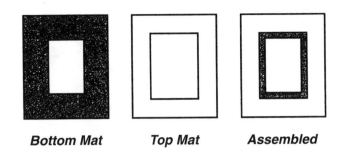

Bottom Mat   **Top Mat**   **Assembled**

Assembling a double mat.

Arrangement of color in multiple mats is also important. The darkest and most saturated colors can overwhelm works if they're used as outer mats. On the other hand, they can be the perfect arresting touch as narrow-bordered inner mats. Conversely, lighter colors and pastel shades usually work best as outer mats.

NOTCHED AND CUTOUT MATS

Notches and cutouts are two of the simplest and most frequently employed variations on conventional matting. A notched mat has a cutaway section, usually centered along the bottom edge of the mat window for the purpose of highlighting a work's title. A cutout is simply an extra, smaller window cut into the mat border for displaying something related to the artwork.

Notched mats are most often used with limited-edition, titled prints. Generally, such prints have portions of the print margins exposed to show the artist's signature and the print number. A notch is then cut into the bottom edge of the window, slightly larger than the print's title.

Cutouts are most often used to display the artwork and another item within the same mat and frame. Wildlife-art prints and stamps are usually displayed this way: for example, the federal duck stamp issued each year in the United States and prints made of the painting the stamp is based on. Some wildlife conservation associations have copied the U.S. government and issued stamps and limited-edition prints as a way of raising funds.

Another use for cutout mats is for displaying documents and related three-dimensional items.

The three mats used with this limited-edition print are notched to show the print's title.

I have seen citations and medals displayed in separate windows in the same mat, and the effect is pleasing. A diploma matted with a small window cut into the mat's bottom border for a Phi Beta Kappa key or similar item is a nice touch.

There seems to be no end to the variety of uses for notches and cutouts. I recently visited a gallery and saw notched mats I didn't like and then attended an exhibit where I saw an unusual cutout mat I liked very much.

At the gallery were some remarqued, limited-edition prints by my favorite marine artist. The matting and framing jobs were flawless, but notches were cut into the lower left edges of the mat windows to display the remarques. Normally, the framer simply exposes enough print-border area to show off the remarque in a conventional rectangular mat window. I did not care for the effect of the off-center notch.

A friend of mine felt just the opposite. He said the remarque notch was striking, that it immediately drew his attention to the remarque. I disliked it for precisely the same reason. To my way of thinking, a viewer's attention should be drawn first to the subject, not to some subordinate detail, such as signature, number, or remarque. But, as I have said before, that's just one person's opinion.

The unusual cutout mat that caught my eye had a large, horizontal rectangular window for displaying a fine print of a pair of ring-necked pheasants flushing in the foreground, while a stagecoach rumbled by in the background. On each side of the main mat window was a narrow vertical window cut the same height as the main window. Displayed in each was a slender cock-pheasant tail feather. Rather than distract me, the feathers seemed to draw me to the focal point of interest in the print.

When making cutout mats, you must consider the thickness of the item you will fit into the cutout. In the case of stamps or other similarly thin items, you can use single mats if you wish. But for other items, such as medals, you will probably have to build the depth by using multiple mats.

There are several materials suitable for mounting the various items in mat cutouts. Stamps should be mounted with stamp hinges, available at hobby shops. Other paper items can be similarly mounted or attached with any suitable adhesive.

The material you use to mount three-dimensional items will depend on the size and weight of the item and whether or not you want the process to be reversible. Epoxy cement will stick just about anything to anything else—permanently. I like the five-minute epoxy kits that consist of a tube of resin and a tube of hardener. It works fast and holds well. When I want something reversible, I use either silicone sealer or double-sided foam mounting tape. Hot-melt glue also works and is reversible with some materials.

CUTTING OCTAGONAL MATS

The simplest and easiest of the special corner treatments is the octagonal mat. By cutting off each corner diagonally, you end up with an eight-sided mat window instead of the conventional four-sided rectangle. Those extra sides can be as long or as short as you want them, provided that they don't obscure or crowd the work being matted.

You can make small (1/4 inch or 1/2 inch) diagonal cuts in almost any mat for an attractive variation on the traditional squared corners. This is particularly pleasing when done with multiple mats.

For practice, cut a piece of mat board to 8 x 10 inches; then follow these simple steps to cut an octagonal window.

Step 1. Lay the mat board facedown on the mat-cutting surface, set the guide bar at 1 3/4 inches, and scribe four guidelines for the rectangular window.

Step 2. Reset the guide bar at 2 3/4 inches, and scribe short marks across the top and bottom of each line scribed in Step 1.

Step 3. Align the guide bar or a straightedge with the marks scribed in Step 2, and scribe a line across each corner of the mat board, from one edge to another.

Step 4. Align the guide bar or straightedge 1/8 inch outside each line scribed in Step 3, and use the mat cutter to cut along the line.

Step 5. Now set the guide bar for cutting at 1 3/4 inches, and cut along the lines scribed in Step 1, between the diagonal corner lines, to complete your octagonal mat.

Octagonal mat window, Step 2.

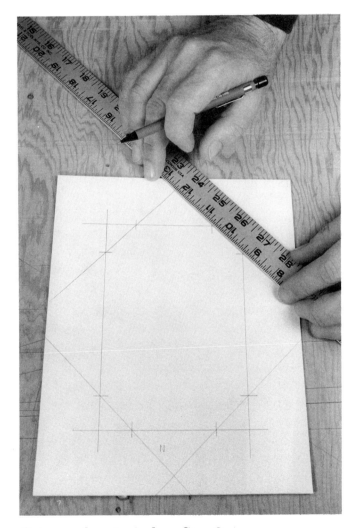

Octagonal mat window, Step 3.

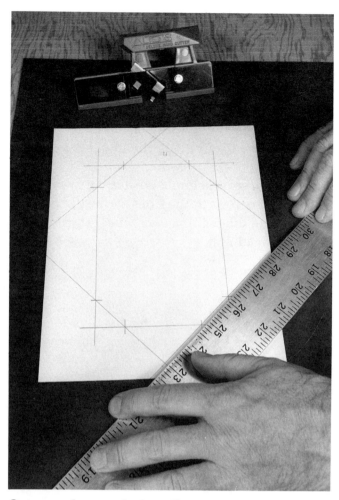

Octagonal mat window, Step 4.

Finished octagonal-window mats.

Zigzag-corner mats, Step 2.

CUTTING ZIGZAG-CORNER MATS

A zigzag corner is a smaller and simpler version of the stepped corner (see below) and can be used with most items suitable for matting. Vary dimensions and measurements to fit your needs, and use zigzag-corner mats wherever they seem to fit.

For purposes of demonstration, I picked a lithograph of a Bill O'Neill pen-and-ink drawing for its standard sizes. The image size is 12 x 18 inches, and the outside dimensions of the mount board and mats are 18 x 24 inches. I decided on three mats: black, white, and Bar Harbor Gray. Here's how to duplicate the steps I took to mat this work:

Step 1. Set the guide bar at 3$\frac{1}{8}$ inches, and scribe guidelines on the back of the inner mat 3$\frac{1}{8}$ inches from each edge.

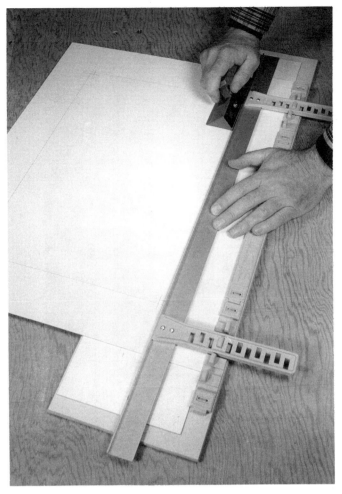

Zigzag-corner mats, Step 4.

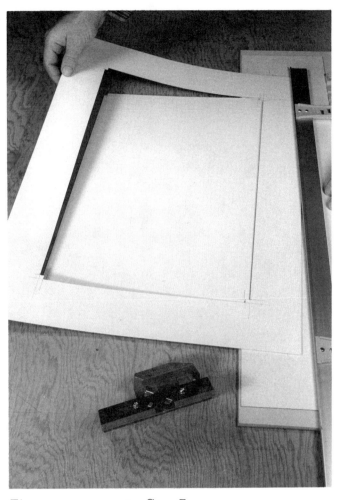

Zigzag-corner mats, Step 7.

Step 2. Move the guide bar to 3³/₈ inches, and scribe lines about 1 inch long across the top and bottom of and perpendicular to each line scribed in Step 1. These lines form the zigzag corners of the mat.

Step 3. With the guide bar set to cut at 3³/₈ inches, use the mat cutter to make the ¹/₄-inch cuts along the lines scribed in Step 2.

Step 4. Reset the guide bar to cut at 3¹/₈ inches, and make the four cuts to complete the zigzag-corner window in the inner mat.

Step 5. Reposition the guide bar at 2⁷/₈ inches, and scribe guidelines on the back of the middle mat at 2⁷/₈ inches from each edge.

Step 6. Move the guide bar to 3¹/₈ inches, and scribe zigzag-corner lines, as in Step 2.

Step 7. Now use the mat cutter and guide to cut the zigzag corners and complete the mat window as with the inner mat in Steps 3 and 4.

Step 8. Set the guide bar at 2³/₈ inches, and scribe guidelines on the back of the outer mat.

Step 9. Move the guide bar to 2⁵/₈ inches, and scribe zigzag-corner lines as you did with the first two mats.

Step 10. Then cut the zigzag-cornered mat window out of the outer mat, as you did with the other mats.

Finished zigzag-corner mats.

Stepped-corner mats, Step 2.

CUTTING STEPPED-CORNER MATS

Of the various special corner treatments, the stepped corner is my favorite and perhaps the most useful. Although it is a bit more complicated than the zigzag corner, it is easier than the notched corner.

To illustrate the techniques, I chose a limited-edition Don McMichael print of a square-rigged sailing vessel with an image size of roughly 11 x 15 inches, which allowed me to cut mount and mat boards to standard 16 x 20 inches. Here's how to cut stepped-corner mats for items of like size.

Step 1. Set the guide bar at 2⅝ inches, and scribe guidelines on the back of the inner mat 2⅝ inches from each edge.

Stepped-corner mats, Step 3.

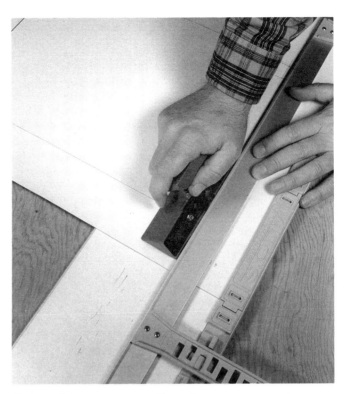

Stepped-corner mats, Step 6.

Step 2. Move the guide bar to 3¾ inches, and scribe lines about 1 inch long across the top and bottom of and perpendicular to each line scribed in Step 1.

Step 3. Reset the guide bar at 2¾ inches, and scribe lines top and bottom about 2 inches long, inside and parallel to the lines scribed in Step 1. These lines will form the stepped corners.

Step 4. Set the guide bar for cuts at 3¾ inches, and use the mat cutter to make the ⅛-inch cuts along the lines scribed in Step 2.

Step 5. Reset the guide bar for cuts at 2¾ inches, and cut along the stepped-corner lines scribed in Step 3.

Step 6. Then with the guide bar set for cuts at 2⅝ inches, make the final cuts to complete the stepped-corner inner mat.

Step 7. Set the guide bar at 2⅜ inches, and scribe guidelines on the back of the outer mat 2⅜ inches from each edge.

Step 8. Move the guide bar to 3½ inches, and scribe lines about an inch long across the top

Finished stepped-corner mats.

and bottom of and perpendicular to each line scribed in Step 7.

Step 9. With the guide bar set at 2¹/₂ inches, scribe stepped-corner lines, as in Step 3.

Step 10. Now use the mat cutter and guide to cut out the mat window as you did with the inner mat in Steps 4, 5, and 6.

Notched-corner mats, Step 2.

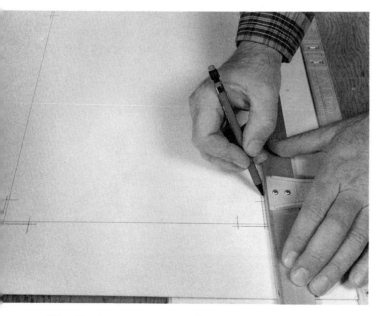

Notched-corner mats, Step 3.

CUTTING NOTCHED-CORNER MATS

Notched corners are less confining and more open than stepped corners and are the most suitable for active subjects. They're a little trickier than the corner treatments covered earlier, but the techniques are worth knowing.

I picked another McMichael limited-edition print to illustrate this matting job, one with an image size of roughly 11 x 14 inches, making it ideal for outside dimensions of 16 x 20 inches. Here's how to cut double mats for any similarly sized picture.

Step 1. Set the guide bar at 3 inches, and scribe guidelines on the back of the inner mat 3 inches from each edge.

Step 2. Reset the guide bar at 4 inches, and scribe lines about 1 inch long across the top and bottom of and perpendicular to each line scribed in Step 1.

Step 3. With the guide bar set at 2⁷/₈ inches, scribe lines top and bottom about 1¹/₂ inches long, parallel to the lines scribed in Step 1. These lines will form the corner notches you will cut out.

Step 4. Move the guide bar to 4¹/₈ inches, and make small marks at the top and bottom edges of the mat board on all four sides.

Step 5. The short cuts along the lines scribed in Step 2 should not be made with the guide bar on the cutting base, as this will create reversed bevels. Instead, lay a scrap strip of mat board on your bench and the mat board on top of it. Align the guide bar with the marks scribed in Step 4, and use the mat cutter to make the ¹/₈-inch cuts along the lines scribed in Step 2.

Step 6. Set the guide bar on the base for cuts at 2⁷/₈ inches, and use the mat cutter to cut along the outside-corner lines scribed in Step 3.

Step 7. Position the guide bar for cuts at 3 inches, and make the final cuts to complete the corner-notched inner mat.

Notched-corner mats, Step 4.

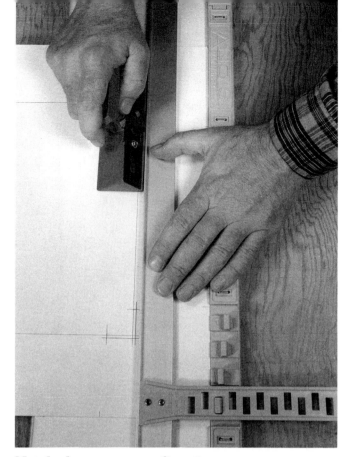

Notched-corner mats, Step 6.

Notched-corner mats, Step 5.

Notched-corner mats, Step 7.

Finished notched-corner mats.

Step 8. Set the guide bar at 2³/4 inches, and scribe guidelines on the back of the outer mat 2³/4 inches from each edge.

Step 9. Reset the guide bar at 4¹/4 inches, and scribe lines about 1 inch long across the top and bottom of and perpendicular to each line scribed in Step 8.

Step 10. With the guide bar set at 2⁵/8 inches, scribe lines top and bottom about 2 inches long, parallel to the lines scribed in Step 8.

Step 11. Move the guide bar to 4³/4 inches, and make small marks at the top and bottom edges of the mat board, on all four sides.

Step 12. Now cut out the corner-notched windows from the outer mat the same as you did with the inner mat in Steps 5, 6, and 7.

CUTTING OVAL-WINDOWED MATS

The oval is second only to the rectangle as a suitable format for matting. It is particularly useful with portraits and can be worked into multi-windowed mats with other oval and rectangular windows.

For high-speed production, there are expensive, pin-registered mat cutters ranging in price from about $800 to well over $1,000, but a person would have to need a tremendous quantity of oval mats to justify such an outlay.

Among the oval mat cutters more appropriate for use in the home or small framing shop, the best buy is, again, a product produced by Alto's EZ Mat. Alto's oval templates come in a kit that sells for about $65 and includes four oval templates and four spacers that enable you to cut twenty different sizes of ovals. The kit also comes with a Model 30 mat cutter and a template for drawing decorative lines and making French mats.

The No. 1 oval template produces a 3 x 4¹/2-inch window in a 5 x 7-inch mat board and is for use with 3¹/2 x 5-inch prints. The No. 2 template is for 5 x 7-inch prints and makes a 4¹/2 x 6¹/2-inch window in an 8 x 10-inch mat board. With the No. 3 template, you can display an 8 x 10-inch print in a 7¹/2 x 9¹/2-inch window cut in an 11 x 14-inch mat board. And the largest template, No. 4., is for use with 11 x 14-inch prints;

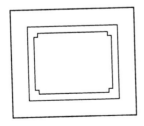
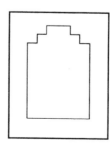
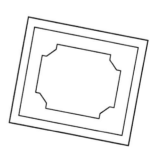

Three other mat possibilities.

it produces a 10½ x 13½-inch window in a 16 x 20-inch mat board.

Spacers, which attach instantly to the mat cutter, are 1/16, 1/8, 1/4, and 3/8 inch. With any of the spacers and any of the ovals, you can cut larger oval windows, either to accommodate larger images or to use with multiple mats.

When using these templates, you will work with the mat faceup, and you will need a scrap piece of mat board or poster board beneath any mat you are cutting.

Templates No. 1 and No. 2 are solid and should be centered on the mat board by eye or with the use of a steel tape or other rule. The two larger templates can be centered the same way or by use of layout lines. To prepare a mat for the No. 3 or No. 4 template, lay a straight-edge or yardstick diagonally across the face of the mat, from one corner to another, and scribe a line about 3 inches long near the center. Reposition the rule at the opposite site corners, and scribe an intersecting line to form an X.

Then, to cut an oval mat window, follow these easy steps.

Step 1. Lay the mat board faceup on a scrap of mat or poster board, and center the oval template on it. Push one of the template tacks into each hole in the template, and tap it into the mat board with the end of the mat cutter handle.

Step 2. Put the mat cutter against the template with two contact points touching the template's outside edge. Make sure the bottom of the cutter is parallel to the face of the mat board when the blade point touches the board.

Step 3. Keeping the contact points touching the template's edge, simultaneously push the cutter forward, downward, and against the template.

Step 4. Move the cutter counterclockwise along the template, making sure the rear of the cutter doesn't drift off the template edge. Cut in several sections. As you round the template, stop and turn the mat for the next section. You should be able to cut the oval out completely in three or four sections.

Alto's Oval Template Kit.

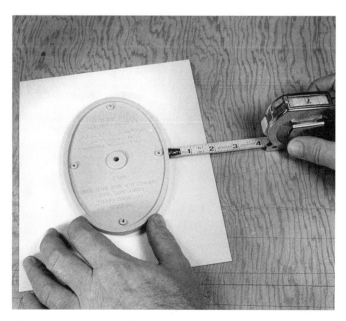

Use a steel tape rule to center the small templates.

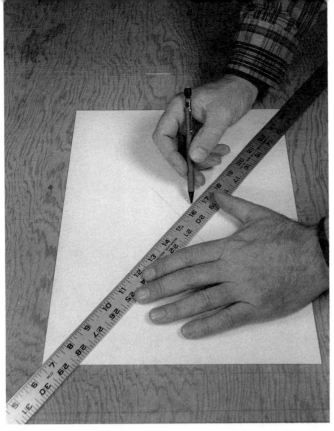

Scribe intersecting diagonal lines near the center of the mat for positioning the large templates.

Cutting oval-windowed mats, Step 4.

Cutting oval-windowed mats, Step 1.

When cutting double oval mats, cut the inner mat first, and use it to make guidelines on the outer mat for positioning the template.

The most important advice I can offer is to concentrate completely. If your mind drifts, so will the cutter, and you'll botch the job. The first time I tried cutting an oval mat window with one of Alto's templates, I did a near-perfect job. Then I got cocky about it and ruined my second attempt.

If you make a bad cut, don't discard the mat, as it is salvageable. Simply attach one of the spacers to the cutter, and make another, larger cut around the template. You'll end up with a mat you can use on another work with a slightly larger image area or one that will be part of a multiple-mat arrangement.

In addition to cutting oval mats, you can use these same templates to add curved accents to rectangular mats. You can give a rectangular mat an arched top or arched top and bottom. And you can also use sections of the templates to guide you in freehand cuts, if you're so inclined.

CUTTING CIRCLES, ARCS, AND OTHER CURVES

For the same reason I don't like square mat windows, I don't care for circular windows. Squares and circles are symmetrical and static, whereas each artwork, photograph, craft item, and other object we frame possesses an inherent tension that dictates a horizontal or vertical presentation inside a rectangular or oval window. Careful examination of any work intended for framing will usually indicate the artist's or artisan's intention and dictate the proper horizontal or vertical treatment. As I've said before, however, that's just one person's opinion. Consider it only a rule of thumb, and remember that you can break a rule when it suits your purposes or preferences. If you like circular windows, by all means, use them.

On the other hand, even if you avoid using mats with perfectly circular windows, don't overlook the usefulness of incorporating the graceful lines of arcs, scallops, and other semicircles into your rectangular, oval, and multiple-window mats. Using a variety of circular household items or tools specifically designed for cutting circles in mats, you can create curved corners,

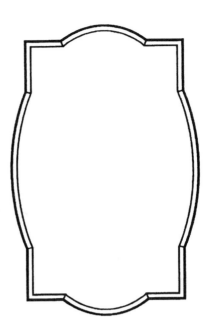

Here's one way an oval template can add interest to a rectangular mat window.

stepped arcs, cathedral mats, scalloped mats, and other designs you find interesting.

You can use oval templates with Alto's Model 30 mat cutter to create a variety of curves, arcs, and scallops. For more circular treatments, use cups, mugs, and bowls of various sizes as templates for cutting radii or semicircles.

Cutting Curved-Corner Mats

Use the following techniques to cut simple curved-corner mats of any size. For practice, cut a piece of mat board to 8 x 10 inches; then follow these simple steps to cut the curved-corner window.

Step 1. Lay the mat board facedown on the mat-cutting surface, set the guide bar at 1³/4 inches, and scribe four guidelines for a standard rectangular mat window.

Step 2. Reset the guide bar at 2³/4 inches, and scribe short marks across the top and bottom of each line scribed in Step 1.

Step 3. Set a coffee mug or similar circular item at one corner, aligned with the guide marks

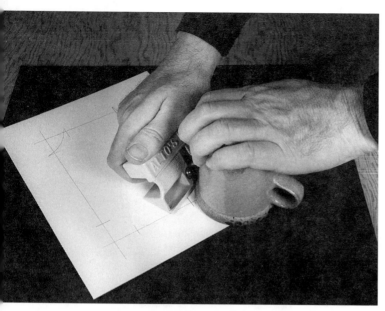

Cutting curved-corner mats, Step 5.

Alto's Model 360 Circle Cutter. PHOTO COURTESY OF ALTO'S EZ MAT.

Cutting curved-corner mats, Step 6.

scribed in Step 2. Then scribe an arc across the corner, from the horizontal guideline to the adjacent vertical guideline. Do the same at each remaining corner.

Step 4. Lay the mat facedown on a scrap piece of mat board or poster board. Set a coffee mug at one corner, aligned with or just outside of the arc scribed in Step 3. Press down firmly on the mug. Position the point of the cutter blade about 1/8 inch outside one of the Step 1 guidelines, and carefully press the blade into the mat board and the cutter toward the rim of the cup.

Step 5. With the cutter firmly against the cup rim, push the cutter along the arc, stopping the blade about 1/8 inch beyond the adjacent Step 1 guideline. Do the same at the other three corners.

Step 6. Set the guide bar at 1 3/4 inches, and cut along the guidelines scribed in Step 1, between the curved corner cuts, to complete your curved-corner mat.

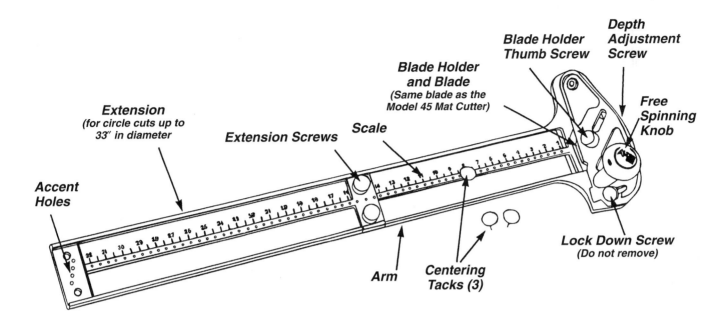

Parts of Alto's Model 360 Circle Cutter.

Using a Circle Cutter

A top-quality circle cutter greatly simplifies the job of cutting circular mat windows, arcs, scallops, and other curves. Alto's Model 360 Circle Cutter is a self-contained system with a cutter head that's similar to the Model 45 mat cutter and uses the same blades. With it, you can cut circles from 1 to 33 inches in diameter, as well as an assortment of arcs, scallops, and semicircular accents and decorations.

Like the Model 45 mat cutter, the Model 360 makes windows and other cuts with 45-degree bevels. Used in conjunction with Alto's Model 4501 Mat Cutting System, the circle cutter greatly expands your mat-cutting and decorating capabilities. The Model 360 sells for about $65 through framing-supply outlets or directly from Alto's EZ Mat (see the Source Directory).

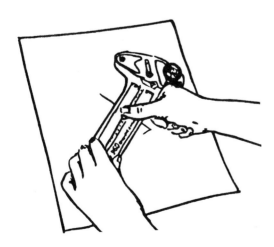

To use the Model 360 Circle Cutter, press the centering tack into the center of the faceup mat board.

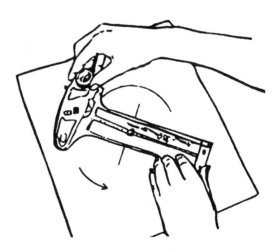

When using the Model 360 Circle Cutter, cut in a counterclockwise direction.

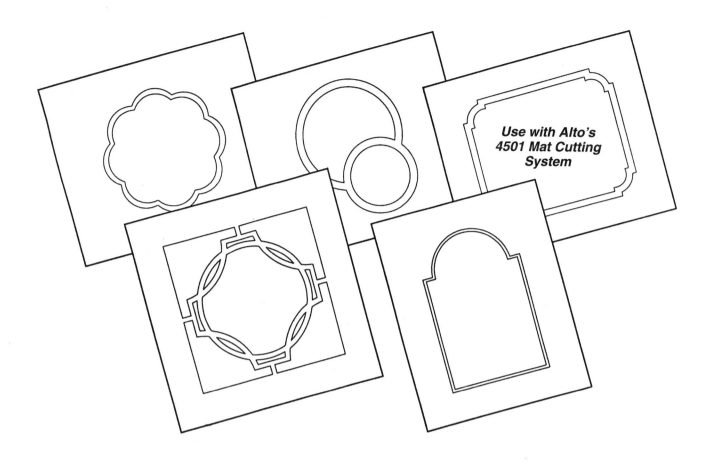

Use with Alto's
4501 Mat Cutting
System

Some of the combinations possible with Alto's Model 360 Circle Cutter and Model 4501 Mat Cutting System.

DECORATING MATS

Mat decoration is a personal endeavor that depends more on individual tastes than on any particular rules. There are various materials and methods for decorating mats, and the decorations range from simple lines or corner brackets to elaborate carvings and cutouts.

The French mat is perhaps the most commonly used decorated mat. In such a mat, lines are used to provide extra borders to set off the matted image. The simplest French mat will have a single line running parallel to the edges of the mat window. More elaborate French mats will display several lines of various widths, and areas between one set of lines might be colored, shaded, or gilded.

Colored or shaded areas are often filled in with watercolor or ink washes. Felt markers can be used, as long as their colors are permanent. Whether you apply color with a brush or marker, there is a chance of running over the guidelines, so apply the color or shading before laying down final lines that will conceal any minor errors.

The French mat is not as popular as it once was, perhaps because of all the easier alternatives, such as using colored or black-cored mats, for achieving similar effects. In its simplest form, however, the French mat is still an attractive way to display some photographs and artworks, particular black-and-white works.

India ink or drawing ink is best for scribing narrow lines on a mat. You can use drafting pens or ballpoint India-ink pens that come with points of different diameters or gauges. For wider lines, graphic tape is best.

Once you have decided how many lines you want and where you want to place them, use a mat-cutter guide or straightedge to scribe light pencil lines on the mat face. If you're using a straightedge, the Boyne Mat Corner Marker can speed things up.

Use an art-gum eraser, kneaded eraser, or draftsman's film eraser to remove pencil lines extending beyond the corners. Then lay down ink lines with pens and an inking ruler to avoid smearing.

Graphic tape, also called graphic-art tape or border tape, comes in a variety of widths and configurations and several colors. Although you might occasionally find uses for the green, yellow, blue, or red tapes, matte black will prove the most useful for white and gray mats. White tape can add a striking touch to a black or gray mat.

Scribing French lines with India-ink ballpoint pen and inking ruler.

Using the Boyne Mat Corner Marker to scribe guidelines.

Scribing guidelines with Alto's mat-cutting guide.

Use an X-Acto knife to miter cut graphic tape at the corners.

Use the X-Acto blade point to lift the end of the tape after cutting it.

Of the various widths the tape comes in, I find 1/32, 1/16, 1/8, and 1/4 inch the most useful for decorating mats.

To use graphic tape, prepare the mat with pencil guidelines, as you would if you were inking the lines. Start the tape an inch or so beyond one corner, and lay it along the guideline just past the opposite corner. With an X-Acto knife angled at 45 degrees, miter cut the leading end of the tape; then do likewise at the other corner. Lay down subsequent tape lines the same way with miters at the corners.

If you cut oval mats with Alto's templates, you can use the special line guide to scribe lines around the oval mat. Scribe the lines either before you cut the mat window or after the cut but before you remove the cutout portion. Holes in the guide are spaced at 1/32-inch increments. The small holes are for pens and pencils, and larger holes for markers. To use, simply put the guide against the outer edge of the oval template, insert the pen or marker into the appropriate hole, and push the guide around the template while applying pressure toward the template. The guide works in either direction.

Companies that make transfer type that you apply to paper with a plastic burnishing tool also make transfer symbols, some of which are useful in decorating mats. You'll find this material at office-supply stores and wherever engineering and drafting supplies are sold. In department stores, check the hobby aisle or department where calligraphy pens and supplies are displayed.

Some framers decorate mats by coloring the mat bevels. Again, be sure to use permanent colors, such as watercolors, India ink, or permanent markers. Always test a scrap piece of mat board to make sure it will take ink or watercolors along the edges without feathering into the surface paper. If you want a black bevel, you can also use black-cored mat board.

Use a small camel-hair brush to apply watercolor or ink to the bevel, or carefully run a felt marker along the bevel. With felt markers, you will have to use a fine-pointed pen to fill in at the corners.

COVERING MATS

There are two primary reasons for covering mats. One is to achieve an effect that is impossible with currently available mat boards. The other is to salvage mats damaged in cutting, coloring, or inking. Don't discard mats with minor damage or surface blemishes; keep them and cover them with any of a number of suitable materials.

Among the many possible materials for covering mats, fabrics—such as burlap and linen—and leather-imitating vinyl are probably the most popular. Con-Tact brand self-adhesive plastic also works well, as it is repositionable, easy to keep clean, and available in a variety of patterns and colors. With most materials, you can use aerosol adhesive, adhesive mounting sheets, or self-adhesive mounting boards.

To cover a mat using an aerosol adhesive, such as 3M Super 77, first cover part of your

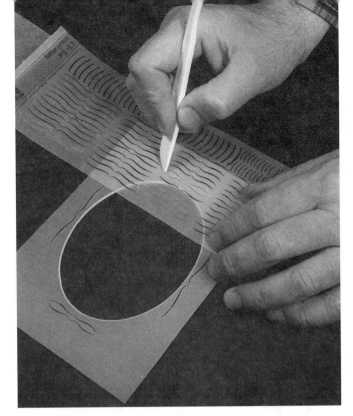

Decorating an oval mat with transfer-type brackets.

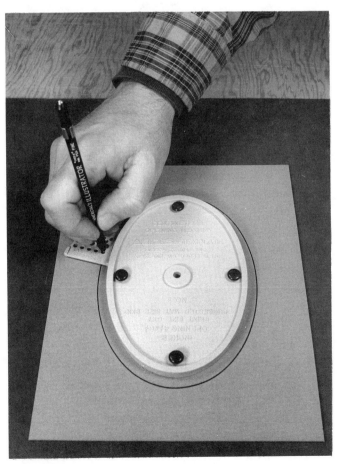

Using Alto's line guide and template to scribe a French line on an oval mat.

Inking the mat bevel with a permanent felt marker.

Mats covered with burlap, vinyl, and Con-Tact.

Covering mats, Step 2.

Covering mats, Step 1.

work surface with freezer paper and masking tape; then follow these steps.

Step 1. Use scissors to cut the covering material about an inch larger on all sides than the mat.

Step 2. Lay the mat faceup on the freezer paper, and apply a coat of adhesive to it. Let it "tack up" according to the manufacturer's directions.

Step 3. Lay the covering material facedown on the bench and the mat facedown on it. Press the mat to the covering material, and make a complete bond with the use of a roller.

Step 4. With a utility knife, make a short diagonal cut from each inside corner of the mat window toward the center. Then cut the center of

Covering mats, Step 3.

Covering mats, Step 5.

Covering mats, Step 4.

Covering mats, Step 7.

the material away to within 1/2 inch or so of the edges of the mat window.

Step 5. Use the utility knife to make a diagonal cut across each outside corner of the covering material to remove excess material down to the mat corner.

Step 6. Lay the mat and material facedown on clean freezer paper, apply a coat of adhesive to the back of the mat, and let stand until tacky.

Step 7. Pull the inner strips of covering material up and over the edges of the mat window, and press them into the mat back. Pull the outer strips up and over the outer edges of the mat, and press them to the mat back. Make sure all material is firmly pressed in place; then let stand until the adhesive cures.

Follow similar procedures to cover mats using adhesive mounting sheets or mounting boards. To cover a self-adhesive board, for example, first lay it facedown, and mark guidelines on the release paper with a permanent-ink pen. Then use a mat cutter and guide to cut out the mat window, turning the self-adhesive board into a mat.

Run a strip of double-sided tape or adhesive transfer tape across the top and bottom and along each side of the board face. Trim the covering material as required, and lay the mat facedown on it. Press the mat to the material to make the bond. Then cut the material as in Steps 4 and 5 above.

Peel the release paper from the back of the mat. Then pull the covering material up and over the mat and window edges, and press in place, as in Step 7 above.

The technique is a little different for covering a mat with Con-Tact sheeting. First, use a straightedge and utility knife to trim the edge of the sheeting to square it, so that at least two edges will square up with two edges of the mat. Unroll enough of the material to cover the mat with about an inch excess, and cut the sheeting with the straightedge and knife.

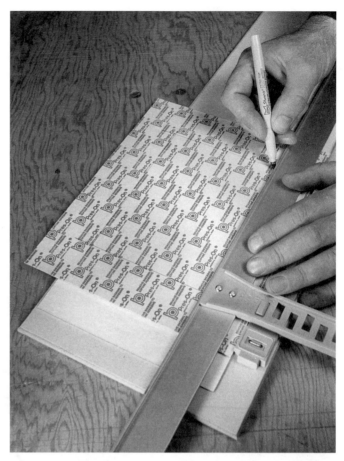

Mark guidelines on self-adhesive board with a permanent pen.

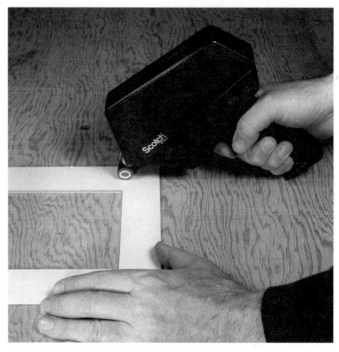

Apply transfer adhesive to the mat face.

Cut covering material slightly larger than the mat.

Cut away center and cut off the corners of the covering material.

Make diagonal cuts from the mat-window corners toward the center.

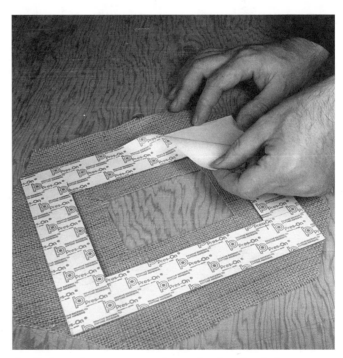

Peel the release paper from the back of the mat.

Press the inner edges of the covering material to the adhesive back of the mat.

Peel the release paper from the back of the sheeting, and carefully lay the adhesive plastic onto the mat, starting at one corner. Align the two squared edges and, working toward the opposite corners, press the material to the mat, repositioning as necessary.

When the Con-Tact is pressed to the mat with no wrinkles or bubbles, lay the mat face-down, and trim the excess along the mat edges with the straightedge and utility knife.

Make cuts in the center of the material as in Step 4 above, and pull the excess sheeting up and over the edges of the mat window and press them to the mat back.

With Con-Tact it is also possible to cover the face of a piece of mat board before doing any cutting. Then simply mark for and cut out the mat window as you normally would. The result is a covered mat with a bevel-cut window.

Covered mats can be used alone or in conjunction with other mats. Those covered with heavily textured materials or distinctly patterned Con-Tact usually look best with smooth-faced inner mats.

Press the outer edges of the covering material to the mat.

Square the cut edge of the Con-Tact with a straightedge and X-Acto knife.

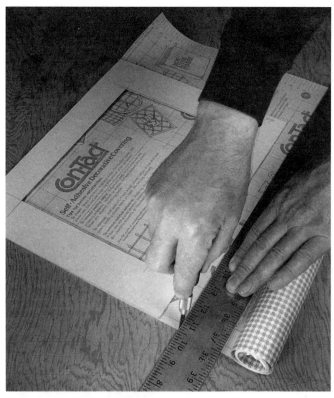

Cut the Con-Tact about an inch larger than the mat.

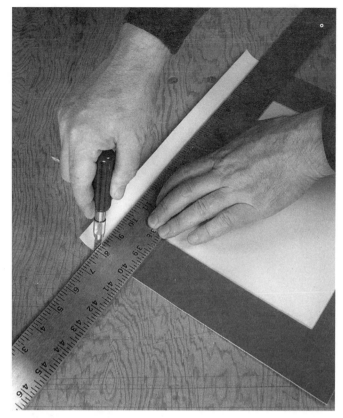

Trim away excess.

Peel the release paper away and press the Con-Tact to the mat face.

Make diagonal cuts from the corners of the mat windows.

VARIATIONS

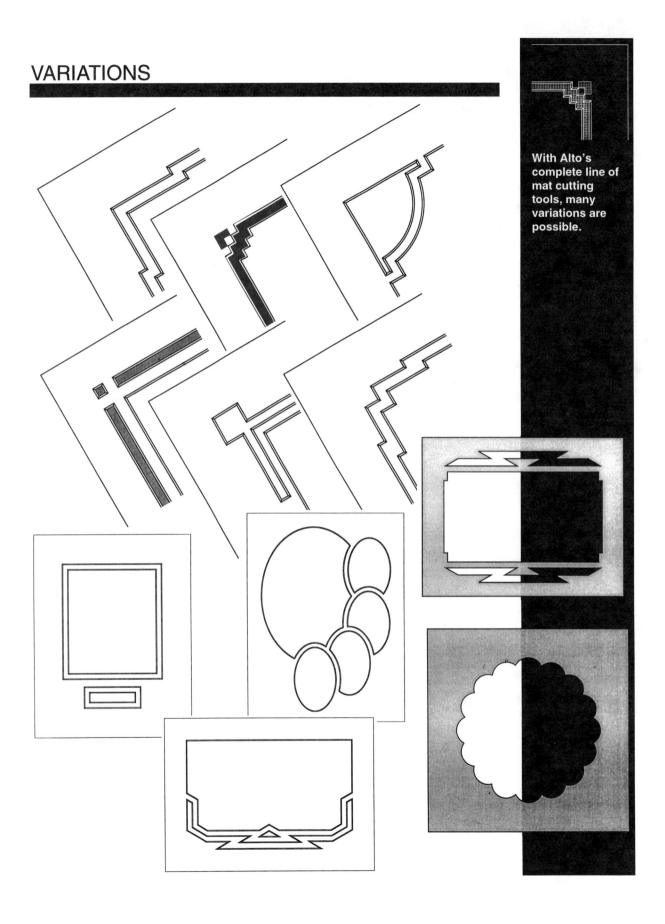

With Alto's complete line of mat cutting tools, many variations are possible.

Then cut away the center portion.

And press inner edges to the back of the mat.

FURTHER READING

Advanced matting topics are far too numerous and lengthy to exhaust in a single book chapter. So for more on the subject, I recommend you phone or write the folks at Alto's EZ Mat (see the Source Directory) to subscribe to that company's bimonthly newsletter, *Cut by Cut*, which offers innovative mat designs and plenty of practical information. There's some talk of eventually discontinuing the newsletter, but I'm told it will remain in publication for at least the next few years. A one-year subscription (6 issues) is $12.

The first thirteen issues of *Cut by Cut* have been bound into a book entitled *Creative Mat Designs: Design Collection #1*, which is available for about $20, plus shipping and handling.

CHAPTER SIX

Framing Materials and Tools

Although a great variety of materials are suitable and useful in building picture frames, the essential materials are few. Some are common and ordinary; others are specialized and peculiar to framing.

Likewise the tools of the trade. Some are so common as to be found in every workshop; others have been designed specifically for framing and aren't likely to be found outside the framer's shop. All of them, even the specialized tools, are easy to master.

ESSENTIAL MATERIALS

Picture-frame moldings come in an endless variety of widths, thicknesses, styles, and finishes. Although most are made of wood, metal moldings are also popular for a variety of applications, and acrylic or plastic moldings have found favor in some quarters.

Both finished and unfinished moldings are available at frame shops and at many artist-supply outlets and department stores. Many home-improvement centers and wood specialty shops also stock wooden moldings.

In addition to moldings made specifically for picture framing, many construction and decorative moldings are useful to framers, and these are commonly stocked at lumberyards and home-improvement centers. There, also, you will find the hardwood and softwood boards and strips from which you can make your own moldings. Unless there are certain cost or other advantages, or you're doing a lot of framing on a regular basis, there's no need to keep a large supply of frame molding on hand. Buying or making it as you need it allows you to pick the right molding for every job.

Of course, you will always have odds and ends of molding and other materials left from various projects, as I do. I also turn many of the wood scraps left from other building products into usable molding. And when I find good buys on moldings or woods I can make moldings from, I lay in a supply.

The fasteners I use most often in framing are brads, and I stock them in 3/4-, 1-, 1 1/4-, and 1 1/2-inch lengths.

For assembling frames and attaching dust seals, among other jobs, you will need white glue or good wood glue. I use Elmer's Professional Carpenter's Wood Glue. This is an aliphatic resin glue that bonds fast, dries clear, and cleans up with water. I watch for sales and buy this glue in quart sizes or larger and then refill an 8-ounce applicator bottle.

Sanding is time-consuming and tedious, so I try to avoid it. But there is always some sanding to do, so I keep 120-grit (medium) and 220-grit (fine) garnet paper on hand to see to most of my sanding needs. For special purposes, I sometimes use coarser and finer abrasives.

An abrasive sponge is good for getting into areas where sandpaper won't reach. I keep a fresh one handy that has a medium abrasive on one side and fine on the other.

I buy stains as I need them, and I always have plenty of leftovers on hand. If you purchase stains only for frames, you will probably want to get them in half-pint cans, unless you're doing a good bit of framing. A little stain goes a long way. What's more, buying in small quantities allows you to experiment with a variety of stains without having to lay out much money.

There are a number of acrylic sanding sealers on the market, but I don't like any of them for frames. Such sealers require light sanding before the application of any final finish. As I said, I try to avoid this boring task whenever I can. Moreover, even simple frames can be difficult to sand.

I seal most of my wooden frames with shellac, which seals very well, dries quickly, and requires no sanding. I usually follow that with a spray coat of satin-sheen polyurethane. When I want a semigloss finish, I use Deft Clear Wood Finish, which is a lacquer that seals and finishes simultaneously. It dries quickly, and two coats are enough for most jobs.

Although I always have shellac on hand, I don't buy it in large amounts because it doesn't store as well as other products. I do watch for sales on aerosol polyurethane and Deft lacquer and stock up on them whenever I can.

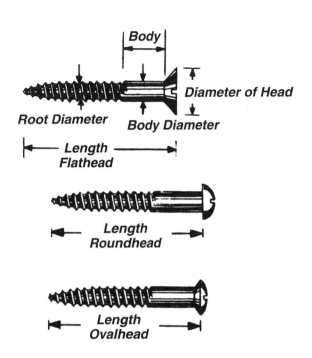

The screw styles used most often in framing projects are flathead, roundhead, and ovalhead.

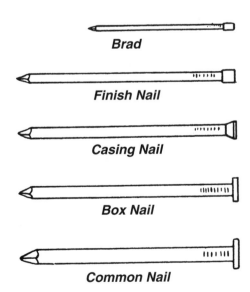

Brads and finish nails are the most common fasteners used in framing. (Other styles are shown for comparison.)

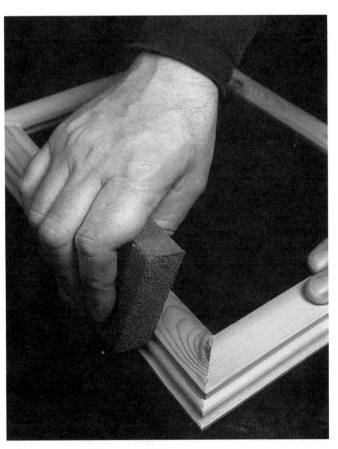

Abrasive sponge gets into frame contours.

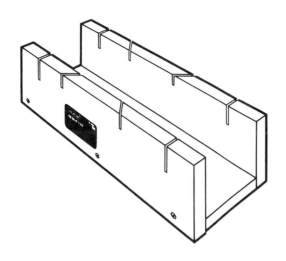

"Jorgensen" hardwood miter box is among the simplest and least expensive available.

The "Jorgensen" Model 63145 6-Angle Miter Box is an inexpensive option for the budget-minded framer.

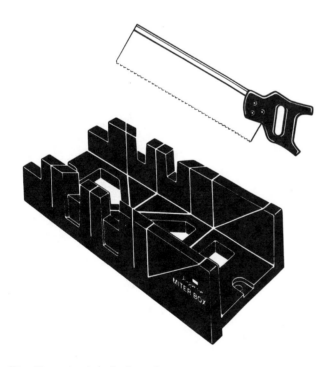

Similar to simple hardwood miter boxes is the "Jorgensen" Model 60115 Plastic Miter Box with a 14-inch backsaw.

Most of the glass I have on hand at any given time is for projects I'm working on or is leftover from earlier jobs. I normally buy glass as I need it and often have it cut to size at the glass shop. If you plan to do any production work in standard sizes, you can save money buying standard-sized glass by the carton.

Kraft paper is the material to use for dust seals. It is commonly available at frame shops and department stores in 30-inch-wide rolls. This is the width I use most, so I usually have a roll or two in my shop. When I need something wider, I buy it at a local frame shop.

Picture hangers regularly go on sale at department stores, so I stock up then and keep a good supply on hand. I buy picture wire by the spool, and I stock screw eyes in several sizes.

Those are the materials required for the craft of frame building. There are a good many others that are useful, either generally or specifically, and I will cover them in later chapters. For now, though, these are the ones you need to know about.

ESSENTIAL TOOLS

The most useful and essential tool in any framer's shop is a miter box. Used with a backsaw, this is the tool that enables you to make those frame-corner cuts at a 45-degree angle. With it, you can also make perfect right-angle cuts. A fully adjustable miter box allows you to cut any other angle in between.

Miter boxes come in a variety of sizes and designs and offer several options you should know about. The simplest are no more than three-sided wooden boxes with saw slits for making crosscuts and left and right miter cuts. This is the cheapest miter box available and is adequate for those who don't wish to invest much in framing tools or have only a little framing to do.

I would urge you, however, to buy the best miter box and backsaw you can afford. Examine what's available and determine which features are most important to you. In addition to wooden miter boxes, there are plastic models, metal ones, and those made of wood and metal.

Some boxes are adjustable, and the ones offering locking stops at the most-used settings are best. My first adjustable box could be set for cuts at any angle between zero (crosscut) and 45 degrees, but it had no positive stops. Consequently, it was not only common for me to be

just slightly off on a cut, but the tool was also impossible to fine tune.

The Sears Craftsman box I have owned for years is a large-capacity metal box, fully adjustable, with locking stops. Perhaps most important, the design offers me the ability to adjust and fine tune the tool for perfect cuts every time. When, from extensive use, the tool starts making inaccurate cuts, I spend a few minutes with a screwdriver and a square making the necessary adjustments, and soon it's operating like a new miter box.

This box accepts 9-inch-wide material for crosscutting and miter cuts material up to 6 inches wide, which means it easily handles all frame moldings with room to spare.

I use a fine-tooth, 26-inch backsaw with this miter box, which enables me to make quick,

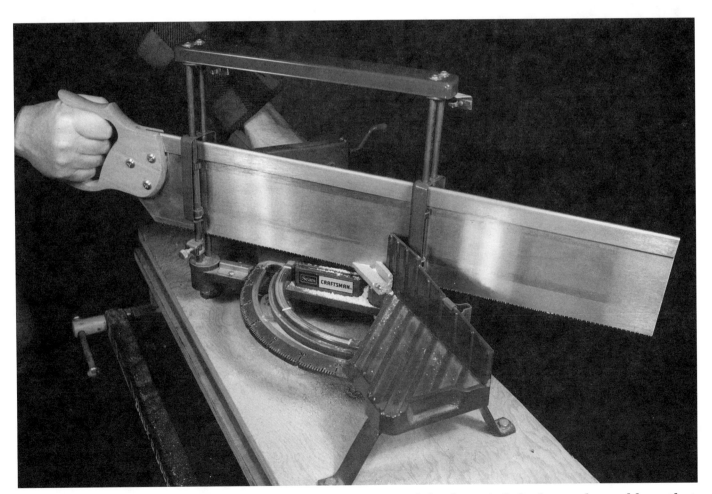

Author's adjustable miter box with locking stops and 26-inch backsaw is bolted to a plywood base that clamps into the jaws of a Black & Decker Workmate.

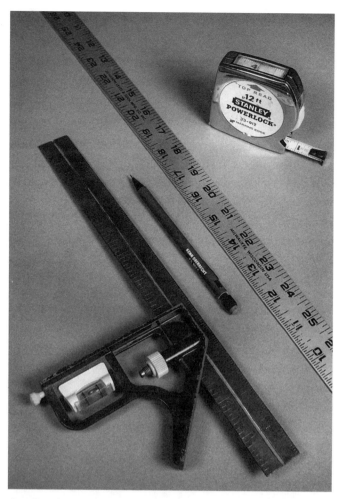

Author's most used measuring and marking tools: combination square, thin-lead pencil, yardstick, and steel tape rule.

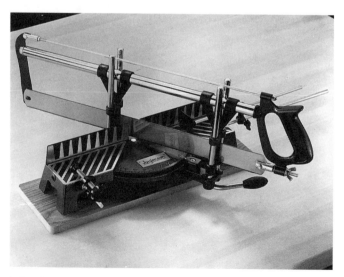

The "Jorgensen" Model 65016 Precision Miter Saw. Photo Courtesy of the Adjustable Clamp Company.

clean cuts in all wooden moldings. The saw rides in ball-bearing guides for smooth operation.

About a year ago, I decided to replace my miter box with a costly model that was advertised to provide all the features I was used to, plus the ability to cut compound miters. It turned out to be a poorly designed, expensive piece of junk that would not make an accurate cut and could not be fine tuned. I returned it and went back to using my old miter box, which I will probably use for years to come.

The simplest miter boxes are available for under $10, and you can pay over $100 for larger models with more features. Miter boxes comparable to the one I own are available for under $100, which includes the price of the backsaw.

If I were in the market for a new miter box today, I would probably buy one of the aluminum self-contained units with saw, clamp, and stops, such as the "Jorgensen" Model 64016 Precision Miter Saw, made by Adjustable Clamp Company. This superior tool features full adjustability and quick-locking settings at 22½, 30, 36, 45, and 90 degrees. The integral saw comes with a standard 14 TPI (teeth per inch) replaceable blade. Also available are an 18 TPI blade for finer cuts in wood and use with aluminum and plastic, as well as a 24 TPI blade that will handle aluminum and brass. The unit lists for about $50, although you'll probably find it for even less at Home Depot and other home-improvement centers and mail-order suppliers, such as Trend-Lines (see the Source Directory).

Measuring and marking instruments are important. I know that some framers like a folding rule as an all-purpose tool, but I prefer a steel tape rule. I also frequently use a yardstick, and mine is aluminum, which is easy to keep clean.

I also use a combination square for a variety of jobs. Most often, I use it to check other tools—miter box, miter saw, table saw, and bench sander—for accuracy. It's useful for measuring right-angle and 45-degree accuracy. It also does various other jobs in the framer's shop, such as serving as a depth gauge for checking cuts when making moldings.

Keep Your Blades Sharp

Just as dull utility-knife and mat-cutter blades do a poor job of cutting and can even be dangerous to use, dull saw blades are inefficient at best and hazardous at worst. Dull blades should be replaced or sharpened as soon as they begin requiring extra effort or showing other telltale signs of dulling.

You can buy saw-sharpening tools and learn how to use them and save a few bucks, but you might be time and money ahead by letting a professional see to the job. A search of the Yellow Pages of your phone directory should turn up the name of a local sharpener. You can also ask the folks at your favorite lumberyard or home-improvement center for a recommendation.

Several years ago, I noticed that I seemed to be working harder cutting molding with my miter box and backsaw. I just blamed it on advancing age, diminishing energy, hard wood, and any other notion that occurred to me and went on sawing and grunting my way through every job. Then it dawned on me that I'd been using that backsaw for more than ten years, had made thousands of cuts with it, and had never sharpened it.

That day, I dropped the old saw off at The Sharp Shop to have its teeth reset and sharpened. Two days later I picked up my saw and couldn't believe the bill the friendly gent handed me: $5.60. As soon as I got back to my shop, I clamped a piece of oak molding in my miter box and cut through it with nearly no effort at all, with a saw that was like new. Believe me, I won't let another year pass without having my favorite saw professionally sharpened. I recommend you do likewise with hand-tool and power-saw blades.

Find out what blades your local sharpener can renew for you and how much it will cost. Then make it a matter of routine maintenance to sharpen or replace any blade that's beginning to get dull. Remember, when you begin to feel that you just can't cut it anymore, maybe it's just a dull blade.

Forget about carpenter's pencils in the frame shop; their lead is too thick for the kind of accuracy you will require. For most of my work, I use a mechanical pencil with thin, soft lead.

Hammers are basic tools, which perhaps explains why they're so often taken for granted and misused. To many, a hammer is a hammer is a hammer, and any one will do. Consequently, we find every kind of hammer imaginable pressed into service in the making of picture frames. The cover of one framing book shows a ball-peen hammer lying next to some brads. Another has illustrations of frame making with a cross-peen hammer. Yet another shows a frame maker driving brads with a riveting hammer. None of these is a nail-driving hammer. Although the ball-peen is considered a general-duty hammer, it is a machinist's hammer and should not be used for driving nails, as its face does not have the proper toe-in for nail driving.

Although the bill-poster's or magnetic tack hammer is meant for driving tacks and small nails, it's not necessarily the best frame maker's hammer, even though it is widely used in this capacity. This is a light hammer, with a head weight of about 5 ounces, which is simply too light for many jobs. What's more, the head is narrow and tapered and will leave quite a dent in frame molding if you miss your mark. You can get into tight places with it, and for that reason some framers like the tack hammer for driving brads into the rear of frames to hold mounted artwork and backing in place. But there are better ways

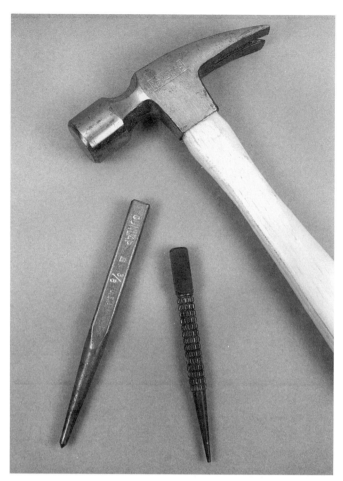

*Author's favorite Vaughan 10-ounce claw ham-
mer, center punch, and nail set.*

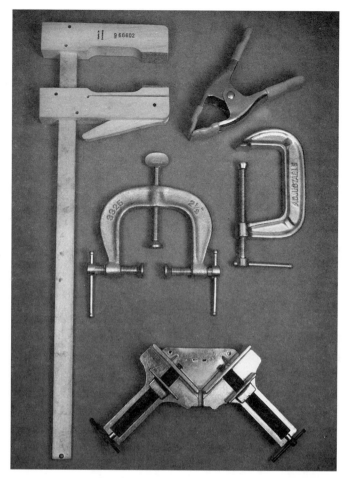

*The most useful clamps for framing projects: bar
clamp, spring clamp, edge clamp, C-clamp, and
corner clamp.*

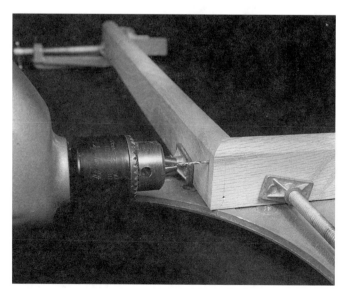

*You'll need an electric drill to make pilot holes in
hardwood frames.*

to do this, especially in hardwood frames, which I
will cover later.

The ideal nail-driving hammer is the claw
hammer, and you will find them with head weights
ranging from 7 to 28 ounces. A 16-ounce claw hammer is usually recommended as an all-purpose
woodworker's hammer, but you will probably want
something lighter for building picture frames.

For years, I owned a 5-ounce tack hammer
and a 16-ounce claw hammer and usually reached
for the latter when I was building picture frames.
The tack hammer was always too light for my
likes, and never felt quite right. While the claw
hammer felt better, it was a bit unwieldy at
times. So I went hammer shopping one day and
tried a number of small claw hammers. One that

Heavy-Duty Corner Clamps

Several manufacturers offer large, heavy-duty versions of the corner or angle clamp. Each has its special features, making it unique in some way. They all share the ability to take on big jobs and handle wide moldings. You should consider owning at least one such tool.

The Can-Do Clamp from MLCS, Ltd., could have as easily been called the "Clever Clamp" for all its nifty features. Its movable jaws with single screw and two swivel points allow it to clamp pieces of different dimensions for any kind of right-angle joinery. In use, the clamp provides ample space for drilling, screwing, and nailing. Oblong holes in its sturdy aluminum frame allow the clamp to be mounted to a workbench. Its big jaws easily handle thick molding and stock up to 2¾ inches wide, making this a top choice for framing jobs of all kinds.

From Wolfcraft comes the heavy-duty but lightweight Quick-Jaw 90° Clamp. This double-screw brute features a push-button release on each screw, which allows instant opening to the clamp's big 2½-inch capacity. Integral holes and slots allow the unit to be clamped to a workbench to function as a bench vise. Jaws are padded to protect wood and other materials from damage, without the use of clamp cushions.

For more information, consult the Source Directory.

WOLFCRAFT's Quick-Jaw 90° Clamp and the Can-Do Clamp from MLCS, Ltd.

felt perfect was a Vaughan 10-ounce No. 9 Little Pro, and it has proved ideal for me. So my advice to you is to do what I did: try a bunch of them, and buy the one that feels best. It will probably turn out to be the best for you.

Not only has the 10-ounce claw hammer proved an excellent choice for driving brads into both softwood and hardwood frame moldings, but it also has enough heft to drive a nail set, which is one of two punches I use in frame building. This is the tool to use for countersinking brad heads and for making pilot holes for screw eyes in softwood moldings. When I occasionally need to make drill-starter holes, I use a center punch.

You should have a pair of slip joint pliers for general duty. With one jaw padded, this tool is also useful for driving brads and for mounting sawtooth hangers on frames.

Long-nose pliers are good for holding tiny brads in places where your fingers won't fit. Most also have wire cutters in their jaws, which you will need for cutting picture wire.

If you will be making frames with hardwood moldings, you will also need an electric drill and bits ranging in size from 1/16 to 1/8 inch for drilling pilot holes for brads and screw eyes.

You will need at least one pair of C-clamps for general duty. They are handy for a variety of chores and come in sizes from about 1 to 6 inches or more. Three-inchers are probably about the best size for most jobs.

Corner clamps are essential, and you will want a set of four. These clamps, also known as miter clamps or picture-frame clamps, hold strips of miter-cut or crosscut molding at right angles for gluing and nailing. You will find them indispensable, and if you do much framing, you might want to invest in a second set.

Keep a damp sponge handy when you're doing any gluing. Damp sponges can damage whatever they rest on, so I installed a metal soap dish on the wall above my workbench, and that's where I keep mine.

HELPFUL BUT OPTIONAL TOOLS

So far, we have covered the tools that are essential to frame building. You *must* have those tools for making frames from manufactured moldings. There are other tools you might find useful in a variety of applications, and some that are essential for making your own moldings. Others simply make framing easier, faster, cheaper, or all three.

Some unfinished manufactured frame moldings and some you can make yourself require sanding. A pad sander will speed up that process. If you own a stationary or bench-type belt and disc sander, you might find that another useful tool, but there's no need to rush out and buy one. Some framers deliberately overcut

Band Clamps for Odd Jobs and More

Band clamps come in a variety of sizes and configurations to handle a wide assortment of framing and other tasks. Most are useful in making unusual frames and holding odd shapes, but they will also secure rectangular frames for joinery. They're the ideal choice for making picture and collector frames with the use of a plate or biscuit joiner and wood biscuits.

An ingenious version from MLCS, Ltd., is the Merle Adjustable Clamp. It's like having an extra set of hands for gluing and clamping all manner of rectangular objects. Integral to the tool are 22 feet of retractable steel band attached to the clamp jaw and three corner saddles. When everything is in place, a twist of the screw handle pulls it all tight. Remove one corner saddle to clamp triangular frames. Remove two to clamp semicircular frames. Remove all the saddles, and the tool becomes a band clamp that conforms to hexagonal, octagonal, and other irregular-shaped frames.

Wolfcraft offers a similar but lighter-duty model that features 13 feet of inch-wide nylon-web belt attached to the clamp's jaw and three removable plastic jaws. Quick-release levers on the clamp's frame allow fast belt feed and adjustment. The unit tightens with a turn of the single hand screw.

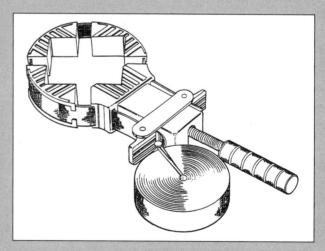

Wolfcraft's Quick Adjust Band Clamp handles a variety of framing jobs.

The Delta 4" Belt/6" Disc Sander is a good choice for the picture framer. PHOTO COURTESY OF DELTA INTERNATIONAL MACHINERY CORPORATION.

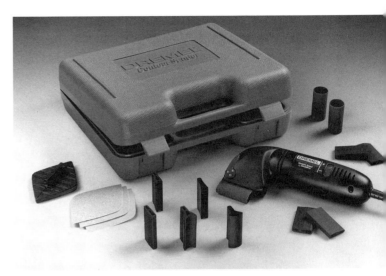

The Dremel Contour Sander Kit is ideal for sanding picture frames and moldings. PHOTO COURTESY OF DREMEL.

their frame pieces by 1/16 inch at each end, then sand them down to finished length on a sanding disc while holding the molding in place with a miter gauge. This makes for clean, precise joints.

Detail and contour sanders are good for reaching the often tight and intricate confines of wood frames and moldings. Ryobi, Sears, and other tool manufacturers offer detail sanders. Dremel makes a fine little contour sander that will see to most frame-sanding chores. Wolfcraft offers an inexpensive kit for converting a quarter-sheet palm sander into a detail sander.

If you plan to produce frames in quantity, you might want to invest in an electric brad nailer. There's nothing faster for driving brads, which come in various sizes and colors to match many frame finishes. The one I own drives and countersinks a 1-inch or 1½-inch brad at the touch of a trigger.

The development of plate or biscuit joiners is one of the most interesting innovations of the past decade or so. Like so many power tools, early models were relatively expensive and found mainly in professional cabinet and woodworking shops, where they revolutionized wood joinery techniques. Since their introduction, however, designs have improved, prices have

Black & Decker half-sheet pad sander.

Black & Decker quarter-sheet palm or pad sander.

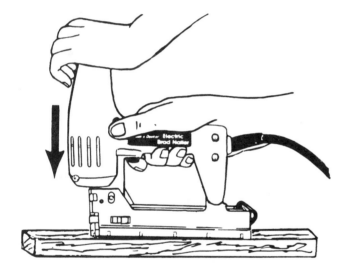

An electric brad nailer drives and countersinks a brad at the touch of the trigger.

Wolfcraft's "Biscuit" Wood Joiner Kit and Ryobi's Detail Biscuit Joiner.

come down, and their popularity has soared among professionals and do-it-yourselfers alike. Some models are available for under $100.

All the major manufacturers and importers of portable power tools now offer biscuit joiners. Some, including Sears, offer kits for converting a router into a biscuit joiner. Wolfcraft has a Biscuit Wood Joiner Kit that converts a 4-, 4½-, or 5-inch angle grinder into a biscuit joiner that's more the shape and heft of the standard tools and, for some applications, easier to handle than a converted router.

A plate or biscuit joiner is a fairly uncomplicated tool fitted with a small, horizontal, circular blade that cuts a semicircular slot into the edge or surface of wood strips, boards, or plywood. To make any joint, simply mark the pieces

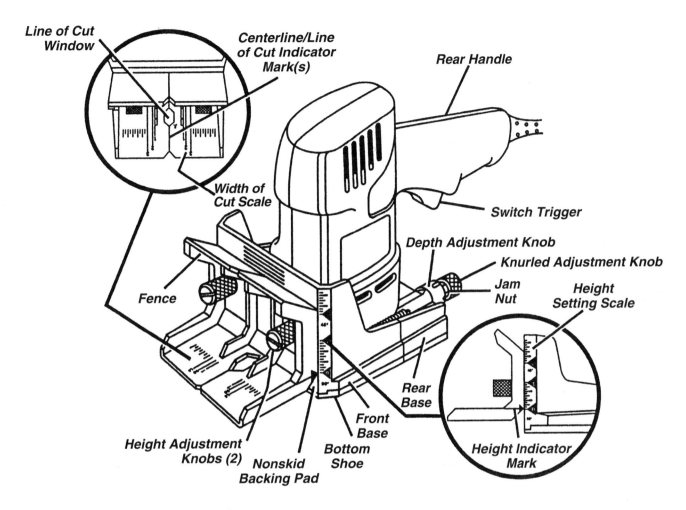

Parts of the Ryobi Detail Biscuit Joiner.

to be joined, and cut an identical slot in each by aligning the tool with the guide marks. Then apply glue to the slots and surfaces to be joined; insert one of the football-shaped, flat wood plates or biscuits into a slot; press the mating piece in place; and clamp if necessary. When in contact with water-based adhesives, such as white glue or carpenter's wood glue, the biscuits begin swelling within minutes. The resulting splined joint is one of the strongest joints possible, and it couldn't be easier to make. Even the inherently weak miter joint achieves superior strength with such tools and techniques.

The value of biscuit joinery to the picture framer should be obvious. What might not be so obvious, however, is that standard-size joiners and biscuits are too big for some framing jobs.

The #0 or smallest standard-size biscuit is 1¾ inches long, so it is useful only with 2-inch or deeper box-style and similar moldings or flat moldings of 2-inch or greater depth. The #10 and #20 biscuits, at 2⅛ and 2⅜ inches, respectively, can be used only with moldings and other wood products exceeding those depths or widths. Nevertheless, wherever they fit, standard biscuit joiners make frame joinery a breeze.

When it comes to smaller moldings, it's Ryobi to the rescue, with its great little Detail Biscuit Joiner. This one cuts slots for tiny biscuits in three sizes, one of which will prove suitable for nearly any frame or liner molding you use. Size R1, R2, and R3 biscuits are only ⅝, ¾, and 1 inch long, respectively, making them ideal for most picture-framing applications. This

A Delta 10″ Table Saw is a good choice for rip-
ping wide stock into narrow strips and making
picture-frame molding. PHOTO COURTESY OF DELTA INTER-
NATIONAL MACHINERY CORPORATION.

The Delta Deluxe 10″ Radial Saw is a superb
tool for ripping stock up to 24 inches wide and
for miter cutting frame sections. PHOTO COURTESY OF
DELTA INTERNATIONAL MACHINERY CORPORATION.

dandy little tool is easy to wield and sells for about $70. I heartily recommend it to anyone who has frames to build.

Some style of stationary or bench-type saw is a valuable asset in any workshop and is worth considering as a frame-making tool. There's an age-old argument over which is the best to buy—a table saw or radial-arm saw. If you already own one or the other, then that's the best one. If you're shopping for one, you must consider how you will use it.

I wrestled with this same problem several years ago and ultimately decided that my first stationary saw should be a table saw, because I was finishing a house we had just built and doing a lot of work with paneling and other sheet stock. I was also going to work on a book of plywood projects, so I needed the wide ripping

ability offered by the table saw. I never regretted my decision, and the table saw turned out to be valuable on many other projects, including making frame moldings.

If I were making the same decision today, however, and wanted a stationary saw mainly for frame-making craft, I think my vote would have to go for the radial-arm saw. Although this saw will not rip stock as wide as the table saw can handle, the materials moldings are made from aren't that wide. What's more, the radial-arm saw is a much better choice for crosscutting and miter cutting. With various attachments this saw can also do all sorts of decorative cuts. There are even heads available that convert a radial-arm saw into a shaper.

A power miter saw is another tool that can make short work of any framing job. It might

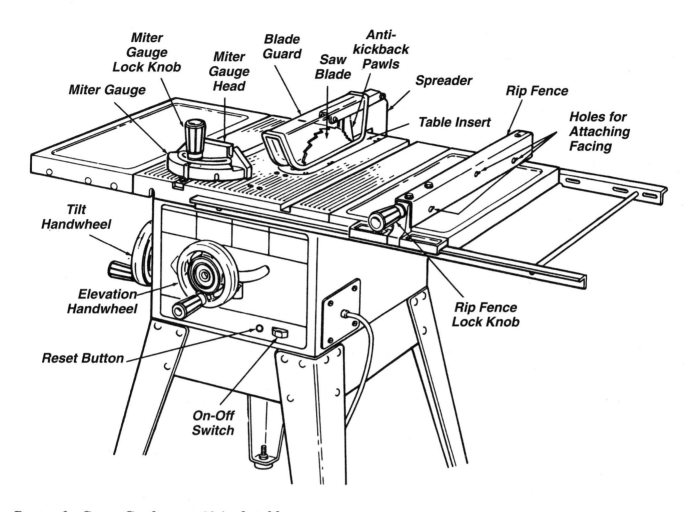

Miter Gauge Lock Knob

Miter Gauge Head

Blade Guard

Saw Blade

Anti-kickback Pawls

Spreader

Rip Fence

Miter Gauge

Holes for Attaching Facing

Table Insert

Tilt Handwheel

Elevation Handwheel

Reset Button

Rip Fence Lock Knob

On-Off Switch

Parts of a Sears Craftsman 10-inch table saw.

not be a tool you would want to consider if you already own or are planning to buy a radial-arm saw, because the latter can do everything the former does and more. But a power miter saw crosscuts and miter cuts frame molding, construction molding, and other wood strips every bit as well as a radial-arm saw and better than a table saw, because it handles long stock with ease. What's more, power miter saws are considerably cheaper than radial-arm or table saws.

Power miter saws have relatively small tables, which can make heavier stock and long strips of wood and molding difficult and potentially dangerous to handle. So you'll need some way to support such material beyond the miter-saw table. You can use any of the various adjustable roller stands made for such purposes or

invest in a portable miter-saw table or stand with integral extension arms. Some miter saws also come with extension arms or can be fitted with optional extensions.

Another option is to build your own miter-saw bench, which is what I did. I built a heavy-duty bench with sliding supports that extend left and right of the bench and support any material I want to cut. I also installed heavy-duty locking casters on the bench legs, which allow me to move the bench anywhere in my shop to accommodate long material.

If your budget doesn't allow you to get into power framing just yet, you can still do so if you own a portable circular saw. Such saws aren't accurate enough on their own for cutting frame molding, but with the right accessories, they can

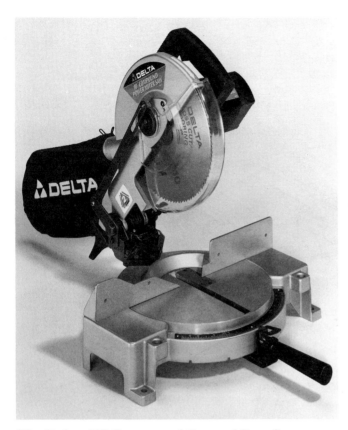

The Delta 10″ Compound Power Miter Saw. PHOTO COURTESY OF DELTA INTERNATIONAL MACHINERY CORPORATION.

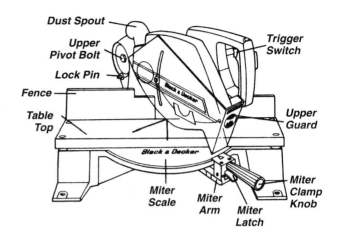

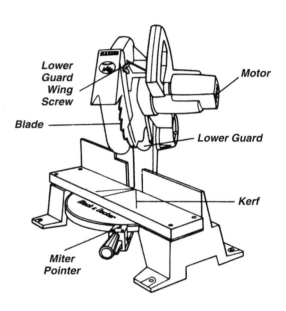

Parts of a power miter saw.

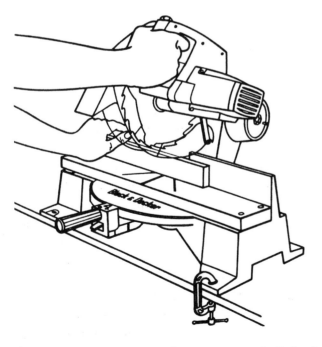

A power miter saw can be permanently bolted or temporarily clamped to a bench or other work surface.

be made wholly adequate to the task. Several products from TRIMTRAMP, Ltd., convert any portable circular saw into an extremely accurate tool, capable of cutting perfect miters.

The TRIMTRAMP Model 125 Three-Fence Miter Table, designed for do-it-yourselfers, can crosscut material up to 16 inches wide in a single pass and will cut miters, compound miters, bevels, and various angles. It easily sets up in minutes on a Workmate or other folding bench and hangs on a wall when not in use. It sells for about $160.

If you own or plan to own any of the power saws I've discussed, you should know that not

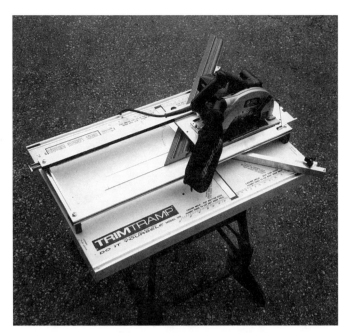

The TRIMTRAMP Model 125 converts a portable circular saw into an efficient tool for cutting frame molding. PHOTO COURTESY OF TRIMTRAMP, LTD.

Delta offers a large selection of carbide-tooth saw blades. PHOTO COURTESY OF DELTA INTERNATIONAL MACHINERY CORPORATION.

all blades are the same. Some are meant for fast cutting where smoothness of the cut is of little or no consequence. Others are designed for slower, finer cutting. You'll find blades designed specifically for ripping, others for crosscutting, and so-called combination blades that do a passable job of both chores. Generally, the fewer teeth a blade has for its size, the faster and rougher it cuts. Conversely, the more teeth a blade has, the slower and finer it cuts.

For cutting frame molding, you'll want the finest-cutting and best-quality blades you can afford. Avoid general-purpose and combination types and any designed mainly for fast cutting. Look for those labeled Fine, Miter, Fine Miter, Trim, Finish, or Plywood.

Standard steel blades are the most economically priced, with 7¼-inch to 10-inch blades running from about $10 to $20. Blades with carbide teeth are usually more than twice the cost of steel blades, and premium carbide blades are more expensive yet. Carbide teeth stay sharp longer, and some carbide blades are specially ground and honed, so they come from the factory sharper than standard steel blades. Often the

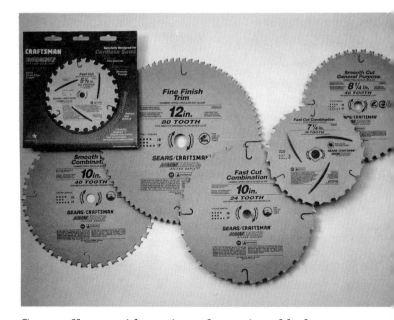

Sears offers a wide variety of premium blades to fit most power saws. PHOTO COURTESY OF SEARS.

Center piece of oak plywood was cut with a top-brand carbide-tipped saw blade (notice the splintered edge). Left and right pieces show entry and exit surfaces with a premium 10-inch, 80-tooth blade.

better carbide blades turn out to be cheaper in the long run than steel blades.

There are so many different makes and designs of blades available now that trying to find the right one or ones can boggle the mind. So spend time studying tool catalogs, buy the best blades you can afford, and keep them sharp and clean.

As power saws are used with wood and wood products, pitch, resin, and adhesives can build up and form a hard coating that dulls blades and causes them to overheat during operation and even warp. Acids deposited by some woods can actually attack the blade and tooth materials. So it's important to keep your blades clean. You'll find bit-and-blade cleaning solutions at home-improvement centers and mail-order suppliers. Easy Off and similar oven cleaners also work.

Although a shaper is an invaluable tool in the professional woodworking shop, where it can turn strips of wood into molding about as fast as they can be fed into the machine, modern routers and router tables have all but replaced them in the home workshop, home-based frame shop, and small picture-framing business. Today's powerful routers are electronic and mechanical marvels that see to an unbelievable range of workshop chores. With top-quality bits available in dozens of useful profiles, routers can turn strips of hardwood and softwood into every kind of molding imaginable. Used with a precision-made, full-featured bench-style or floor-model router table, a router becomes one of the most useful tools in the picture framer's workshop. In 1997, Sears introduced a new line of

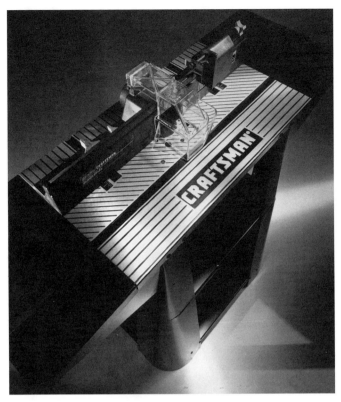

Craftsman Industrial Router Table will see to any picture framer's needs. PHOTO COURTESY OF SEARS.

The Craftsman lineup of 1/4-inch-shank routers includes models with 1 1/2, 1 3/4, and 2 horsepower. PHOTO COURTESY OF SEARS.

router tables that, coupled with one of the Craftsman 1/4-inch-shank consumer routers or 1/2-inch-shank industrial-rated routers, has something to fit everyone's needs.

For the small home workshop and do-it-yourself picture framer, Craftsman Benchtop and Deluxe Benchtop router tables are easy on the budget, at about $45 and $65, respectively. The framer interested in high-quantity molding production can't go wrong with a Craftsman Industrial Router Table—either the benchtop model or the stationary table with stand. These units are loaded with professional features any framer will appreciate. The benchtop model sells for about $120 and the stationary model for about $170.

If you already own a router, you'll be pleased to know that these tables, with the addition of an adapter plate, will accept all models. If you're shopping for a router and watching your budget, take a look at the Craftsman 1 1/2-, 1 3/4-, or 2-horsepower 1/4-inch-shank routers, with prices ranging from less than $60 to just under $100. It's possible for

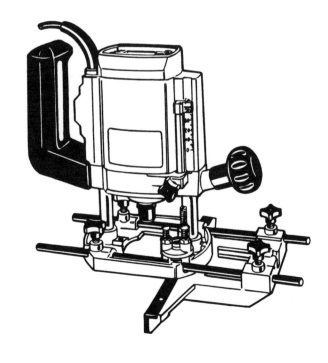

The Swiss-made Elu plunge router.

An Elu Benchtop router table and Elu electronic plunge router.

Black & Decker Workmate.

the economically minded framer to have a router and table setup for just a little over $100.

To match up one of the industrial tables with the right power source, take a look at the 1/2-inch-shank Craftsman Industrial Plunge Routers, available in single-speed 2-horsepower and variable-speed 3 1/2-horsepower models. The single-speed model sells for about $185 and the variable-speed unit for about $240. Each comes with both 1/4-inch and 1/2-inch collet assemblies to accept the two sizes of router bits.

For my setup, I coupled the Craftsman Industrial 2-horsepower router with the stationary table and its stand and accessories, which Sears calls the Craftsman Industrial Router Table Center. With heavy-duty steel table extensions added to an already spacious die-cast aluminum table, the surface area was doubled, enabling the unit to handle any size wood I want to shove through it.

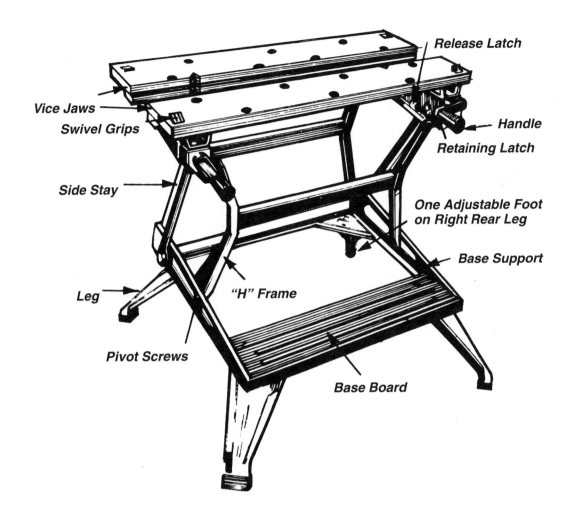

Vice Jaws

Swivel Grips

Release Latch

Handle

Retaining Latch

Side Stay

One Adjustable Foot
on Right Rear Leg

Base Support

Leg

"H" Frame

Pivot Screws

Base Board

Parts of a Black & Decker Workmate.

Two other features I especially like are the keyed safety switch with dual electrical outlets and the integral 2½-inch dust port. I keep the router power cord plugged into the switch. When I set up to make molding, I also plug the power cord of my wet/dry shop vac into the switch and attach the vacuum hose to the dust port. I need only flip one conveniently located switch to turn on the router and shop vac simultaneously, allowing me to make molding while keeping my shop relatively free of wood chips and dust. I also like the dual capability of the router. As I build my collection of the heavier-duty ½-inch router bits, I'm also able to use my sizable assortment of ¼-inch bits, simply by switching collet assemblies, which takes only a minute or so and requires only a Phillips screwdriver.

One optional tool so useful that I consider it essential in my own shop is the Black & Decker Workmate, which the manufacturer bills as a portable work center and vise. When this item was first introduced, I lived in an apartment and decided this would be an ideal accessory on many jobs, especially because it could be folded for storage. Since then, I have lived in two different houses, each with a large shop and big workbench, but I still use my Workmate on nearly every job. In fact, I own two of them and wonder how I ever got by without them.

I use the Workmate by itself or in conjunction with my other tools and accessories. My miter box, for example, is mounted on a plywood base made to fit the Workmate jaws. Whenever I need it, I clamp the base into the jaws of the

The Portable Quick-Clamping Workbench III from Wolfcraft. PHOTO COURTESY OF WOLFCRAFT.

Workmate and in seconds it's ready to use. In this way, my miter box is as stable as if it were mounted permanently to a bench, but it can be moved anywhere and can handle stock of any length because of this portability.

It's also possible to set up other bench-type tools for use with the Workmate or other folding workbenches and tables. For example, before buying my stationary bandsaw, I owned a benchtop bandsaw that I simply C-clamped to the Workmate whenever I needed to use it. I also had a benchtop drill press bolted to a ply-

wood base that I secured between the jaws of the Workmate. Similarly, for years I used an Elu router and router table mounted to a plywood base that easily clamped to the handy Workmate.

Other companies also sell folding workbenches and work tables. Sears, for example, offers the Craftsman Portable Clamping Worktable and the Deluxe Tilt-Top Workbench. Wolfcraft's contributions to this category include Quick-Clamping Model 6194 Workbench II and Model 6189 Workbench III.

CHAPTER SEVEN

Framing with Commercial Frames and Moldings

Some very competent framers have never built a frame in their lives. Others build frames, but for one reason or another use only commercially made moldings. With either approach, a person can still save money and do a good job of protecting, preserving, and displaying framable items.

Among the reasons for using ready-made frames is a lack of frame-making tools. Although frame making requires relatively few tools, if you're just starting out you need not wait until you have a fully equipped framing shop to get to work. In fact, it's probably best to start by buying matting and mounting tools and learning how to use them first; then buy ready-made frames until the proper framing tools are on hand.

Similarly, if you have no interest in making your own moldings or are simply waiting until you can buy the necessary tools, you can easily begin making frames with commercial moldings and a minimal tool investment. Most of us probably start out making frames with commercial frame moldings, and even after we own the tools for making our own moldings, we continue to use ready-made frames and store-bought moldings whenever it makes sense.

Ready-made frames are commonly available in standard sizes—from 4 x 5 to 24 x 36 inches—at department stores, discount stores, drugstores, some lumberyards and home-improvement centers, artist-supply shops, photography-supply stores, and frame shops. Some frame shops even stock frames in odd sizes—such as 5 x 9, 9 x 13, and 10 x 14 inches—and in some fractional sizes. Moreover, some frame suppliers custom-build frames or cut frame sections to customers' specifications for surprisingly reasonable prices.

Frames often go on sale at various outlets, sometimes even below cost. Keep an eye out for such sales, and stock up on the sizes you use most.

Likewise with commercially made moldings. Recently, a lumberyard where I deal began phasing out most of the picture-frame moldings in stock and marked them down to about a third of their original prices. It doesn't take a genius to figure out what to do in such a situation; I bought nearly every piece of molding they had. One of my favorite commercial moldings had been costing me $8.80 for an 8-foot strip, or $1.10 a foot. The close-out price was $3.20 for each 8-footer, or 40 cents a foot.

FRAMING WITH METAL AND ACRYLIC

Metal-section frames, usually made of aluminum, are popular for framing photographs, posters, and all sorts of artwork. Their lean, clean lines lend them to numerous applications and assure users that they will never overwhelm the works they frame. They come in all standard sizes, ready made or in kit form, or can be cut to any desired size.

These frames offer excellent protection to the works they contain, yet they are easily dismantled and reassembled with no more than a screwdriver. (Some don't even require that.) Consequently, these frames are often favored by photographers and artists who exhibit their works at museums and galleries and must frequently change their show items about. For sim-

Nielsen and Intercraft metal-section frames.

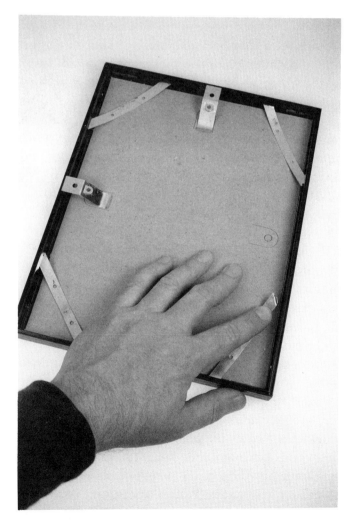

*Intercraft frame comes with four spring clips
and two hanger clips that install by hand.*

ilar reasons, they're popular in the home wherever changeability is desired.

The most readily identifiable metal frames are those with highly polished or brushed metallic finishes—namely, silver, brass, and bronze. But anodized frames are now available in dozens of colors and shades. In fact, an attractive way to use the colored metal frames is to match frame color to inner-mat color in a multiple matting.

These frames also now come in a number of different depths and shapes, from shallow to deep, from flat to curved. Hanging hardware is available in several configurations, from snap-in eyes for use with picture wire, to sawtooth hangers that require no wire.

Intercraft offers metal-section frames in standard sizes that are available through many retail outlets. This is an extremely easy frame to use, as it requires no tools to install photographs or artworks. Each frame is equipped with four spring clips that span the corners and hold mats, work, and backing securely in place against the glass. Two hanger clips are also provided, one on a long section and one on a short section, for vertical or horizontal use. These clips are also removable.

Most typical of the metal- and acrylic-section frames are those made by Nielsen and distributed mainly through frame shops and mail-order suppliers. The frames come assembled or in kit form, or cut to any length.

Molding sections are held together at the corners with two-part corner braces with integral setscrews. The setscrews are tightened to hold the sections together and loosened to dismantle the frame or change the contents. Contents are held in place with spring-tension clips.

To install artwork in and assemble one of these metal-section or similar acrylic frames, just follow these easy steps.

Step 1. Insert a two-part corner brace into one end of one of the mitered frame sections and the other end of the brace into the adjacent frame section. Tighten the setscrews until the two pieces are secure. Attach another frame section the same way to the opposite end of the section you started with.

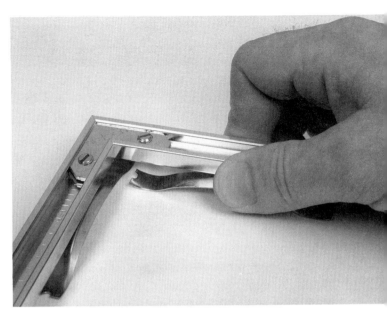

Assembling the Nielsen frame, Step 3.

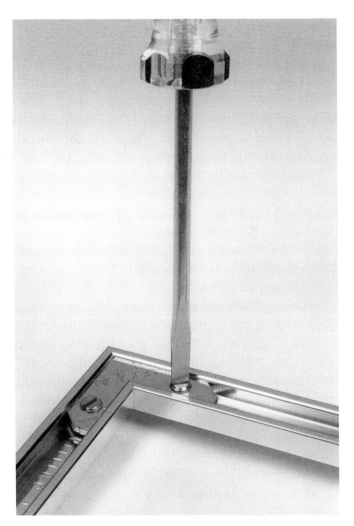

Assembling the Nielsen frame, Step 1.

Step 2. Carefully slide the clean glass, mounted photograph or artwork, and backing into the partly assembled frame, and attach the remaining two corner braces and frame section with the setscrews.

Step 3. With the frame facedown, position two spring-tension clamps on the backing near each frame section—eight in all. Press each clamp down with your thumb, and slide it under the rear lip of the frame.

Step 4. Attach snap-in or screw-type eyes and picture wire, or snap a sawtooth hanger into the rear of the top frame section, and your frame is ready for hanging.

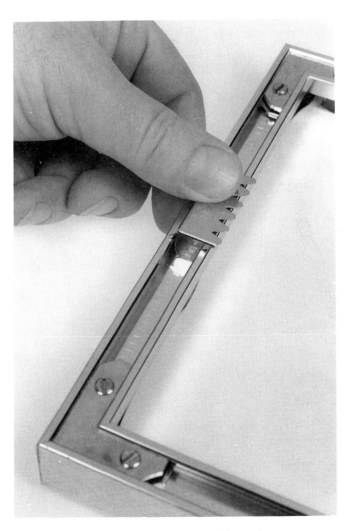

Assembling the Nielsen frame, Step 4.

You can, of course, cut your own metal moldings to fit your needs, if you have the right tools. For metal, you will need a metal-cutting blade for a power miter saw or one of the special backsaws with interchangeable blades for wood and metal. But there's really little need to invest in such equipment. You can usually get these frames cut to size at frame shops, and at many shops the charge is nominal or nothing at all.

FRAMING WITH COMMERCIAL WOOD MOLDINGS

You will find commercially made wood moldings in dozens of sizes and shapes at lumberyards, home-improvement centers, some discount and department stores, and frame shops, as well as through some mail-order sources. They come finished or unfinished; the latter is always cheaper and often the better choice.

Prices vary widely from source to source, sometimes for no apparent reason. So it's wise to shop around. In fact, it's a good idea to locate all the molding sources in your immediate vicinity and spend some time comparison shopping.

Usually, the larger and more intricate the molding, the more expensive it will be. Prices for unfinished moldings generally range from about 50 cents to $3 or so a linear foot. The simplest finished moldings usually run at least $1.50 a linear foot, and prices increase dramatically with the size and complexity of the molding. At some frame shops, it's not uncommon to find finished

Ordering Frames and Moldings by Phone, Fax, or Mail

We call them mail-order houses or companies—those outfits with warehouses and catalogs chock-full of items of every description—but these days most of us order by phone or fax, not by mail. The reason is simple: phone and fax are fast; mail is slow. Moreover, with toll-free lines, most of our electronically placed orders travel free. Snail mail, as it's called in cyberspace, requires postage. For one reason or another, a few folks might prefer ordering supplies and materials by mail, and that option is available to them. From some companies, we can even order catalogs and products by e-mail.

Among the reasons for shopping by phone, fax, or mail, convenience probably tops the list. It's easier to find the items we're after, and the catalog companies offer a much greater selection than many of us are able to find locally. So we end up usually saving time and often saving money.

In the Source Directory you'll find a number of companies offering picture frames and frame moldings. I suggest you phone for their catalogs and spend time getting familiar

The Champagne series of frames from Graphik Dimensions, Ltd. PHOTO COURTESY OF GRAPHIK DIMENSIONS, LTD.

moldings costing $4 to $6 or more per foot, which is one of the best reasons I can think of for making and finishing your own.

Most unfinished and many finished moldings are sold in 6- and 8-foot lengths and sometimes 4-foot strips. If you have reason to buy any of the most expensive finished moldings, though, insist on buying it by the foot to avoid expensive leftovers.

Making frames from any of these moldings is easy, but there are a few tips and tricks that will help make it even easier for you. The steps that follow demonstrate how to cut frame sections with mitered ends and how to joint these sections to make a frame. If you have never done any framing, this is the most important method

you will learn, because these are the same techniques you will use to make all miter-joined wood frames and liners. What's more, you can apply what you know about picture framing to many other projects.

The size of the work to be framed determines the inside dimensions of the frame, and molding width determines outside dimensions. Because of humidity and temperature fluctuations, framed works expand and contract. To keep them from buckling, allow extra room inside your frames by making them 1/8 inch larger than what you're framing. For example, if your mats, mount board, and glass are 11 x 14 inches, the inside dimensions of your frame should be 11 1/8 x 14 1/8 inches. That means your molding should

with the companies and all the products they offer.

One supplier I've dealt with for years with total satisfaction is Graphik Dimensions, Ltd. In the company's catalog you'll find more than 150 styles of wood moldings, in a great variety of widths and finishes, from which you can choose custom-made frames or ready-made frames in all standard sizes. The company's metal-section frames come in more than a half-dozen styles and dozens of colors and finishes, ranging from brushed matte to high-gloss lacquer. Canvas and shadowbox frames are also available. Graphik Dimensions frequently adds new frames to its already extensive selection. The company fills orders promptly and its prices are good.

The best source of commercially made wood picture-frame and liner moldings I know of is XYLO, Inc. You will certainly want to order that company's catalog so you can browse through it and check out the full-size profiles of more than 200 frame and liner moldings of every size and shape imaginable. Well, that's not entirely true; the folks at XYLO regularly imagine new designs and add them to their catalog.

The Imperial series of frames from Graphik Dimensions, Ltd. Photo courtesy of Graphik Dimensions, Ltd.

Sources of Cheap Frames

Cheap frames are getting easier to come by all the time. Increasingly, department stores, discount stores, and major drug-store and other chains are offering imported frames at rock-bottom prices, often as special sale items or loss leaders. Keep an eye out for these opportunities, and stock up when you find good buys on reasonably well-made frames.

Where I live, and I suspect elsewhere as well, all kinds of inexpensive picture frames from Mexico and other Pacific Rim countries are showing up at most of the usual frame outlets at bargain prices. Most of the cost of any commercially made frame is labor. When frames are made in countries where labor is cheap, the resulting product is also cheap.

Recently, a nearby department store advertised a sale on frames in standard sizes from 5 x 7 to 16 x 20 inches. In one display, I found solid-oak 8 x 10-inch frames, complete with glass and easel backs, priced at two for $5. Similar oak frames in 11 x 14 inches were $3; 16 x 20s were $4.

I can't build frames for that. At any local outlet, unfinished oak moldings of comparable size would cost me as much as the entire assembled frame. In fact, the frame shops in my community charge more than $2.50 for an 8 x 10 easel back alone.

Naturally, I sorted through the displays and filled a shopping cart with these frames, then stacked them on shelves in my workshop for future use. I've already used several for wall frames and just added the bonus easel backs to my inventory.

At many of the places where such frames are made, quality control and final inspection of finished products are lax or nonexistent. Consequently, seemingly identical frames in the same sale displays often vary in degree of craftsmanship, and some exhibit flaws. Intensity of wood stains and quality of finish coats differ from one frame to the next. So you will want to carefully inspect frames and pick the most evenly stained and flawlessly finished ones you can find. Likewise, check painted frames for any problems.

Most such frames are joined at the corners with small staples. Make sure the staples have met their mark and that joints show no gaps. In your shop, you can use matching wood filler, putty sticks, or hot-melt shellac sticks to fill the staple holes.

Don't overlook opportunities to buy used frames at good prices. Some might require repairing, rebuilding, or refinishing, but if the price is right, you can end up making good deals. Sources of used-frame bargains include auctions, estate sales, garage sales, flea markets, secondhand stores, and some antique shops.

have a rabbet of at least 3/8 inch deep (or a lip 3/8 inch wide).

When you buy molding, you will need more than might be apparent at first. You will be cutting miters at each end of each frame section, which means there will be some waste. The general rule is to take the width of the molding and multiply it by two for each frame section, or by eight for any conventional four-sided frame, and add that to the section lengths. The saw kerf doesn't amount to much—about 1/8 inch with most blades—but that too must be considered. So for the eight cuts necessary, you'll need to add another inch.

To frame your 11 x 14-inch work with a 2-inch-wide frame molding, then, you would need

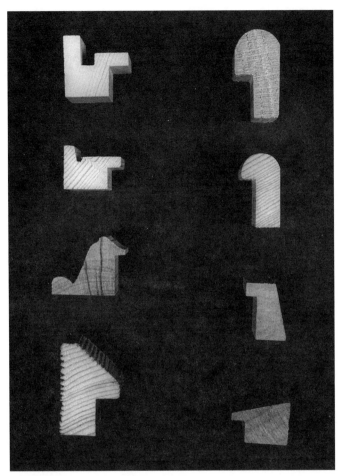

Profiles of a few of the many commercial wood frame moldings available.

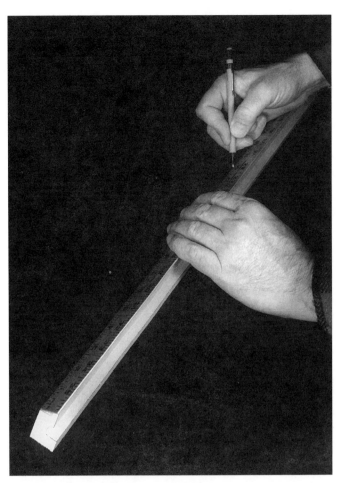

Building a wood frame, Step 2.

two sections at 11⅛ inches and two at 14⅛ inches, or 50½ inches. To that, you will add eight times the molding width, then tack on an inch for the saw kerfs, for a total of 67½ inches. It's smart to add a little for good measure, so you might as well buy a 6-foot strip.

The more expensive the molding, the more careful you have to be about these measurements. If you do much framing at all, you'll find eventually that you will keep certain favorite moldings on hand all the time, and if you make your own moldings, you will accumulate plenty of stock, as well as the raw materials for making more as you need it.

Once you've found the right molding for your picture and have bought as much as you will need, it's time to make the frame. For purposes of illustration, we'll use the 11 x 14-inch dimensions we've

been discussing, but the same techniques apply to any size frame. Here's how it all goes together.

Step 1. Lay the frame molding faceup or facedown in your miter box with the rabbeted (lipped) edge toward you. Clamp the molding to the miter-box table or fence with a pair of cushioned spring clamps. Then cut one end off the molding at a 45-degree angle.

Step 2. Align one end of a yardstick with the inside edge of the miter cut, along the rabbet, and mark for the next cut at 14⅛ inches. Then make that cut at a 45-degree angle, opposite the first cut, to form one frame section.

Step 3. Cut the end off the molding strip as you did to begin with in Step 1. Now lay the strip

Building a wood frame, Step 3.

back to back with the frame section you cut in Step 2, and align the mitered ends. Using the frame section as a guide, mark the molding strip for another cut, and cut a second section to 14¹⁄₈ inches.

Step 4. Following the same procedures as in Steps 1, 2, and 3, cut two more frame sections to 11¹⁄₈ inches each. Lightly sand any rough edges at the miter cuts, and you're ready to assemble the frame.

Step 5. Apply a thin but even coat of wood glue or white glue to one end of a long frame section, and clamp a short section to it with a corner clamp.

Step 6. Apply glue to the other end of the long strip, and clamp the other short strip to it. Then glue and clamp the remaining long strip to the ends of the short strips.

Step 7. At one corner of the frame, drive a small brad through a long section into the end of a short section. Nail the remaining corners identically, countersink the brads with a nail set, and let the frame stand with clamps in place for an hour or overnight.

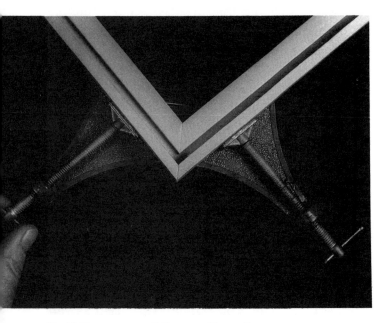

Building a wood frame, Step 5.

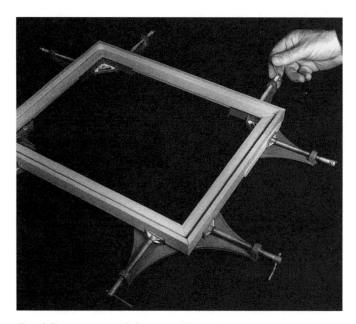

Building a wood frame, Step 6.

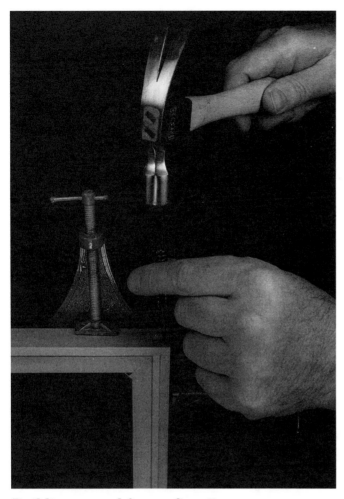

Building a wood frame, Step 7.

Finished frame.

In large moldings, drive two brads at each corner—one near the rear edge, and the next from the opposite direction and near the front edge.

Excess glue may seep from the assembled miter joints. Wipe it away with a damp sponge.

That's all there is to cutting and assembling a wood frame. When the glue has set, the frame is ready for finishing. If you're using finished molding, you're ready to frame your picture.

BUILDING FRAMES WITH A BISCUIT JOINER

You can build frames even faster and more efficiently with the aid of a biscuit joiner. With box moldings deeper than 1³/₄ inches, you can use a standard-size joiner and #0, #10, or #20 biscuits, depending on the depth of the molding. Similarly, you can use a standard-size joiner

and biscuits with flat-style moldings wider than 1³/₄ inches. Or you can use the Ryobi Detail Biscuit Joiner, as I did in the accompanying photographs, to build frames with molding of any size.

Biscuit-Joined Box-Style Frame

Building strong frames from commercial box-style molding or any you make yourself (see chapter 8) is easy with the aid of a biscuit joiner. The trickiest part is securing the molding to a solid work surface for cutting the biscuit slots, but that's a simple matter if you have one or two C-clamps or hold-down clamps. Here's how:

Step 1. Use a miter box and backsaw or appropriate power saw to cut four frame sections to length with 45-degree angles at the ends.

Biscuit-joined box-style frame, Step 3.

Step 2. Lay a frame section, outside (long) edge up, on the edge of a Workmate top or other suitable work surface, with the molding's rabbet down. Secure the section to the Workmate with one or two cushioned C-clamps or hold-down clamps.

Step 3. Use a combination square to mark the top center of each end of the frame section. Then, with the joiner's blade depth set for the appropriate size biscuit (#R3 in the accompanying photographs), align the fence with the centered guideline, and cut the biscuit slot. Do likewise at the opposite end of the frame section and at both ends of the other three sections.

Step 4. Apply wood glue to the slot and one end of a frame section and to the slot and mating

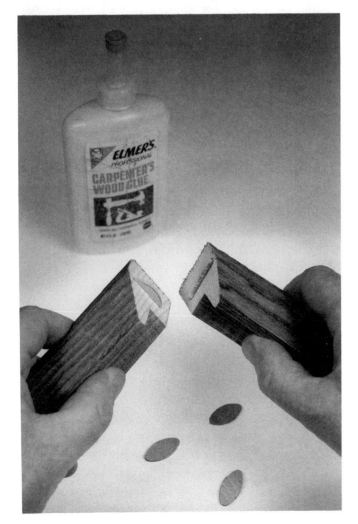

Biscuit-joined box-style frame, Step 4.

Biscuit-joined flat-style frame, Step 2.

end of the adjoining section. Push a biscuit into the slot in one glued section, and join the mating section to it.

Step 5. Glue and join the remaining three corners the same way, and clamp the frame together with a band clamp or four corner clamps. Wipe away any seeping glue with a damp sponge, and let the frame stand until the glue sets.

Biscuit-Joined Flat-Style Frame

Building frames with a biscuit joiner and flat-style molding is slightly different from, but just as easy as, making box-style frames. Just follow these simple steps:

Step 1. Cut the four frame sections to size with a miter box and backsaw or an appropriate power saw, creating the usual 45-degree angles at the ends.

Step 2. Lay the frame sections facedown, and use a combination square to find and mark the center of each piece at the mitered ends. Then join the mating frame sections, and use a straightedge to scribe a pencil line across each corner at the center marks.

Step 3. Secure a frame section to the top of a Workmate or other suitable work surface with one or two cushioned C-clamps or hold-down clamps, with the mitered end extending an inch or so beyond the edge of the work surface. Set the joiner fence for a 90-degree cut, align it with the guideline scribed in Step 2, and cut the biscuit slot. Cut another slot at the opposite end of the frame section and at each end of the other three sections.

Step 4. Apply glue to the slot and one end of a frame section and to the slot and one end of its mating section; then join the two sections. Glue and join the remaining sections the same way, and clamp the frame with a band clamp or four corner clamps. Wipe away any seeping glue with a damp sponge, and let the frame stand until the glue sets.

Biscuit-joined flat-style frame, Step 3.

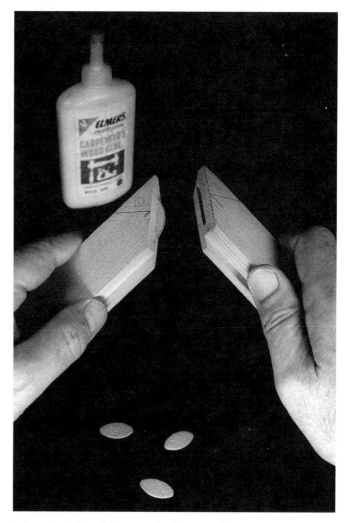

Biscuit-joined flat-style frame, Step 4.

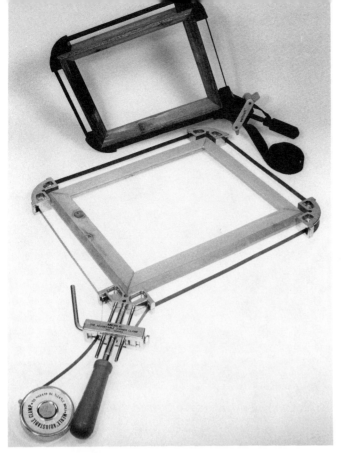

Biscuit-joined box-style frame secured in a Wolfcraft band clamp (top) and biscuit-joined flat-style frame in a Merle band clamp from MLCS.

MAKING AND INSTALLING LINERS AND FILETS

A liner is a narrow strip-frame that fits inside a larger frame, and a filet is narrower yet. Liners are usually painted, covered, or textured, and filets are often gilded or painted silver or gold. Some filets are even made of metal and are left natural.

Both liners and filets are used primarily with oil paintings, acrylics, batiks, and other works that are customarily framed without glass and mats. Liners serve much the same visual purpose as a mat, separating the work from its frame. Filets serve a similar but subtler purpose.

You will find liner moldings stocked with frame moldings at most outlets. You can also make your own. You can paint or texture your own liners, but if you want to use a covered one, you would probably do best to buy finished liner molding at a frame shop.

Cut and assemble liners the same way as frames. When using a liner, cut it 1/8 inch larger

Fabric-covered liner separates the image from the frame, much the way a mat does.

Gold-colored filet provides a subtle, narrow border for this large oil painting in a massive frame.

Commercially made easel backs fit most frames up to 11 x 14 inches.

than the work you're framing, but then make the frame only 1/16 inch larger.

Build the liner first; then make the frame to fit the liner. To install the liner, lay the frame facedown and the liner inside it. Then toenail brads through the liner into the back of the frame molding. With most frames, two brads per section should suffice.

If you want to use a filet and make it yourself, cut it 1/8 inch larger than the artwork. Then make the liner 1/16 inch larger than the filet and the frame 1/16 inch larger than the liner.

FREESTANDING FRAMES

Freestanding frames—those meant to stand on their own on a table, desk, or shelf—are available in several varieties, commonly in sizes from 3 x 3 to 11 x 14 inches. They're mainly for dis-

playing photographic portraits and family snapshots and are made of plastic, metal, or wood. You'll find freestanding frames in great assortments of styles and sizes at most department stores, or you can make your own from many commercial frames and moldings or moldings you make yourself.

Easel Backs

One of the oldest styles of freestanding frames is the familiar easel-back frame. You can turn almost any frame up to 11 x 14 inches into an easel-back frame by simply adding an easel back to it. An easel back is no more than a sturdy backboard to which a necktie-shaped stand is attached, usually with a hinge.

Some framing books offer directions for making easel backs, but I don't know why anyone

A pair of small brass hinges will turn two frames into a freestanding hinged frame.

Making hinged frames, Step 3.

would want to. Although they're easy enough to make, they're terribly time consuming and rarely as efficient as those you can buy. Well-made easel backs are readily available at framing-supply and mail-order outlets in standard sizes, from 3 x 5 to 11 x 14 inches, ranging in price from under $1 to about $3 or $4. They're even cheaper in quantity.

There's nothing to turning any portrait or snapshot frame into an easel-back frame. Simply buy an easel back with the same outside dimensions as everything else that goes in the frame—glass, mats, and mount boards—and make it the last item to be stacked in the frame. Secure it with glazing points, and you're done.

Hinged Frames

Hinged frames are another popular freestanding style. They come in double or triple configurations, made of metal, plastic, or wood. You can make your own wooden hinged frames from many styles of commercial frames or those you make yourself. You'll need frames made with flat-sided molding, and box-style are the best.

For a double frame, you'll need two frames and a pair of small brass hinges. For a triple frame, use three frames and four hinges. You'll find small brass hinges—two or four to a pack, with screws—at hardware or department stores and home-improvement centers. Sizes 5/8 x 3/4 and 3/4 x 1 inch will take care of your needs.

Ten Tips for Building Better Wood Frames

1. When cutting molding with a miter box and backsaw, move the saw in smooth, even strokes, being careful to keep the blade teeth running parallel to the miter-box table. A rocking saw motion results in uneven miters.

2. Although it's possible to measure and mark frame sections individually, it's best to use one section to mark the cut for its opposite section. A measurement that's only slightly off will create gaps in the miter joints, but if opposite pieces are identical— even if the first one cut was slightly over or under the desired length—the joints will be tight.

3. Don't horse the backsaw when cutting molding. Use only enough pressure to cut through the molding in a reasonable time. Usually the weight of the saw provides sufficient pressure. If it takes too long to cut most moldings, your saw probably needs sharpening.

4. Use a thin-lead pencil when marking moldings for cutting. Thick lead, such as in a carpenter's pencil, can cause your cut to be as much as 1/16 inch off.

5. Saw teeth are staggered, left and right of the blade. Always align the teeth slanting toward the pencil mark along the edge of the mark and you won't have problems with inaccurate cuts.

6. When assembling wood frames, dry clamp them before gluing and nailing. That is, carefully align the pieces and clamp them together with corner clamps. Then loosen one screw in one clamp, remove the piece, apply the glue, and reclamp it. This way, the clamps serve as guides to ensure accurate clamping.

7. Don't overnail; use only as many brads as necessary. In some small moldings, one brad in each corner is sufficient. In some thin liner or filet moldings, there's no room for brads. So just glue and clamp. All the brads do anyway is hold the frame pieces together as the glue cures. So if you wish, you needn't use the brads at all. If you have only one frame to build and you have four corner clamps, just glue and clamp, and don't worry about joints coming loose. Glue dries stronger than wood.

8. Wipe seeping glue away from frame joints immediately and completely. Any glue left on the face of an unfinished frame will show up when the frame is stained, as the glue will not take the stain.

9. When assembling frames with hardwood moldings, you should mark the corners where the brads will go, punch drill-starter holes with a small center punch, and drill pilot holes slightly smaller in diameter than the brads. This will make the brads much easier to drive and will prevent the wood from splitting.

10. When using small brads with narrow moldings, use long-nose pliers to hold the brads if you can't grip them adequately with your fingers. You can also wedge a brad between the teeth of a comb and hold the comb instead of the brad.

To turn any pair of matching frames into a hinged frame, just follow the directions below. For a triple frame, attach another frame to the double frame with another pair of hinges. The frames used in the photographs were oak box-style frames, 5 x 7 inches.

Step 1. Use a combination square to scribe guidelines across a side section of a frame 1½ inches from the top and bottom corners. Do the same on the mating side of another identical frame.

Step 2. Align a hinge below the top guideline, and use the hinge as a template to mark the frame for screw holes. Do the same at the bottom guideline and at both spots on the other frame.

Step 3. With a center punch and hammer, punch drill-starter holes at the spots marked. Then carefully drill pilot holes for the screws with a ⅛-inch twist-drill bit.

Step 4. Lubricate the screws with silicone spray or soap, and attach the hinges to one frame with a Phillips-head screwdriver. Then join the two frames with the remaining screws, and your hinged frame is ready for adding portraits or snapshots.

CHAPTER EIGHT

Making Frame Moldings

As I said in the introduction to the previous chapter, a good many competent framers, for one reason or another, use only commercially made moldings for making frames. I certainly have no quarrel with them, and in fact recommend the use of commercial moldings to anyone new to picture framing and their continued use when they meet your needs or can be had at the right price. But for several reasons, I strongly urge all readers to seriously consider making their own frame moldings.

First, making moldings is a great learning experience. Once you find the various materials at your disposal and begin turning them into useful moldings, you will gain new insights into the craft. Ideas will breed more ideas. And you will rarely, if ever, face a framing problem you can't solve.

You will also save tremendously in many ways. You will discover that some of the cheapest wood products can be turned into the finest picture frames. By staying alert for good buys on raw materials, you will be able to lay in supplies when prices are at their lowest.

If you're a woodworker, you will be able to use many of the scraps from other projects to make picture-frame moldings. With these random lengths of molding on hand, you can put a frame together when you have an extra twenty or thirty minutes you might otherwise waste.

Some moldings are simply made of strips of material glued together to form the necessary rabbet or lip characteristic of all picture-frame moldings. Others require power tools. If you are already a woodworker, there's a good chance you currently own or plan to buy the necessary tools. So making frame molding is just one more use you can put them to.

BEST WOODS FOR FRAMING

Many woods are good for making frame moldings. Among the most popular softwoods are pine, fir, hemlock, cedar, and redwood. Favorite hardwoods include poplar, oak, walnut, birch, cherry, mahogany, and maple. No doubt you will soon begin to favor certain woods for their beauty, suitability, availability, and cost. Depending on where you live, you will probably find other species that are locally popular, such as ash, hickory, myrtle, and alder, to mention only a few.

So-called exotic woods from all over the world are usually only available at wood specialty shops. Although most are too expensive for use in frame making, you might want to experiment with some from time to time or buy small quantities that you can use for inlays to decorate moldings made of cheaper domestic woods.

You will find an amazing variety of colors, patterns, and degrees of hardness in the woods of the world. Between the extremes of white and black are woods that are blood red, purple, yellow, green, blue, and every shade of brown imaginable. Some are coarsely grained and heavily textured; others are smooth, almost waxy, and as finely grained as marble. There are woods that are extremely light and so soft they can be gouged with a thumbnail, others so dense, heavy, and hard as to seem petrified.

You really don't have to possess a wealth of knowledge about woods to buy them wisely and make frame moldings from them. If you're new to woodworking, you should learn a bit about sizes and grades and how the mills treat the wood before it reaches your retail outlet. The salesperson at your local lumberyard or home-improvement center should be able to answer all your questions and lead you to the right products. So don't be afraid to ask. Most of these folks are experts, and there's nothing experts like more than showing off their expertise.

Even when you have gained some knowledge of woods and their characteristics, there is still no substitute for close physical examination of the wood products you are considering buying. Also, nosing around a lumberyard will often lead you to other materials and good buys. So spend some time at local lumberyards and home-improvement centers just prospecting. Keep a notebook handy to jot down dimensions, prices, and other pertinent information.

Lumber comes in such well-known sizes as 1 x 2, 1 x 6, 1 x 10, 2 x 2, and 2 x 4, to mention a few. These are *nominal* rather than actual sizes, and most of the lumber you use will be nominal 1-inch and 2-inch stock. Although 1-inch and 2-inch lumber start out at those thicknesses, they're reduced to 3/4-inch and 1 1/2-inch thicknesses, respectively, during the drying process and when their broad surfaces are milled. As the remaining two sides are finished, they are similarly reduced, so a 1 x 2 is actually 3/4 x 1 1/2 inches. A 1 x 3 is 2 1/2 inches wide; a 1 x 4 is 3 1/2 inches; a 2 x 2 is 1 1/2 inches by 1 1/2 inches. In other words, from rough board to finished product, 1-inch-thick stock is reduced by 1/4 inch and 2-inch stock by 1/2 inch. Widths are reduced by 1/2 inch through 7 inches (actually 6 1/2 inches). Beyond that, they are reduced by 3/4 inch. So a 1 x 8 is 7 1/4 inches wide; a 1 x 10 is 9 1/4 inches wide; and a 1 x 12 is actually 11 1/4 inches wide.

Hardwoods are sometimes sold the same way, or might be labeled according to actual widths and thicknesses expressed in quarters. The designation 4/4 is expressed as "four quarters," and 8/4 is "eight quarters." These are 1-inch and 2-inch thicknesses, respectively. This is the language generally used in the mills, and it often finds its way into retail outlets as well.

Most lumber and moldings are sold in lengths of 6, 8, 10, 12, 14, and 20 feet, with 8-footers being the most common. Hardwoods are sometimes available in standard lengths and are also available in a variety of random lengths.

I have read a number of books on lumber, wood products, and woodworking and have been told by the authors that our system of lumber grading is meant to help us in our selection of woods for various purposes. It is not meant to confuse us—they keep telling me. But grading and grading language might differ according to manufacturing association designations or U.S. Department of Commerce standards. There are certainly differences among the various wood products and how they are graded among the regions of the country, and even from one mill to another or one inspector to another. What's more, when a load of wood arrives at a retail outlet, the owner's opinion of it might differ from how the grader saw it. It's not easy to sort all this out, but I will try.

First, grades might be expressed numerically, alphabetically, or literally. Numerical gradings, best to poorest, are 1 to 4. Alphabetically, they are A to D, and literally they go from clear to common.

Clear lumber is the most nearly flawless and most expensive. *Select* grades have more and larger knots than clear lumber but often possess more character as a result of the knots and attractive grain and are therefore often better for natural finishes. What's more, they're cheaper. *Common* is the cheapest. Depending on its numerical grading, it might range from lumber with numerous knots and other minor blemishes to wood that is full of loose knots, knotholes, and pitch pockets.

Construction, standard, utility, and *economy* are all grades of common lumber and coincide with No. 1, No. 2, No. 3, and No. 4 grades. No doubt, you will come across other designations, such as *stud grade* or *shop grade,* and more other variations than you care to know, such as the vague designation *standard-and-better*. If it's something you're not familiar with, ask for a translation. And always examine the product closely before you buy it.

Another term you'll come across is *K.D.*, which stands for kiln dried and is the way most lumber is dried these days. Some is air dried, but this is a more time-consuming, less efficient process. What's more important to know is that some lumber is sold "green," which means it has not been dried.

Here's one rule in picture framing you should never break: buy only dried, preferably kiln-dried, wood for making frames. Green or wet wood shrinks as it dries and might also warp, crack, and split. Such woods can also be dangerous to work with, as they can bind up power saws and cause kickback.

Green lumber is cheaper than dried lumber, but the savings aren't worth the potential problems and hazards. Furthermore, you're going to be able to make frame moldings so cheaply from kiln-dried stock that you won't need wood that's any cheaper.

The two woods I use more than any others for making frame moldings are oak and pine. Oak is my favorite hardwood, not only because of its inherent beauty, but also because it is easy to work with. In fact, in many ways, it's like a softwood. It is easy to rip, drill, rout, and sand. Yet it also exhibits the strength and durability of hardwood. I also like walnut and mahogany for similar reasons.

The pine I use is kiln-dried No. 4 common that I buy in fairly large batches. What I look for are the boards that others don't want—those with the character that others view as flaws. Most of what I buy is 1 x 4 stock, although I sometimes find wider boards that fit my needs. Then I rip most of this stock into 1 x 2s that I sort and store for later use.

In any batch of pine, I end up with greatly varied material for moldings. Strips of clear or nearly clear wood I keep mainly for making router moldings. Some of the pine will be deeply colored brown or even red, and I sort those for striking frames that will be finished naturally.

But the bulk of it—the so-called blue pine, the material honeycombed with borer holes, and the pieces full of knots and pitch pockets—I use for making rustic frames in various sizes and configurations. And all these pine 1 x 2s that I end up making so much molding from cost me a mere 12½ cents a foot.

And that's not a sale price. I pay 25 cents a foot for each pine 1 x 4 that I turn into two 1 x 2s at 12½ cents a foot. Believe it or not, I have made frame molding for less.

Several years ago, the folks at a local lumberyard had a big stack of 1 x 12 incense cedar they wanted to get rid of to make room for other products that would move faster. They put it on sale for 15 cents a foot, and I hauled off a pickup-truck load. I used much of it for shelving and various building projects, and I still have a good bit on hand. Recently, I started ripping 1 x 2s from it and making picture-frame molding. I can get six 1 x 2s from each board, which means the cedar I'm making frame molding with cost me 2½ cents a foot.

USING CONSTRUCTION MOLDINGS

The most abundant and widely available moldings are construction moldings, used mainly in house building but also in woodworking projects. It's usually construction moldings that give the finishing touch to carpentry. And some of these are also useful to the frame builder for making frame moldings.

For several reasons, I won't attempt to cover all the construction moldings or even all the ones suitable for picture framing. First, there are just too many to deal with. More important, though, is that many of them differ considerably from East to West, so I will cover only some of those that are common throughout the country.

In the East, most construction moldings are made of clear pine. In the West, they are generally clear hemlock or white fir. There are hardwood construction moldings available—mainly oak, mahogany, and birch—but they are expensive. Nevertheless, some are ideal for certain framing jobs.

A major difference between eastern and western construction moldings is style. The older

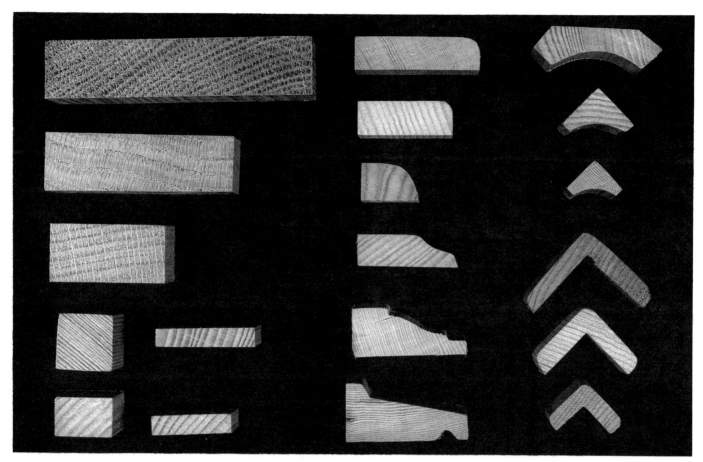

Common stock and construction moldings used in making frames: (left) *1 x 4, 1 x 3, 1 x 2, ³/4-square, part-ing bead, and two sizes of lattice;* (center) *two sizes of bullnose stop, base shoe, ogee stop, shingle molding, and drip cap;* (right) *ceiling cove, two sizes of cove molding, and three sizes of outside corner molding.*

styles of the East are more ornamental and deco-rative, exhibiting their colonial heritage. In the West, styles are simpler and relatively unadorned. Of course, there is some crossover and some mold-ings that are used universally.

The simplest of all are not really moldings at all, but strips of various configurations smaller than 1 x 2; they are usually found stocked with the moldings. Parting bead, ³/4-square, and lat-tice are three that are useful in framing.

Parting bead is no more than a strip of wood with dimensions of ¹/2 x ³/4 inch. Similar is the ³/4-square, which, as the nomenclature suggests, is a strip of wood with dimensions of ³/4 x ³/4 inch. Both parting bead and ³/4-square can be turned into simple, narrow frame moldings by merely routing a rabbet along one edge with a straight router bit. Such moldings are useful for framing

certificates and other items that are often dis-played in simple, narrow frame moldings.

Parting bead and ³/4-square are also used in conjunction with other moldings and with com-mon stock to create frame moldings. Often the different strips are simply glued together to form frame molding.

Lattice is ¹/4-inch-thick stock that comes in widths of 1, 1¹/8, 1⁵/16, and 1⁵/8 inches and can be ripped to narrower widths to suit your purposes. Lattice can be used in various glued moldings and to make simple slat-style frames. It is also good for making floater frames for photographs.

Base shoe is ¹/2 x ³/4-inch molding with one corner rounded over. It can be turned into an at-tractive certificate-frame molding by simply rout-ing a rabbet along one edge. It is useful in glued moldings and functions well as a liner molding.

Bullnose stop is similar to lattice but is larger and has one corner slightly rounded over. It's 7/16 inch thick and comes in widths from 3/4 to 15/8 inches. Use this molding with other moldings and common stock, or use it by itself for slat and floater frames that are a bit more decorative than those made with lattice.

The smallest ogee stop is 3/8 x 3/4 inch. Other sizes are 7/16 inch thick and range in width from 11/8 to 15/8 inches. With an ogee molded along one edge, this molding is good for use with other moldings and for making liners.

Shingle molding is 5/8 inch thick and 11/2 inches wide. It is a decorative molding and one of the most useful for the picture framer. It can be used with other material in the construction of complex frames. You can also slap together a good-looking molding by ripping a 1 x 2 or other inch-thick stock to a 11/4-inch width, then gluing that to a strip of shingle molding. Rout a rabbet into the thick end of shingle molding, and it can be used by itself as a frame molding.

Drip cap is another useful molding that comes in several sizes; 3/4 x 15/8 inches is the most common. This one, too, works with other moldings and common stock, or it can be used by itself as a deep or shallow molding, depending on how the rabbet is routed into it.

Cove moldings come in a variety of configurations and sizes. The most useful are 1/2 x 1/2-inch cove, 3/4 x 3/4-inch cove, and 5/8-inch-thick ceiling cove that's 15/8 inches wide. The smaller cove moldings make attractive liners and are useful for decorating larger frames. Both cove and ceiling cove work well in glued moldings and in some shadow-box frames.

Outside corner molding comes in three sizes: 3/4 x 3/4, 1 x 1, and 11/4 x 11/4 inches. It's among the most useful of the construction moldings in making a variety of frames and related items, such as bulletin boards, pegboard organizers, and calendar frames.

One of the easiest construction moldings to convert to frame molding is brick molding. This is large molding, 15/16 inches thick and 2 inches wide. To make an attractive frame molding, you need only rout a rabbet into its narrowest edge.

There's no substitute for experience, so as I have recommended before, visit your local lumberyards and home-improvement centers, and spend some time in their molding departments. Find out what is available in your locale, and imagine how these moldings might be used to make frames. Try various combinations to find out what works.

SAW MOLDINGS

If you own a bandsaw and no other stationary or bench-type power saw, you can use it to make a few simple frame moldings. Of course, you can rip stock to be used with construction moldings. You can also tilt the saw table and fully bevel one of the narrow edges of 1 x 2 stock. Then rip other 1 x 2 strips (or any nominal inch-thick stock) to strips 11/4 inches wide. Glue these to the beveled strips with the beveled edge creating the lip of the rabbet. This simple molding can be

With a router or table saw you can turn brick molding into frame molding.

Brick-molding frame.

You can rip 1 x 2 from wider stock with a table saw.

used alone or in conjunction with other material. Attach corner molding to the outside edge for an attractive frame molding.

Far more useful than the bandsaw, though, are radial-arm and table saws, with the latter shaking out a little ahead for its ease of setup for various ripping jobs. The following moldings can be made with either a radial-arm or table saw, although directions are for the table saw. If you already own a radial-arm saw, you know how to use it and will have no trouble making these moldings.

Box Molding

After ripping your favorite inch-thick wood into 1 x 2s, remove the blade guard to perform the following steps. Exercise extreme caution when operating the saw without the blade guard. Follow all the manufacturer's safety precautions,

and be sure to use push blocks to move material along the fence and over the blade.

Step 1. Set the table-saw fence 1/4 inch from the *far* teeth of the blade, and set the blade for a 1 1/4-inch depth.

Step 2. Stand a 1 x 2 on its narrow edge on the saw table, with a broad side against the fence. Then use push blocks to run it over the blade.

Step 3. Reset the fence 1/4 inch from the *near* teeth of the blade, and reset the blade for 1/4-inch depth.

Step 4. Lay the 1 x 2 on a broad side, with the ungrooved narrow edge against the fence, and use push blocks to run it over the blade.

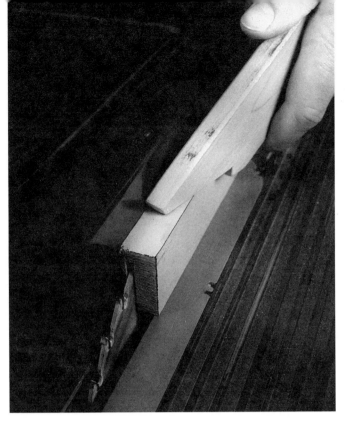

Box molding, Step 2.

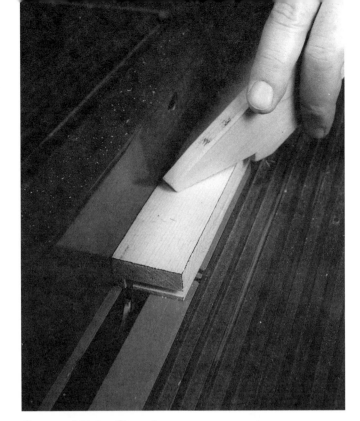

Box molding, Step 4.

Step 5. Lightly sand the strip to remove any slivers or smooth out any rough spots, and your box molding is ready for framing.

Flat Molding

The flat molding is just as simple as the box molding, except that it is rabbeted on a narrow edge instead of a broad edge to make a shallow molding. Again, exercise extreme caution with the saw, following the manufacturer's safety precautions, and use push blocks to move the material.

Step 1. Set the table-saw fence 1/4 inch from the blade's *near* teeth, and set the blade for a 1/4-inch depth.

Step 2. Stand a 1 x 2 on its narrow edge on the saw table, with a broad side against the fence. Then use push blocks to run it over the blade.

Step 3. Reset the fence 1/4 inch from the *far* teeth of the blade, and reset the blade for a 1/2-inch depth.

Step 4. Lay the 1 x 2 broad side down on the saw table, with the grooved edge against the fence, and use push blocks to run it over the blade.

Box-molding frame.

Flat molding, Step 2.

Flat-molding frame.

Flat-molding, Step 4.

Step 5. Sand the strip, as required, to smooth any rough edges and remove slivers, and your flat molding is ready for use.

Grooved Molding

To make a single-grooved molding, start with 1 x 2 stock and set up the table saw as in Step 1 of the flat-molding directions. But before making the first cut for the rabbet, run the face side of the 1 x 2 over the blade to cut a groove 1/8 inch wide and 1/4 inch deep. Now turn the 1 x 2 over, with the face surface up, and follow Steps 2 through 5 to complete the molding.

To make a double-grooved molding, set the saw up the same way as above. Make one pass to cut the first groove 1/4 inch from one edge. Then turn the 1 x 2 so the opposite narrow edge is against the fence, and with the face down on the table, run the piece through again, creating a second groove 1/4 inch from the other edge. Now turn the 1 x 2 over and complete the molding, as above.

You can cut grooves wider than 1/8 inch by simply moving the fence to different distances from the blade and passing the 1 x 2 over the blade to remove more material. Of course, you can also adjust the blade to cut shallower grooves. I don't recommend cutting any deeper than 1/4 inch, though, for structural reasons.

Beveled Molding

You can tilt your saw blade to bevel the outside edge of either box or flat molding. You can also bevel the inside edges if you wish. You might want to combine techniques by putting a slight bevel on one or both face edges of the flat molding after you have grooved the face.

ROUTER MOLDINGS

If I had to decide on which power tool to recommend first—a table saw or a router and router table—I would be hard pressed to make up my mind. I would hate to be without my table saw; I use it for most of my moldings. But it's possible to make a great assortment of moldings with a router and router table, and the combination is cheaper than a table-saw setup.

Grooved-molding frame.

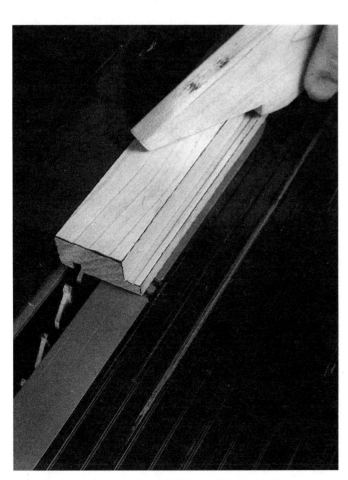

Cutting a groove in molding with a table saw.

Author uses his Craftsman Industrial Router Table, mated with a Craftsman Industrial Router, to turn 1 x 2 stock into frame molding.

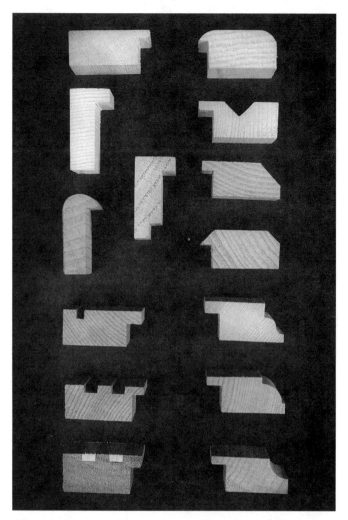

The author used a router and router table to make all these moldings from 1 x 2 stock.

Making J-molding with a router and table.

You need some way to rip boards into 1 x 2s, which are the most useful strips for making frames. But you can also buy 1 x 2s, in which case you could get by without a power saw, or you could get wider stock ripped at the yard or by a friend who owns a table or radial-arm saw.

I guess you're the only one who can decide. Meanwhile, I'll tell you about what you can accomplish with a router set up for making picture-frame moldings.

If you already own a router, you will find router tables from several manufacturers available through tool and hardware outlets, discount stores, and mail-order suppliers. Simply make sure that the table you are buying will fit your router.

If you plan to buy a router specifically for making frame moldings, then look for a router and table combination. Sears offers fine routers and tables, as do several other manufacturers. Visit hardware and department stores and home-improvement centers, or study tool catalogs to find the right combination for you.

Although you can use various sizes of stock to make frame moldings with your router, you will probably find the 1 x 2 the most useful size. If you need a smaller or narrower molding, either rip 1 x 2 or inch-thick stock to any desirable width under $1\frac{1}{2}$ inches, or use parting bead or $\frac{3}{4}$-square for the narrowest moldings. If you want something wider, use 1 x 3 or 1 x 4. I doubt that you will want anything wider than molding made with 1 x 4.

To avoid putting undue stress on your router motor, overheating bits, and damaging the wood you're working with, make all but the shallowest cuts in several passes. For example, instead of trying to rout out a $\frac{3}{8}$-inch cove or groove in one step, set the bit for a $\frac{3}{16}$-inch depth and make the first pass. Reset the depth at $\frac{3}{8}$ inch, and make a second pass to remove the rest of the material.

All router moldings shown in this section, incidentally, were made with 1 x 2 stock.

Box Molding

Tighten a $\frac{1}{2}$-inch or $\frac{5}{8}$-inch straight bit into your router's collet, and adjust for a $\frac{1}{4}$-inch-wide, $\frac{1}{4}$-inch-deep cut. With a 1 x 2 broad side down on the router table, run it over the bit to rout a 1/4 x 1/4-inch rabbet. Move the router 1/4 inch out from the fence, and make another pass. Continue moving the router in 1/4-inch increments until you have made five passes, resulting in a 1/4 x 1 1/4-inch rabbet. The molding will be L-shaped, with a 1/4-inch lip. It can be used by itself as a box molding, or in conjunction with other moldings for more complex frames.

J-Molding

To make a J-molding, start by routing a box molding from 1 x 2. Replace the straight bit with a 3/8-inch-radius corner-round bit, adjusted for about a half-cut.

Stand the box molding on its unrouted narrow (face) edge, with its broad surface against the fence. Run the strip over the bit. Rotate the strip, and round over the lip edge.

J-molding frame.

Finishing J-molding with a pad sander.

Making flat molding with a router and table.

Straight bit.

Set the bit for its full 3/8-inch depth, and repeat the process to fully round over both face corners. Then clamp the molding in a Workmate or woodworker's vise, and use a pad sander to finish rounding the molding face with 120-grit sandpaper.

Flat Molding

Use a 1/2-inch or 5/8-inch straight bit to make the flat molding. Set the bit for a 1/4-inch-wide, 1/4-inch-deep cut. Lay a 1 x 2 broad side down on the table, and run it over the bit to create a 1/4 x 1/4-inch rabbet. Move the bit up 1/4 inch and

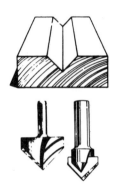

V-*groove bits.*

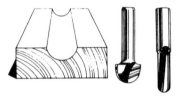

Round-nose bits.

Align the bit with the mark on the end of the molding.

Graphik Dimensions, Ltd., offers a wide range of moldings and frames at wholesale prices. PHOTO COURTESY OF GRAPHIK DIMENSIONS, LTD.

The Tuscany and Symphony lines are custom-made frames available from Graphik Dimensions, Ltd. PHOTO COURTESY OF GRAPHIK DIMENSIONS, LTD.

Graphik Dimensions' Slimwoods are narrow moldings, available in nine variations and cut to customers' specifications. PHOTO COURTESY OF GRAPHIK DIMENSIONS, LTD.

Town & Country frames from Graphik Dimensions, Ltd., are rustic, custom-made frames in an assortment of barn-wood and driftwood finishes. PHOTO COURTESY OF GRAPHIK DIMENSIONS, LTD.

One professional framer charged $250 to frame this humorous, cartoon-style poster. The author did the same job for $56, paying full retail for all components.

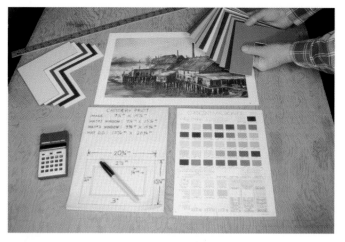

Making careful plans and taking good notes are just two of the steps toward achieving professional results in any framing job.

Mat sample corners are great aids in picking the right mat combination for any work.

When mounting and matting lithographs, watercolors, and other works on paper, use removable transparent tape to temporarily position the works on mount boards.

The author uses an adjustable metal miter box and a 28-inch backsaw to cut moldings for most frames.

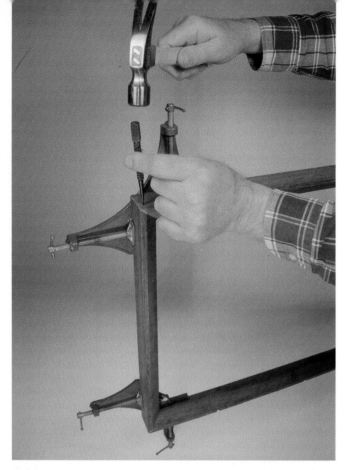

Corner clamps are essential tools for assembling wood picture frames.

Corner clamps come in various sizes and designs to accommodate moldings of any size. Shown are large-capacity, heavy-duty clamps from Wolfcraft and MLCS, Ltd. (top left and bottom right) *and two styles of standard-size clamps* (top right and bottom left).

A glazier's tool is the ideal accessory for securing works inside wood frames. Other options include a tack hammer and brads (top left) *and brad driver* (bottom).

Anyone can make drum-tight dust seals by following the simple directions in chapter 10.

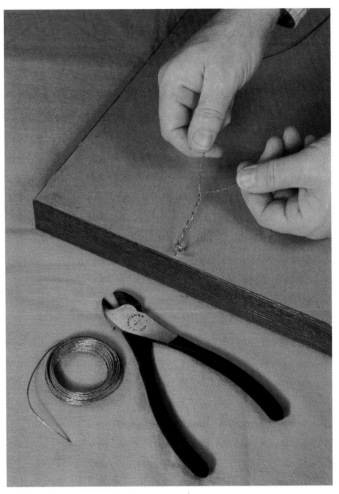

The final step in making most wood frames is installing screw eyes and picture-hanging wire. (See chapter 10 for details.)

Metal-section frame moldings come in a wide variety of colors and configurations. Sectional frames go together quickly with a screwdriver.

Mat and frame corner samples are great aids in deciding on the best mats and frames for most works.

Use push pins to position and stretch needle-work on 3/8-inch foamboard, prior to matting and framing. (See chapter 4 for details.)

Finished mounted and matted needlework is set inside an attractive lacquered frame from Graphik Dimensions, Ltd.

Krylon Metallic Spray Paints are ideal for finishing and refinishing wood and metal frames. Shown left to right are silver, copper, gold, and brass finishes.

Plasti-Kote's Fleck Stone and Formby's Granite Stone Finish impart interesting colors and textures to simple wood frames. Shown left to right are Plasti-Kote's Mineral Spring finish and Formby's mauve, forest green, and desert sand finishes.

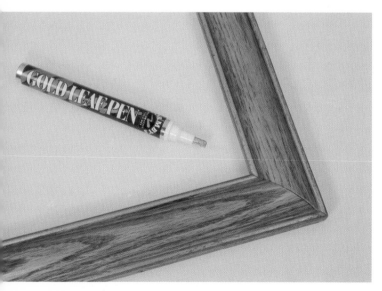

Formby's Gold Leaf Pen is handy for touching up or adding gold accents to wood and metal frames.

The most popular freestanding frames are easel-back and hinged frames. Learn to make your own by following the directions in chapter 7.

Greeting cards and note cards are excellent sources of cheap or free art for many decorating applications. Just mount, mat, frame, and display them throughout the home.

Calendar art is another source of cheap or free framables, ranging from fine-art and folk-art reproductions to exquisite photographs.

This calendar art, entitled "Nail Apron," made a handsome addition to the author's work area when mounted, matted, and framed for less than $15.

The traditional way to display sets of artwork and photographs is with matching mats and frames. For variety, use identical styles, but try mixing mat and frame colors and finishes.

Not all frames require miter-cut corners. Make this handsome lap-joint frame by following the directions in chapter 13.

This canvasback decoy carving by Artist Royal Cook is secured in a shadow-box mount and mat, as described in chapter 18.

A lacquered frame from Graphik Dimensions, Ltd., finishes this proof by the artist Christopher "Dutch" Mostert in the author's collection.

make another pass, leaving a 1/4 x 1/2-inch rabbet and 1/4-inch lip.

This molding is used as is for making a simple, shallow frame, or it can be used in conjunction with other moldings. This is also the basic configuration to begin with when making the router moldings that follow.

Grooved Moldings

You can use several different bits for making grooved moldings. The straight bit you used to make the rabbet will make a broad groove in the molding face. A narrower straight bit will make smaller single and multiple grooves. A V-groove bit will make V-shaped grooves at various depths.

To make a centered groove on the molding face, start by setting a combination square at 3/4 inch and make a centered pencil mark on one end of a strip of flat molding. Lay the molding on the router table, and move the router until the bit is aligned with the guide mark on the end of the molding.

Always start shallow. Not only will this make the routing easier, but a shallow groove might turn out to be all you want. You can always make it deeper, but you can't correct a groove that's too deep.

To make a double-grooved molding, use a combination square to mark one end of a piece

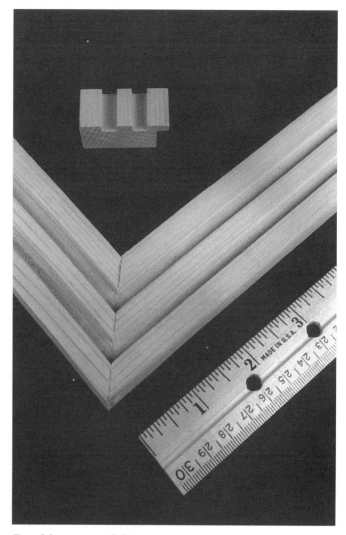

Double-grooved frame.

Making double-grooved molding.

Making V-grooved molding.

V-grooved frame.

of molding ¼ inch from one narrow edge. Put that edge against the router-table fence, and align a ¼-inch straight bit with the guide mark. With the bit set for a ⅛-inch depth, lay the molding facedown and pass it over the bit to create a ¼-inch-wide, ⅛-inch-deep groove. Rotate the molding so the opposite edge is against the fence, and make another pass to create a second groove.

A ⅜-inch V-groove bit is the ideal size for a 1 x 2 flat molding. With it, you can make ⅛-inch to ¼-inch single and double grooves, and ⅜-inch centered grooves.

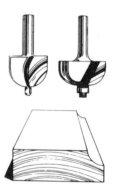

Cove bits.

Making coved molding.

Coved-molding frame.

Coved Molding

This is not a cove molding, as discussed in the earlier section on construction moldings. Rather, this is a picture-frame molding with a cove routed into it.

To make the molding, start with the flat molding, facedown on the router table. With a 3/8-inch-radius cove bit set for about 3/16 inch, run the molding over the bit to rout a cove into the edge opposite the rabbet. If you want a deeper cove, set the bit for full depth, and run the molding through one more time.

Beaded Molding

You will see in the profile of this molding that when fully beaded the routed edge has two sharp corners. As you produce this molding in steps, though, you will end up with a different molding on each pass over the bit. Note the different effects you can accomplish at different depth settings, and choose the one you prefer.

Use a 3/8-inch-radius beading bit, set for a 1/8-inch depth. Lay the flat molding facedown on the router table, and run it over the bit. Reset the router for a 1/4-inch depth, and make another pass. Finally, set the router for full depth and make one last pass. You can even make subsequent deeper passes for different effects entirely. Experiment.

Roman Ogee Molding

Start with a 5/32-inch-radius Roman ogee bit, and use it as you would the beading bit on flat molding. Set the router for a 1/8-inch depth, lay the molding facedown on the table, with the edge to be routed against the fence, and run it over the bit. Then continue resetting the depth in 1/8-inch increments and noting the effect of each pass. Pick the one you like.

Beading bits.

Making beaded molding.

Beaded frame.

Making Roman ogee molding.

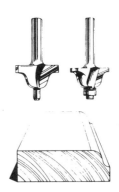

Roman ogee bits.

Rounded Molding

Corner-round bits come in various sizes and can be used at different depths, much the way beading and ogee bits are used. To simply round over one or both front corners of a molding, though, you must limit the depth of cut to the radius of the bit.

Earlier, I used a 3/8-inch corner-round bit to make the J-molding. You can use the same bit to round over the unrouted face corner of flat molding to a depth of 3/8 inch. You can round over both face corners, but you should not go the full depth on the molding lip, as you will lose material if you do.

Roman ogee frame.

Making rounded molding.

As with other bits, round over the corners in at least two steps. With a 1/4-inch corner-round bit, though, you can set it for full depth and make one pass on each face corner for a fully rounded molding. The molding shown was rounded this way with a 1/4-inch bit.

Beveled Moldings

You can do shallow beveling with the 3/8-inch V-groove bit used for making V-grooved moldings. But if you want to bevel the face edges deeper, use a 1/2-inch chamfering bit.

As with other bits, take off about 1/8 inch with each pass, until you achieve the effect you desire. You can bevel one or both face edges. If you bevel the molding lip, be careful not to go so deep as to change the width of the molding lip.

Other bits are useful in making frame moldings, as are various sizes of the bits covered

Corner-round bits.

here. The ones demonstrated, though, are probably the most generally useful and are certainly good ones to start with.

Be sure to browse at your local tool and hardware outlets to find out what is available.

Rounded frame.

Making beveled molding.

Making double-beveled molding.

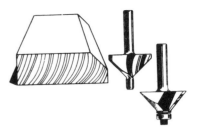

Chamfering bits.

And when you own a few bits, do some experimenting with them to find out what they will do. Combine some of the techniques covered here. For example, try a centered V-groove on the face of a double-beveled molding. Add a straight groove to a beaded or Roman ogee molding. Work with some wider stock. Glue up thicker, more complex moldings.

Beveled frame.

Double-beveled frame.

There's no end to what you can accomplish, once you turn your imagination loose.

DECORATIVE FRAME MOLDINGS

The more framing you do, and the more you think about framing and study the work of other framers, the more ideas you will come up with for making your frames distinctive. You will find various materials—vinyl, leather, cloth, cork, acrylics, Formica, twine, rope, and others—that you can use for decorating frame moldings. Keep in mind, though, that decorating frames is like cooking with garlic: a little goes a long way, and you can overdo it.

I don't think it's a good idea to just decorate frames willy-nilly. Try to match the frame to the subject, if not entirely, at least partly. You won't always be able to do so, but some frames can be suggestive. A frame can even blend with a room's decor, though it needn't and probably shouldn't match the drapes or carpet.

Be subtle in your approach to decorative frame moldings, and if you might err, do so on the side of conservatism and you'll stay out of trouble. Think about what you are doing and what you hope to accomplish. Remember that the art is the object of interest, not the frame. The frame should complement the art, prepare the viewer for the subject, and keep the viewer interested. It should never distract the viewer or distract from the work.

There is really no end to the materials you can use to decorate frames or to the methods and ma-

terials you can use to add flair to some frames. I have seen bead-covered frames that I really didn't care much for, but I'm sure others liked them, or no one would have spent all that time gluing beads. I remember seeing several shells in a frame

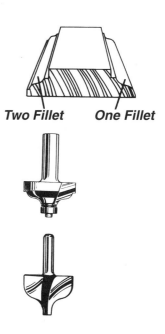

Two Fillet   **One Fillet**

Ogee bits with fillets.

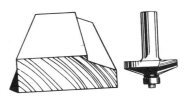

Raised-panel bit.

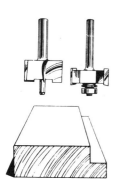

Rabbeting bits.

Classical bit.

Making Router Moldings Without a Router Table

If you own a router but haven't yet bought a router table, you needn't let that keep you from making picture-frame moldings with your router. Several techniques will allow you to do so. Depending on how your shop is equipped, one of these ought to work for you.

The first method requires only a router and the right kind of bits. A router edge guide will enable you to use any kind of bit. Some routers come with edge guides; for those that don't, edge guides are available as optional accessories. In the absence of an edge guide, you should use piloted router bits, the best of which have integral ball-bearing pilots. Edge guides and bit pilots allow the user to rout along the edge of a

Rabbeting the edge of a board with a router.
Photo courtesy of Sears.

strip or board while using the edge itself to keep the router on track.

Start by clamping each end of an 8-foot strip of 1 x 2 or wider wood (depending on how wide you want your molding to be) to a sawhorse with a pair of C-clamps or bar clamps. With a piloted rabbet bit, start as near the left end of the strip as the clamp allows, and rout from left to right along the strip until you reach the clamp at the opposite end. Make as many passes as necessary to rout the rabbet to the necessary depth.

Turn the strip over and clamp it to the sawhorses. Then with a piloted decorative bit, rout the outside edge of the strip the same way, making as many passes as necessary. Cut the unrouted ends off the strip, and your molding is ready to be cut into frame pieces.

If you own a bandsaw, you can quickly make strips of flat molding. Use your router and a rabbeting bit to mill a rabbet along one edge of an 8-foot 1 x 10 or 1 x 12. Set the bandsaw fence 1 1/2 inches from the near teeth of the blade, and run the rabbeted edge of the board through the saw to create one strip of flat molding. Rout another rabbet along the sawed edge of the board, and rip another strip with the bandsaw. Continue in this manner until you have used up the board or made as much molding as you need.

If you own a table saw, you can easily make decorative moldings using similar techniques. This time, clamp the wide board to sawhorses, and use a piloted decorative bit to rout one edge. Make as many passes as necessary. Then use your table saw to rip a 1 1/2-inch-wide strip from the decorative edge. Rout another decorative edge on the wide board, and rip that the same way. Continue doing so until you've used the whole board or made as many strips as you need for a project or want for inventory. Then use the table saw to cut a rabbet along the unrouted edge of

With the Rabbet-Master Kit from Jesada Tools, you can make a half-dozen different size rabbets, from 1/8 to 1/2 inch. PHOTO COURTESY OF JESADA TOOLS.

each strip according to the directions found earlier in this chapter under Saw Moldings (see page 127).

You'll find router bits and accessories at most tool outlets, including the various mail-order suppliers listed in the Source Directory. One of the largest selections of top-quality router bits and bit sets, including piloted bits, is available from Jesada Tools. The company also offers the Rabbet-Master Plus, a unique bit kit consisting of one high-quality bit and a set of interchangeable ball bearings of different sizes, allowing the user to make seven different cuts with a single bit.

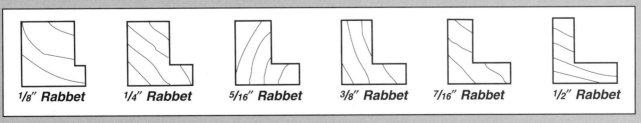

| 1/8" **Rabbet** | 1/4" **Rabbet** | 5/16" **Rabbet** | 3/8" **Rabbet** | 7/16" **Rabbet** | 1/2" **Rabbet** |

Profiles of rabbets that can be made with the Rabbet-Master Kit from Jesada Tools.

Sisal rope in ¹/4-inch and ³/8-inch diameters comes in 50-foot spools.

that was covered with hundreds of tiny shells. Too much of a good thing, I thought at the time.

On the other hand, I once saw a small frame made from a flat molding that was covered with hundreds of tiny seashells all glued into a fascinating mosaic. All that was in the frame was a mirror. I liked the effect and wished I had the patience to sit long enough to glue all those shells in place.

Of course, much of this is a matter of taste, but I do think that there is a limit to the use of highly decorative frames and some rather loose guidelines you can use. The more decorative the frame is, the simpler the subject should be. And what could be simpler than a mirror? In that case, the shell-covered frame *was* the subject.

Many decorative materials at your disposal are fairly subtle and unobtrusive. Formica and other similar acrylics, for example, are often effective when cut in strips and glued to frame moldings. White, off-white, charcoal, and black are the best colors for general use.

Leather and leather-imitating vinyls are also noncommittal, but can be used evocatively. While wood-and-leather moldings work well with many different subjects, I think they are particularly striking in use with western art, a genre enjoying great popularity today.

Making Rope Moldings

Frames decorated with rope are also fairly universal in their adaptability, but these, too, suggest certain subjects or motifs to me—marine art in particular. Rope-and-wood moldings also work well with western art and pastoral scenes.

Rope also changes any molding or frame dramatically without being overwhelming, because it mainly changes the texture and pattern of a molding, rather than color or bulk. Rope is also easy to use in framing. And for these reasons, it is one of the most useful of all decorative items.

Sisal and Manila hemp ropes are the best for use in making picture frames. Both are coarse, natural-fiber ropes that stain well and are easy to work with. You will find these ropes at variety and hardware stores, where they are available in several diameters and are sold by the foot. Some sizes are also available in small spools you might want to keep on hand. I buy ¹/4-inch and ³/8-inch sisal rope in 50-foot spools. When I need a larger diameter, I buy it by the foot for a specific project.

With rope, it's best to decorate the frame rather than the uncut molding. You can stain the frame first, then attach the rope, or attach the rope and stain frame and rope together. If you stain the frame and not the rope, the two will contrast, and the rope will be more noticeable. If both rope and molding are stained, the effect is subtler. The choice is yours.

Rope can be used with some commercially made moldings or moldings you make. Use ¹/4-inch rope with moldings that have ¹/4-inch grooves, such as the double-grooved molding

Use a utility knife or razor-blade scraper to cut 1/4-inch rope at a 45-degree angle, run a bead of glue along 1/4-inch grooves, and press rope into grooves.

When glue sets, pry nail heads up with a screw-driver, and pull nails out with pliers.

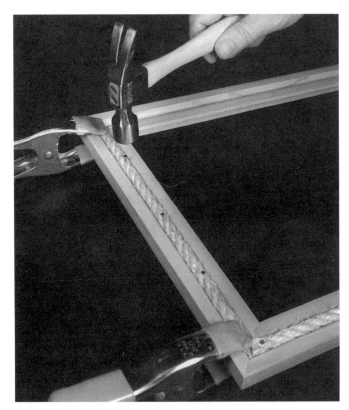

With a V-grooved frame, run a bead of glue along the groove, clamp the rope in the groove, and tack the rope with wire nails.

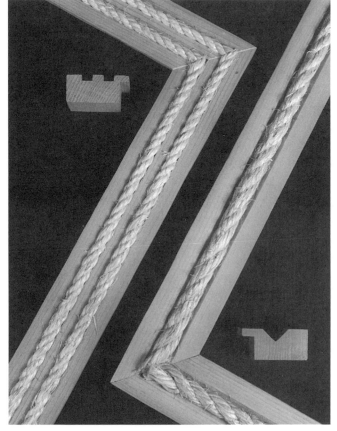

Finished rope frames, ready for staining.

Three styles of decorative molding.

Using Carved or Pressed Moldings

In the molding department of your favorite home-improvement center and at some department stores, you will find carved or pressed moldings that are used for decorative purposes in various woodworking and finish-carpentry projects. Some are also useful in making frame moldings.

These decorative moldings are usually 1/4 inch thick and come in various widths, from about 3/4 to 11/2 inches, and lengths of 6 or 8 feet. Most can be glued to the face of nominal 1-inch-thick stock cut to the same length. The 3/4-inch molding can also be used on the 3/4-inch edge of nominal 1-inch-thick wood.

If you prefer, you can inlay the molding. Use a straight bit on a router attached to a router table to rout a groove in the face of the frame molding, making as many passes as necessary to accommodate the width of the molding to be inlaid. For a flush inlay, simply match the depth of the groove to the thickness of the decorative molding. For a different effect, make the groove slightly deeper. You can also cut grooves with a table or radial-arm saw.

To attach the decorative molding, apply wood glue to the groove, and clamp the decorative molding in place. If you don't have enough clamps, lay a strip of parting bead or 3/4-square on top of the inlaid decorative molding, and tightly wrap masking tape or rubber bands around everything about every 12 to 15 inches. Let stand until glue sets, and the molding is ready for cutting.

Making Inlaid Moldings

Contrasting woods also make attractive inlays. Rather than make long strips of such moldings, though, I prefer to use scraps leftover from various projects. The Micro Wood I use for many of my laminating jobs is hardwood that comes in 1/8-inch and 1/4-inch thicknesses and 24-inch strips of various widths from 1/8 inch to 3 inches. I always have a lot of odds and ends of this material on hand in such species as oak, walnut, cherry, and maple. I use various species of hardwood in nominal inch-thick stock and always have random lengths in the scrap bin.

shown earlier. The molding deeply grooved with a 3/8-inch V-groove bit is ideal for use with 3/8-inch rope. You can also rout a 1/4-inch or 3/8-inch cove into the edge of a frame molding, and attach 1/4-inch or 3/8-inch rope along that edge.

To attach rope to a frame, first cut one end of it at a 45-degree angle with an X-Acto knife. Lay it along the groove of one section of the frame, mark it for the second miter cut, and cut it. Cut the rope for the remaining three frame sections the same way.

Use wood glue or five-minute epoxy to attach the rope to the frame. If you have enough spring clamps, use them to hold the rope in place until the glue sets. Or you can temporarily tack the rope to the frame with brads or small wire nails. When the glue has set, pull out the nails with pliers.

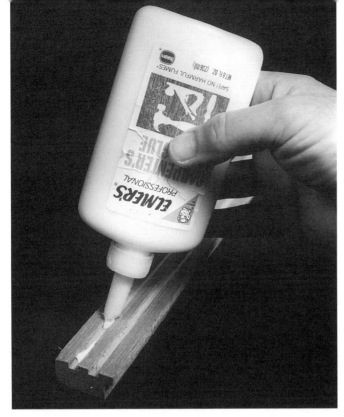

Applying glue to double-grooved molding.

Sanding molding smooth with a belt sander.

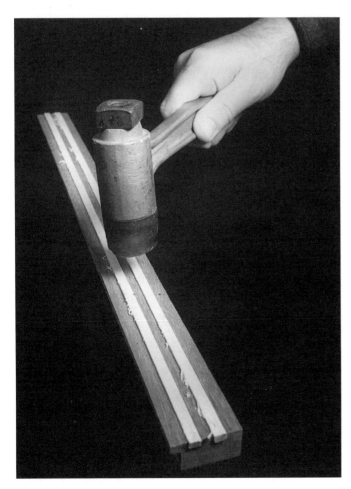

Tapping maple strips into grooves with soft-faced mallet.

Maple and mahogany inlaid frame.

Always a Frame in the Making

I enjoy making frames, especially from my own moldings. Perhaps what I like most is that the gratification is almost instant and comes in several phases of the framing process. I get a kick out of turning a strip of 1 x 2 into an attractive frame molding and another out of turning that molding into a handsome and useful frame.

After a hard day at the computer keyboard or in the studio or darkroom, I welcome the opportunity to relax for a few minutes or a half-hour in my workshop. But I'm certainly not going to build a cabinet or refinish a table in that length of time. I can in that half-hour, though, turn out up to 100 feet of frame molding, or cut the sections for several frames, or build an entire frame, or build two if I use sections cut earlier.

I keep a list of items that need framing, and I often have framing to do for others. And I make frames in standard sizes that I'm always able to use or sell. When I just feel like cutting some frame sections, I do so, binding each set of four with rubber bands and storing them on shelves in the shop. When I feel like building frames simply for therapy, I usually work with these "kits" I keep on hand. Or sometimes I just go through the scrap bin, looking for lengths of leftovers that I can turn into moldings and frames.

I'm sure once you begin making your own moldings and building frames from them, you'll be doing the same kinds of things. In your shop, as in mine, there will always be a frame in the making.

There are certain woods that work well in combination. I like oak with walnut inlays, walnut with oak inlays, maple with cherry inlays, and mahogany with maple inlays.

To make the molding in the accompanying photographs, I made a double-grooved molding from scraps of mahogany 1 x 2. I used a 1/4-inch straight bit to rout 1/8-inch-deep grooves. I then used a bandsaw to rip some scraps of 1/4-inch maple Micro Wood to a width of 3/16 inch.

Then I cut them to match the length of the mahogany scraps.

Next, I ran a bead of glue along each groove in the mahogany, tapped a strip of maple into it with a soft-faced mallet, and let the molding stand until the glue dried.

I sanded the face smooth with a belt sander and medium-grit belt. When I later made the frame, I sanded it with a pad sander and 120-grit and 220-grit sandpaper.

CHAPTER NINE

Finishing and Refinishing Picture Frames

Considering all the woods suitable for picture framing and all the ways there are to finish these frames, I could fill a book with a discussion on the various finishing methods and materials. Consequently, to allow but a chapter on the subject means I must leave out some information and include only what I deem to be most important.

I know I'm asking for trouble—or at least an argument—but mainly what I am leaving out of this discussion is what some professional framers and authors of framing books consider to be most important: all their gessos, patinas, and gilds and how to use them.

I'm a woodworker, not an artist. So I finish my frames with woodworkers' techniques and materials. I am also a busy person who values his time, spare and otherwise. So what I look for in the finishing or refinishing of any frame is the quickest way to get the job done right. And frankly, many of the methods covered in other books and used by some professional framers seem terribly time-consuming and a bit old-fashioned.

That these methods are covered adequately elsewhere is good enough reason to exclude them here. Nevertheless, I recognize that there will be a few readers who either do not entirely agree with me or simply wish to know about the other ways to finish frames. So I will direct them to the book *How To Make Your Own Picture Frames,* third edition, by Hal Rogers and Ed Reinhardt (Watson-Guptill Publications, 1981). This book was first published in 1958 and includes the materials and techniques that were widely used then. The book will tell you how to

mix gessos and patinas, how to cut in and build up texture, and how to tone and gild.

Just as many new mounting and matting products and techniques developed in recent years have provided us with many more options, so have some of the wood-finishing products and methods. What's more, there are a few old standbys worthy of rediscovery, and some that are particularly suitable for finishing picture frames.

FILLING AND PATCHING WOOD FRAMES
The kind of wood patch or filler to use on any frame depends on the type of finish you plan. If you will be painting the frame, use spackling paste. If you plan to stain the frame, use a stainable wood filler, such as Zar Wood Patch, Dap Wood Dough, or Plastic Wood. For natural finishes, hot-melt shellac sticks are best.

With most frames, the only patching you will need to do is to fill brad holes at the corners. On some frames, even those can be left unfilled. If you have a miter joint that refused to come together completely (and all of us face that problem from time to time), you can fill that too.

You can use spackling compound that mixes with water for patching frames that will be painted, but the latex paste that comes in a can is much quicker and neater to use, and it's always ready. You can use a putty knife to fill brad holes with spackling paste, or you can work it in with a finger. Either way, build it up slightly above the molding surface, as it will shrink as it dries.

With simple, unadorned frames, you can patch gaps in miter joints with spackling paste and the

149

If you plan to paint a frame, fill and patch with spackling paste.

Zar Wood Patch is a neutral-colored latex filler that dries fast, is easy to sand, and takes a stain.

putty knife. Where contours of the molding pose problems, work the paste in with your finger, and wipe away all excess. In areas that will be difficult or impossible to sand, use your finger to completely smooth the paste and remove as much as possible.

Some years ago, my day's mail included a sample tube of Zar Wood Patch, which I put on my bench as a reminder to give it a test next time I had any filling to do. Since then I have come to prefer this filler for many jobs on items that will be stained and varnished or lacquered. The paste is the consistency of peanut butter and doesn't seem to dry out, as other fillers do. It goes on as easily as spackling paste, but takes a stain as readily as the plastic wood fillers do. What's more, I have found no need to thin it, and it doesn't seem to shrink as other fillers do. It dries fast and is as easy to sand as spackling paste. Apply it with putty knife or fingers, as you would spackling paste.

The bad news about the plastic wood fillers, such as Dap Wood Dough, is that they aren't quite as easy to apply as spackling paste or Zar Wood Patch. They will shrink some as they cure, and in time they will dry out in the container. The good news is that you can easily get around the shortcomings. Dap is relatively cheap; it cures hard, stains easily, and comes in wood-tone colors as well as natural. This is a good filler to use on frames you plan to finish naturally without staining.

Dap Wood Dough in "natural" will darken somewhat with the application of oil, shellac, polyurethane, or lacquer, so it fairly well disappears when you use these finishing materials. The "natural" product will also take stains. The colored wood-tone products are the best to use on specific species that will be finished without stains. I keep Dap Maple Wood Dough on hand, for example, for patching maple frames that I don't plan to stain. Likewise with Mahogany and Red Cedar Wood Dough, both of which also work well with the various shades of redwood.

With most rustic or roughly finished frames, you needn't worry about patching, but if the frame is to be finely finished, then all flaws should be removed or hidden. Small pitch pockets, cracks in and near knots, tiny borer holes, and the like must be filled. For frames that will be naturally finished, the best material to use for these blemishes is hot-melt shellac sticks.

The sticks are available in a wide array of colors and hues to match most woods perfectly. You can apply the material with a heated putty-knife blade, or you can buy one of the electric burn-in knives designed for such purposes, which are available by mail for about $20 or so.

To patch any hole, crack, or other imperfection, touch the heated blade of the applicator to the end of a color-matched shellac stick, and transfer the melted material to the flaw in the frame. Smooth the shellac with the hot blade, and remove any excess. Let the shellac harden for a minute, and it is immediately ready for sanding.

Dap Wood Dough is available in natural and various wood tones. Keep it thinned and workable with solvent.

SANDING AND PREPARING FRAMES FOR FINISHING

The best way to save time and enjoy sanding is to avoid it entirely. For most of us, sanding is a tedious chore, but with some moldings and frames it is necessary. It is the way to achieve the finest finish, and it's a way to correct mistakes.

There is a little sanding to do on just about every wood frame, but rustic frames and those made with prefinished moldings require the least. After you cut frame sections, the miter cuts often have tiny splinters on the saw-exit surfaces. Gently sand these edges with 120-grit sandpaper to remove the splinters.

Moldings are not always consistent in width and thickness. Moldings you make yourself and those that are manufactured commercially can be slightly off, keeping your miter joints from matching perfectly. When the width of two adjoining sections differs slightly, always match the inside corners and allow the resulting overhang at the outside corners. Then when the frame is assembled, simply sand down the overhang.

Similarly, when molding thicknesses vary slightly, the face or rear surface of one section will be higher than that of the adjoining section. During assembly, align either the face or rear surface, depending on the intricacy of the mold-

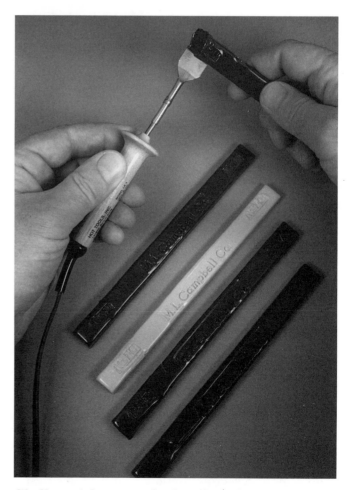

Shellac sticks are melted and applied with an electric burn-in tool or a heated putty knife.

A 3-inch pure-bristle paintbrush makes a good dusting brush.

When you want the finest finish—perhaps to simulate the superb hand-rubbed oil finish used on some furniture and gunstocks, or the rubbed lacquer look—continue sanding with the pad sander and 320-grit waterproof sandpaper. Then hand sand with 400-grit waterproof sandpaper, and polish with #0000 steel wool.

On some frames you will want sharp corners and edges; on others rounded corners and edges are better. Round over the corners and edges as you sand, beginning with the 120-grit step. A 1/4-sheet palm sander is handy for this operation, as it is easy to handle and to rock back and forth along a sharp edge to round it over.

To sand corners and other confined areas in any frame, fold a sheet of sandpaper and sand with the creased edge. Another handy item for sanding tight spots and contours is an abrasive sponge. Buy one with a medium-grit abrasive on two sides and fine-grit on the other two sides. Some flap-sanding attachments that fit grinders and electric drills are good for sanding intricate moldings, but I don't recommend them for use on softwood moldings, as they will remove too much material and ruin the molding.

Detail sanders or attachments and contour or profile sanders are good tools for reaching confined places in many wood frames. Sanding contours are available for hand sanding in tight spots.

During the sanding operation, you must clean frame surfaces frequently to check your progress. I carry a 3-inch, pure-bristle paintbrush in a back pocket when I'm in the shop. This is my dusting brush, and I don't use it for any other purpose. With it, I dust the surfaces I'm sanding and inspect them closely. In this way, I know when I have removed scratches and have achieved a consistent smoothness with any particular grit, which is my signal to change to a finer abrasive or stop sanding altogether. With such open-grained woods as oak, walnut, and mahogany, a brush is the only efficient tool for cleaning sanding dust from the grain.

When I have finished sanding any frame, I use the dusting brush and a vacuum cleaner to thoroughly clean the frame. Then, just before applying any stain, oil, paint, polyurethane, or

ing, and sand the other surface smooth when the frame has been assembled.

Only rarely should any frame require coarse sanding, unless you wish to use coarse abrasives to create texture. When you do need to remove a good bit of material quickly, though, as in the case of inlaid moldings where the inlays might be 1/16 inch or more above the molding surface, use a belt sander and 80-grit belt to sand the surface smooth and flat. If you don't own a belt sander, use a pad sander and 80-grit sandpaper.

Next, sand the surface with a pad sander and 120-grit sandpaper until all scratches left by the belt sander are gone. Follow that with a sanding with pad sander and 220-grit sandpaper. You will rarely need to go to any finer abrasive than this.

lacquer, I wipe down all surfaces of the frame with a tack cloth.

You can extend the life of any tack cloth by "snapping" the dust out of it frequently and storing the cloth in an airtight container to keep it from drying out and losing its sticky characteristics. I keep mine in a Ziploc plastic sandwich bag.

STAINING FRAMES

Most natural-wood frames that won't be painted should be stained before the final finish is applied. Of course, some woods and inlaid frames require no stain. Black walnut, teak, redwood, and a number of other dark woods look best without staining. And some rustic frames should be finished sans stains. With many woods, however, stains bring out the beauty of the wood and enhance the character of the frame.

Stains come in a variety of colors and shades, and their colors will vary further depending on the kinds of woods they are applied to. For example, a Medium Walnut stain looks one way on oak, quite another way on pine, and different yet on cedar. Paint stores, department stores, and home-improvement centers where stains are sold display charts or boards with actual samples of woods treated with various makes and colors of stains. These can help you make decisions about what kinds of stains to buy. But even with such assistance, you should always test every stain on a sample of wood that matches the wood of the frame you plan to stain.

Eventually, you will settle on a few favorite woods and a few favorite stains, and you'll know without experimenting and testing what the right combination is. As I said earlier, I use pine and oak more than any other woods for my framing jobs. Similarly, I have a few favorite stains and other finishes that I use on most frames. Occasionally, though, I try out a new stain or finish, or one that's new to me. Or I work with different woods. Then I always test the stain and wood.

Most of the stains you use will be transparent oil-base stains that require no thinning. Different colors of these stains can be mixed for even greater diversity and variety.

You can also use different colors of oil-base stains in consecutive steps to achieve different effects. For example, apply one of the wood-tone stains—such as medium walnut, cherry, golden oak, or fruitwood—to an open-grained wood, such as oak. After sufficient penetration, wipe it dry with paper towels, and let it dry overnight. The next day, apply a coat of Fuller O'Brien Pen-Chrome #640-13 Platinum stain, being sure to work it into the grain with a brush. Wipe the frame dry, and let it stand overnight. The result will be a lightly frosted finish that is quite attractive in picture frames. You can slightly tone down the effects to suit your tastes by polishing the frame with #0000 steel wool.

Such oil-base stains can be applied with a brush or rag, but for picture frames, I suggest using a brush to get into all the corners and

Apply stains to frames with a brush.

crevices. After frames are stained, clean brushes with paint thinner, turpentine, or mineral spirits.

Most manufacturers recommend applying the stain and letting it penetrate and dry overnight, but this might darken a frame too much. So I suggest you apply the stain, let it penetrate for about ten to fifteen minutes, and wipe the frame dry with paper towels. Let the frame stand overnight, and determine then if additional staining is required. You can always apply more stain if it's needed; it's quite a chore to lighten a frame that's too darkly stained.

Don't assume that because two or more manufacturers offer stains in identical tones or shades that they are identical in their effects on any particular wood. For example, several companies offer stains they call English Oak, and each is at least slightly different from the others. For me, the one that comes closest to what I think English Oak ought to look like is Fuller O'Brien Pen-Chrome #640-11 English Oak.

When I apply this stain to frames made of red oak and wipe it off in ten or fifteen minutes, it darkens the oak to a color that can best be described as an aged brown with hints of charcoal gray residing in the open grain and pores. This is precisely my interpretation of English oak— what I expect it to look like.

This is not to say that other English oak stains are inferior. Rather, they produce different results that don't meet my expectations. Only by experimenting with different brands and colors of stains can you discover those that meet your needs and expectations. For that reason, I always recommend buying stains in small containers until you find the ones that work best for you.

Once a frame has been stained and allowed to dry, it is ready for sealing and final finishing. Although you can store the stained frames until you're ready to finish them, it's best to finish them immediately, or at least seal them before storing them.

THE DANISH OIL TREATMENT

There are a number of oil-and-resin finishes on the market today, and all will work well on picture frames. I suggest you start with Watco Danish Oil Finish. It's easy to use, is available in the widest variety of colors, and produces a superb finish. And for many frames, this is the final finishing step.

Watco finishes include natural, light walnut, medium walnut, dark walnut, cherry, fruitwood, and golden oak. You can also mix colors for a broader range of effects. For example, I use a half-and-half mixture of natural and medium walnut on inlaid frames of oak and walnut.

Although the various Watco finishes share common characteristics, they should be treated like other stains as regards the different colors and their effects on various woods. Experiment and always test any Watco and wood combination you haven't tried before.

Use a brush to apply a liberal amount of Watco Danish Oil Finish to a picture frame. Let the oil penetrate for thirty minutes, applying more to spots that absorb the oil and dry faster. Then apply another liberal coat, and let stand for fifteen minutes. Wipe the frame dry, and let stand for twenty-four hours.

Such open-grained woods as oak and walnut will bleed excess oil from their pores after being finished with Watco Danish Oil Finish, producing sticky, often discolored spots on the frame surface. Don't rub these spots with rags or paper towels; the friction will only compound the problem. Instead, let the frame stand until the spots dry completely; then take them off with #0000 steel wool.

If you plan to use the frame with an oil painting, acrylic, batik, or anything else where archival or conservation methods aren't required, the final step is wet polishing with wax. Brush on Watco Satin Wax, and lightly wet sand the frame's exterior surfaces with 600-grit waterproof sandpaper or polish with #0000 steel wool. Let stand ten minutes, and buff with a soft cloth.

For conservation framing, the frame must be sealed. But before applying any sealer, lacquer, varnish, or polyurethane over Watco Danish Oil Finish, let the frame stand for seventy-two hours, and do not apply the Watco Satin Wax.

Clean brushes with paint thinner or mineral spirits. Rags used during the Danish Oil treatment should be thoroughly soaked with water before discarding to prevent spontaneous combustion.

As great as the Watco products are, their container caps leave a lot to be desired. They're the kind of childproof caps that only children can open. We adults must use pliers and the appropriate language, and then when the container is opened, it's impossible to pour the stuff without making a mess. So be sure to lay newspapers on the floor of your work area, and wear old clothes or a shop apron. As my neighbor, a professional wood carver, says, "You have to love Watco; why else would you put up with their containers?"

SEALING WOOD FRAMES

Sealing a wood picture frame provides a barrier between the frame's contents and the acid in the wood—a necessity in conservation framing. Sealing also prevents the leaching of natural resins and moisture in the frame. Even properly cured or kiln-dried wood has a moisture content of 15 to 19 percent, and temperature fluctuations can cause this moisture to percolate to the frame surface and discolor the finish.

Although some finishing materials, such as Deft Clear Wood Finish, seal and finish in one step, others don't adequately seal the wood, or work better when a sealer is applied first. Even paints applied over raw wood can be stained by leaching resins and moisture. So it's a good idea to seal before painting as well.

Although most varnishes and polyurethanes will seal the wood, sealers dry much faster. So you will save time by applying a sealer and then a finish coat, instead of two finish coats.

Acrylic sanding sealer is popular as a base coat for polyurethane, as it will be dry and ready for sanding in two or three hours. The problem is it must be sanded before the finish coat is applied, which can be difficult with the more intricate frame moldings.

Shellac is an excellent sealer, and nothing dries faster. What's more, it need not be sanded before the finish coat is applied. For those reasons, I use shellac almost exclusively for sealing frames.

You can brush on shellac or spray it on, and either method works well with picture frames.

Shellac can be brushed on or sprayed on. It thins and cleans up with denatured alcohol.

Apply a thin base coat, let it dry, and you're ready to apply the final finish. You can thin shellac and clean paintbrushes with denatured alcohol.

PAINTING FRAMES AND LINERS

Modern paints are a joy to work with. The odorless latex flat and semigloss paints can be mixed to match nearly any hue. They dry without leaving brush marks, and clean up with water.

These are the paints to use for many frames and most liners. When you are trying to match the liner to a color in a painting, stop by a paint store or home-improvement center and check the paint chips that show the various color mixtures available. When you find the right one, have the paint mixed at the store, and it's ready to use. Apply two coats to the sealed liner.

Use paint-sample chips to find the precise colors, and have them custom mixed.

High-gloss enamels and lacquers make fine finishes on some frames. If this is the sort of finish you're interested in, prepare the frame by sanding it to the finest finish described earlier in the chapter. Seal it with shellac, and lightly burnish the shellac with #0000 steel wool. Then apply high-gloss enamel or lacquer and let it dry. Burnish again with steel wool, and apply another coat.

Simulated stone finishes from Formby's and Plasti-Kote add interest to frames.

Although these glossy finishes can be applied with a brush or sprayed on, brush-on lacquers are sometimes hard to find. What's more, both glossy enamels and lacquers are available in aerosol cans that are ideal for finishing frames.

Some of the rust-inhibiting enamels for metal are also useful for painting wood frames. Some dry to a flat finish, while others dry to a high gloss.

Modern metallic-finish paints—gold, silver, bronze, copper, and the like—are a vast improvement over their predecessors. Use these for simulating metal or for painting liners, filets, and molding edges in lieu of gilding.

Simulated stone finishes provide other interesting options for some frames. Plasti-Kote and Formby's are two brands of such finishes. Plasti-Kote offers kits in several colors, each containing an aerosol can of the finish and a can of clear final finish. Formby's Granite Textured Stone Finish comes in aerosol cans in such colors as decor blue, desert sand, forest green, salt and pepper, mauve, and peppermint. The company recommends applying a final coat of Formby's clear satin or gloss finish, which is sold separately.

CLEAR FINISHES

Although I have worked with many different kinds of varnish, polyurethane, and lacquer over the years, I have settled on a few that have served me well. I like those that dry fast to a keen, uniform finish without showing every tiny bubble or speck of dust.

Most of the clear finishes I use are available in brush-on form, but I mainly use aerosol cans now for their convenience and the ease of even application. Clear finishes dry to dull matte, satin sheen, semigloss, or glossy finish, depending on the type of material you use. The finishes on most of my frames are either satin sheen or semigloss, or occasionally dull matte. When I want a semigloss clear finish, I skip the sealing step and apply three coats of Deft Clear Wood Finish, which seals and finishes simultaneously. For those who like a glossy finish, Deft is available in glossy.

For other clear finishes, I start with shellac to seal. Over that I apply an even coat of dull matte or satin sheen polyurethane, depending on the finish I want.

REFINISHING OLD FRAMES

For some frames—namely those you have found at garage sales, flea markets, and secondhand stores—finishing is mainly a matter of refinishing. Part of the refinishing process is the removal of the original finish.

Although some finishes can be removed with abrasives, chemical finish removers are better for picture frames, as they will get into hard-to-reach places and take off the finish without removing wood.

With some chemical finish removers, the old finish is softened, then scraped off with a putty knife. Another type allows you to hose off the old finish with a garden hose, and this is the better choice for picture frames.

You will find such finish removers stocked with the paints and other finishing materials at hardware, department, and paint stores and most home-improvement centers. Read the labels to find the one that best suits your needs.

Sometimes I find old wood frames that require very little in the way of refinishing. I brush them to remove dust, then wash them with Murphy's Oil Soap. I lightly and quickly rinse them, trying to avoid soaking the corner joints or any exposed wood surfaces, and wipe them dry at once. Then I let them stand overnight to thoroughly air dry.

With painted frames, often all that's needed is a fresh coat of paint. It's also possible to paint naturally finished frames, but if the finish remains fairly well intact, it may need only a little minor repair and touch-up. I carefully examine such frames under good, bright light, looking for nicks, scratches, dents, chips, and other imperfections.

Many nicks, scratches, and other minor defects in the finish that expose bare wood are easily covered with a variety of materials. I stock a good assortment of wood stains in small cans and often am able to match original finishes with

Two of the author's favorite finishes are Deft Semi-Gloss Clear Wood Finish and satin sheen polyurethane. A plastic gun handle that snaps to the can makes application easier.

them. I also keep various colors of wood putty and hot-melt shellac on hand for such purposes. I have even used color pencils, shoe polish in several shades, and felt-tipped pens and markers to hide surface blemishes on picture frames.

For touching up gilded frames or adding gold highlights or accents to other frames, I use Formby's Gold Leaf Pen, which is similar to a felt-tipped marker and as easy to use. The broad, pointed tip lays down broad or narrow lines of quick-drying gold paint and allows the pen to be used like a calligraphy pen. At a sidewalk art sale some years ago, I found an original oil painting I liked in a nicely finished oak 16 x 20-inch frame that seemed to need a little something added. Recently, I used the Formby's pen to gild the inner and outer beads of the frame. The subtle touch was just what the frame needed.

I occasionally pick up old metal portrait frames at garage sales, flea markets, and second-hand stores. When I get them home, I dismantle them, put the glass aside for later attention, and check any backing materials, which often include easel backs. If the easel backs are badly damaged or too worn, I discard them. Some require only a good cleaning.

I use a stiff-bristled brush to clean old metal frames with hot, soapy water. I sometimes enlist the aid of a toothbrush for getting into small places. Then I rinse the frames in hot, running tap water, towel dry them, and use a hair dryer to completely dry them.

Before painting any metal frame, I wipe it with a cloth dampened with clear, distilled vinegar to remove any fingerprints and oils left from handling the frame, which might prevent paint from adhering to it. I also suspect that the acetic acid in the vinegar gives the metal surface some bite that helps paint stick to it.

Once the frame is clean, dry, and ready, I apply two coats of Krylon Metallic Spray Paint: usually gold or brass, but sometimes copper or silver. I then clean and dry the glass and install it, along with a new or refurbished easel back. What I end up with is a frame that looks new.

KEEP IT SIMPLE

The simpler you keep the finishing process, the more time you will save and the more you will enjoy it. And you don't need to spend tedious hours, days, or weeks trying to achieve the ultimate finish on any frame.

You needn't be an expert on every kind of finishing material available or every technique known. In fact, if there is a secret to success, it has to be simplicity. Experiment and test as a way of finding the best products for your purposes, and when you find a few that work well, stay with them and learn all their characteristics.

CHAPTER TEN

Glazing, Installing, and Displaying Framed Works

Essentially, there are two types of framable works: those that get framed behind glass or acrylic, and those that don't. Ordinarily, we frame mounted and matted originals and reproductions behind glass or acrylic, as well as some three-dimensional objects, and delicate items that require glazing to protect them from dust and other damaging elements. Conservation framing calls for the use of glass or acrylic. We also glaze some artworks on paper that we frame without mats. Oil paintings, acrylics, batiks, and similar works, however, should be framed without glass. With photographs, glazing is optional.

Most of the framable items found in the average household should be glazed, so it's important for any framer to learn how to work with the various glazing tools and materials and how to pick the right type of glass or acrylic (Plexiglas is a brand of acrylic) for any particular job.

For most framing, you will probably want to use either standard picture glass or nonglare glass, both of which are 1/16 inch thick. For very large works, you might need the added strength of window glass, but use this material only if you must. It is thicker, thus heavier, and is not manufactured to the same exacting standards as picture glass and nonglare glass. Consequently, it might exhibit bubbles and other flaws.

Acrylic or plastic glazing material offers some advantages and disadvantages. Some framers prefer it for glazing large works because it is lighter than glass. But the product isn't always as flat as glass, especially if it has not been handled and stored properly. It is not so susceptible to breakage as glass, but it scratches easily, so you must exercise more care in handling and cleaning it. Acrylic also builds up static electricity so that dust and lint cling to it.

Perhaps acrylic is most useful in framing color photographic prints, which are prone to damage from ultraviolet (UV) radiation. Ultraviolet is present everywhere in natural and artificial light and causes photographic dyes to fade. By using a specially formulated ultraviolet-filtering acrylic in front of a print, you can greatly prolong the print's life. This product filters more than 90 percent of the harmful rays.

Acrylic is usually more expensive than glass. It is cheaper in large sheets that you cut yourself, but is also available at some outlets in standard sizes. Sometimes the precut material ends up being cheaper in the long run, because you can save time using it.

An alternative is to use a sheet of ultraviolet-filtering polystyrene behind picture glass. This material is only .040 of an inch thick, filters about 75 percent of the harmful radiation, and comes in standard sizes, from 8 x 10 to 16 x 20 inches.

There are special processes for coating color photographic prints with a special UV-inhibiting lacquer or overlaminating them with special UV films. Such services are available from many commercial photo labs. Check with a local lab or photography dealer, or write to Meisel Visual Imaging, the lab I use (see the Source Directory).

The advantages of using these processes are several. First, they save time, as someone else does the work. Although the cost works out to be

PRECUT GLASS Standard Sizes (in inches)
8 x 10
9 x 12
11 x 14
12 x 16
14 x 18
16 x 20
18 x 22
18 x 24
20 x 24
22 x 28
24 x 30
24 x 36
26 x 32
30 x 40
36 x 48

more than that of the polystyrene filter sheets, these processes save time and provide the only practical way I know of to frame prints without glazing while protecting them from UV rays.

The biggest decision you'll have to make in glazing most works, though, is whether to use picture glass or nonglare glass, and here only you can be the judge. For some reason that continues to baffle me, many professional framers adamantly oppose the use of nonglare glass in *any* framing job. The reasons they give are that the nonglare glass diffuses light and thereby gives the illusion of softening the image or reducing clarity. They further argue that mats only compound the problem, because the farther the glass is from the image, the greater the reduction of clarity. Moreover, they warn that works viewed obliquely or from askance are obscured by nonglare glass. Finally, they point out

Print on left is under nonglare glass, and print on right under standard picture glass. Notice the distracting reflections on the latter.

that picture glass seems to improve clarity and color saturation.

Of course, all this is true, but these arguments dissolve like sugar in water when the surface of ordinary picture glass reflects so much light as to obscure the work behind it. The commonsense approach to glass selection is to examine each framing job individually and pick the glass most suitable for the medium, the matting, and the area where the work will be displayed.

Nonglare glass does, indeed, slightly diffuse light, which will cause an apparent loss of clarity in some works and some media. It seems to be more of a problem with some watercolors (but not all) and intricately detailed pen-and-ink works. It also seems to work admirably with lithographs, serigraphs, and other reproductions. It's an excellent choice for glazing diplomas, certificates, and other documents. And it is ideal for many landscapes, scenics, and portraits, regardless of whether or not reflections would pose problems with standard glass.

I often use nonglare glass with single and double mats and have used it with triple mats on large works. I would not recommend using it with more than two mats on small works that are normally viewed at close range or more than three mats for larger works. But then, I double mat most works I frame and rarely ever use more than three mats, so I simply don't have a problem with extreme reduction of clarity.

No work is meant to be viewed at a sharp angle, so that argument is specious. If you look at a work head-on, you will have no problem with distortion, regardless of the type of glass used.

With some works, such as certain watercolors, drawings, and black-and-white photographs, standard picture glass does seem to offer more clarity. I have trouble accepting the notion that it provides better color saturation, because display techniques and ambient light play major roles there and can affect any work.

In short, determine what sort of glass best fits the work. If you're framing a color photograph that you want to last, you might need UV-filtering acrylic. If you're planning to hang a collection of prints in a bright area where reflec-

tions obscure them, you will probably want to use nonglare glass. Where reflections are not as severe, you might still want to use nonglare glass, and that's your prerogative. If you prefer standard glass, that's fine too. And standard might prove best for some works. Just don't let someone else's unfounded prejudices influence you.

I keep at least one sheet of each type of glass on hand at all times. Then, if I'm not sure what kind of glass will be best for any work, I try it with each type. I also check the room where the work will hang if I'm not sure how reflections will affect it. If you do the same, you needn't worry about picking the wrong glass.

GLAZING TOOLS AND TECHNIQUES

There is really no need to ever cut a piece of glass yourself, but I recommend learning how to do it, for several reasons. First, it's an easy enough skill to learn and requires little in the way of tools. It can prove to be worthwhile, and you can usually save money over the long run. What's more, if you know how to cut glass, you can salvage usable pieces from larger ones that have been chipped, cracked, or broken.

Picture glass and nonglare glass are available in standard sizes, from 8 x 10 to 36 x 48 inches. Where precut acrylic is available, it usually comes in standard sizes from 8 x 10 to 20 x 24 inches. You'll save time and money using this precut material, so when you can, try to make your framable items conform to standard sizes. Some odd-sized works can be made standard by cutting mats to standard outside dimensions.

With certain popular sizes, you can save by buying a large sheet of standard-size glass and cutting it into several smaller sizes. For example, if you need a number of 8 x 10-inch pieces of glass, keep in mind that you can easily cut four from a single 16 x 20-inch piece.

Whenever you need a piece of glass or acrylic that is not standard size, you must either buy a larger sheet and cut it yourself, or have it cut at the glass shop. Sometimes the cutting charge is so small that it's hard to justify cutting your own. So you'll just have to use your own judgment.

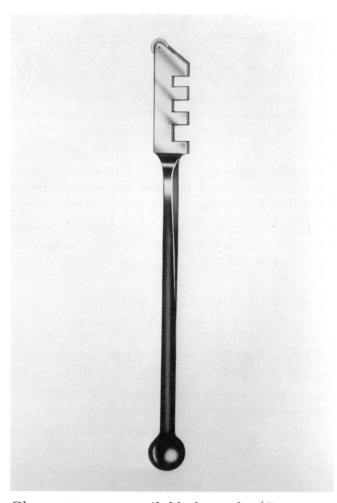

Glass cutters are available for under $5.

Scribe guidelines on freezer paper.

Glass size in any framing job is determined by the outside dimensions of the mounted work. So you simply cut the glass the same size as the mount board and mats.

To cut your own glass, you will need a good glass cutter. They range in price from about $2 to $15, and they all work the same way. You will also need a solid working surface, a straightedge, and a few other items you probably already have around the house or shop.

One of the easiest ways I have found to cut glass is to mark a sheet of paper with guidelines instead of the glass. Start by taping a sheet of freezer paper to your bench or table top. Scribe a line across it, near one end. This is your edge-alignment guide. After determining where your cut should be made on the glass, scribe a second line parallel to the first at that distance. Scribe a third line 1/8 inch beyond the second, or whatever distance is dictated by the width of your cutter head.

Pour a little kerosene or turpentine into a small container, and keep it nearby for lubricating the cutter head. (Make sure you have a strip of masking tape running the length of the underside of your straightedge to keep it from slipping on the glass.) Align one edge of the glass along the first line you scribed on the freezer paper. Align your straightedge on the third line. Dip the cutter head in kerosene, and scratch a line in the glass along the second line scribed on the paper. Keep your elbow stiff, and move the cutter by moving your upper body backward in one fluid motion.

There are several ways to part the glass along the scratched line. Some simply tap the underside of the glass at one end of the line, then grasp the glass with thumbs and forefingers near the edge, and snap it in two. You can also align the scratched line with the guide mark on the upper jaw of a pair of glazier's pliers, squeeze the plier handles, and thereby part the glass along the line. A third way is to lay a pencil on your work surface, position the glass atop it, and align the pencil with the scratched line. With your hands on the glass, a few inches left and right of the scratched line, press down-

Cutter should make a continuous hissing sound as you scratch a line into the glass.

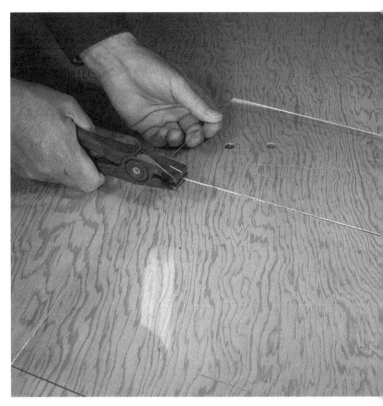

You can use glazier's pliers to snap glass in two.

ward quickly but gently, and the glass will part along the line.

Glass edges are quite sharp, so handle them carefully. Run the glass under warm water to flush away tiny glass particles. Then mix a cup of detergent ammonia in two quarts of warm water, and use this to wash away kerosene and fingerprints. Rinse with warm water, and dry with paper towels.

Cutting acrylic is no more difficult. For this job, substitute an acrylic-cutting knife for the glass cutter, and don't bother with freezer paper, because you can scribe cutting marks or lines onto the protective paper or plastic covering the acrylic.

When you have scribed your cutting marks or lines, align a straightedge along the first one, and draw the point of the knife along the line. Repeat the process as many times as necessary to cut nearly all the way through the acrylic—usually three or four passes for picture-frame acrylic.

Lay a length of dowel 3/4 inch in diameter (or larger) on your bench. Lay the acrylic on top of

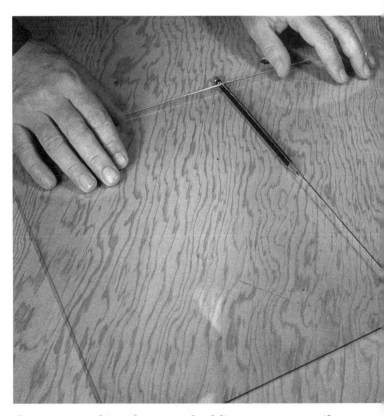

Or you can align the scratched line over a pencil and press down on the glass to snap it in two.

Folding acrylic knife.

you find any, remove them with 120-grit sandpaper. Then wipe the edges clean with a damp sponge or rag. Remove the protective paper when you're ready to install the acrylic in the frame.

INSTALLING MOUNTED WORKS

Most of the works you frame behind glass will probably be matted. Remember that one of the functions of a mat is to provide the necessary air space between the glass and the surface of the work. So if you're framing something without a mat, you must take other measures to provide that important air space.

I'm amazed by the number of unmatted works I see framed right against the glass, and I have seen such shoddy work in some pretty highfalutin galleries. One in central Oregon springs to mind, because it was a spendy spot meant to tempt the well-to-do tourists who frequent the area. I was looking at a collection of color photographs that were only a small cut above okay. The frames were mediocre, and the prints were sandwiched

it, and align the cut with the dowel. Put your hands on top of the acrylic on each side of the cut, and press down quickly to snap the piece in two. Then make subsequent cuts the same way.

Before removing the protective paper or plastic from the acrylic, inspect the edges for burrs. If

Use a straightedge and acrylic knife to score the acrylic in several passes.

against the glass without mats. The only thing outstanding about any of the prints was the price.

I would have been perfectly contented to mosey on, but some silver-tongued dandy cornered me and began expounding on the many virtues of the photographs and the photographer. For all I know, it was the photographer himself. After his tediously long-winded spiel, I said, "Well, that's all fine and wonderful news for someone who doesn't know a photograph from an epitaph, but I'm afraid the ignoramus who framed this collection has rendered it worthless."

He sputtered and choked and asked, "Why would you say such a thing?"

"Simple," I said, "look here." I brought him up for a close inspection and pointed to one of the prints that was exhibiting damage obviously caused by condensation on the inside of the glass. It had laminated the print surface to the glass, and I was sure the rest of the prints were already suffering similar damage or soon would be. "These photos don't have a plug-nickel's worth of collector's value," I told him, and all he could do was agree with me.

Photographers or people who frame their photographs are some of the worst offenders when it comes to this damaging practice. Perhaps the reason is that photographs are mounted and displayed without mats. Sometimes photographs are simply mounted to mount boards, either flush or with borders, and are displayed without glass or frames. Fine. Sometimes, photographs are framed and displayed without glass. Fine. But if they're framed behind glass without mats or spacers, not so fine.

As a general rule, don't let any work you're framing touch the glazing material. There are, however, some notable exceptions to the rule. Some framing techniques call for contact, but in such cases I can only recommend using works that have no potential collector's value.

For example, sometimes photographs and posters are displayed with so-called frameless frames: hardware that's used to sandwich glass, work, and backing material without the use of a conventional frame. If the work is of little or no commercial or sentimental value, then by all

Then align the scored line on a dowel rod, and snap the acrylic in two.

means display it against the glass if you wish. But if you want to preserve and protect it, mat it first.

For works displayed in conventional frames without mats, a simple product is available that's easy to use and provides the necessary air space between glass and artwork. Framespace is an archivally safe plastic material that can be cut with scissors to fit on the edges of picture glass or acrylic. It comes in white, black, or clear. If you're framing without mats, this is the material I recommend for providing that important air space and protecting the work from condensation and other damage. Another similar and equally adequate product goes by the name Innerspace.

By the time you're ready to install any work in a frame, the frame should be finished. To pro-

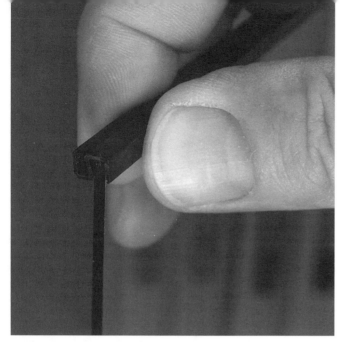

When framing behind glass without mats, use Framespace to provide the necessary separation between glass and the work.

One style of glazier's points can be pushed in with a screwdriver or a putty knife.

tect the finish, spread a piece of felt, carpeting, or other protective material on your work surface. Clean the frame to remove any dust and lint, and lay it facedown on the protective material.

Then everything simply gets stacked inside the frame: glass (with spacer, if necessary), mounted and matted work, and backing if required. Backing material should be cut the same size as glass, mats, and mount boards, and you should use backing with any large works that might require the added support the backing can offer.

Once everything is stacked in the frame, hold it in place by hand, and gently lift the frame for inspection. Carefully examine the glass to make sure there are no pieces of dust or lint on the inside surface. If there are, there's nothing to do but take everything out and clean the glass again.

When you're satisfied that all is clean and ready for the finishing touches, it's time to secure everything inside the frame. For this, you can use either brads or glazier's points. In the case of the latter, either buy the kind that you can press in with a screwdriver, or you will need a special tool specifically designed for the task.

You can tap brads into the inside surface of the frame molding with a hammer. If that's the method you will use, you might need a pair of

You can squeeze brads into molding with the end of a nail set.

long-nose pliers to hold the brads. You should also C-clamp a strip of wood along one edge of your work surface, atop the protective material. Then brace the facedown frame against this strip as you tap the brads into the molding.

An alternative is to squeeze the brads into the molding by hand with the aid of a nail set. Grasp the nail set in your hand, and press its flat side against the head of a brad. Loop your thumb over the molding, and press toward the brad to squeeze it in. This method works best with softwood moldings.

For hardwood or softwood moldings, you can use a tool specifically designed to seat brads. Known as a brad squeezer or brad setter, this tool is adjustable for different sized moldings and brads. One jaw is rubber-covered to prevent marring the finished frame.

For narrow moldings, you can make your own brad squeezer with a pair of slip-joint pliers. Cover one jaw with self-adhesive foam weather-stripping tape to protect frame finishes, and put the other jaw against the brad head. Then simply squeeze the brads into the molding.

If you will be doing much framing, or if you would rather use glazier's points, invest in a glazier's tool, which is loaded and used much like a staple gun. With the tool positioned on the backing, and against the inside of the frame

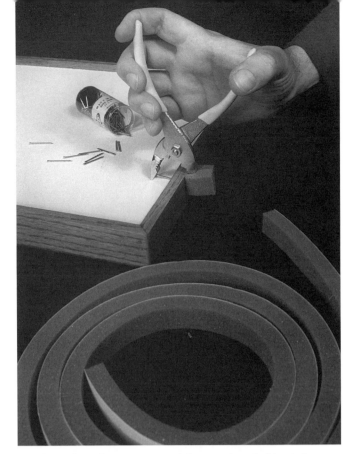

Make a brad squeezer with a pair of slip-joint pliers with one jaw padded.

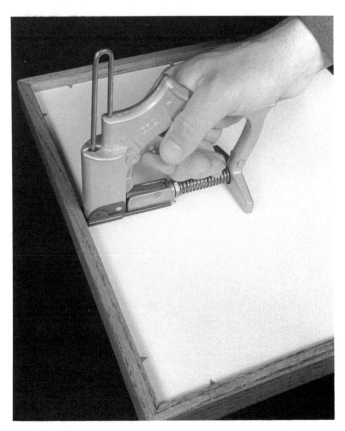

A glazier's tool drives glazier's points quickly and efficiently.

A brad squeezer or brad setter in use.

Apply an uninterrupted bead of wood or white glue to the rear edge of the frame.

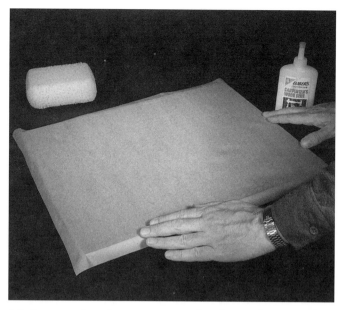

Make sure kraft paper completely seals rear of frame.

On wide moldings, spread glue with a finger or paper towel. Then dampen kraft paper with a sponge.

molding, you drive a diamond-shaped glazier's point every time you squeeze the handle.

Whether you use brads or glazier's points, you must drive enough to hold the work securely in place. For the smallest works, that means at least two per side, or eight in all. The larger the work, the more you will need spaced along each side of the molding—a half-dozen or more per side in the largest works.

ATTACHING DUST SEALS

There are several ways to attach dust seals. My favorite way calls for a piece of kraft paper cut slightly larger than the frame and attached with white glue or carpenter's wood glue.

With the frame facedown, I run a narrow bead of glue along the rear edge of the frame, and spread it evenly with a folded paper towel (you can use your finger if you prefer). I let that stand while I completely dampen the kraft paper with a sponge. Then I lay the frame, glued side down, onto the damp paper, press it firmly in place, and carefully turn it over. I examine the entire rear edge to make sure the frame is completely sealed, and I press the paper in place wherever necessary.

I then let the frame stand until the paper dries completely. As it dries, it shrinks and tight-

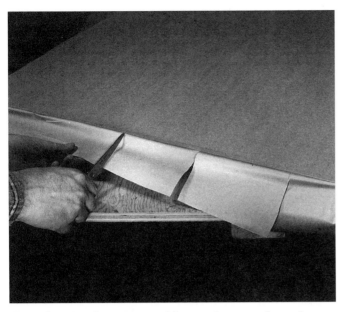

Cut slits in the excess of large dust seals to keep them from buckling.

One way to trim a dust seal is with the frame faceup, using the molding as a guide.

ens. Properly attached, a dust seal will become taut as a tom-tom.

Large dust seals can buckle as they dry, so I cut slits into the excess that extends beyond the frame edges. This relieves pressure and allows the seal to cure perfectly.

There are several ways to trim the seal. One way is to lay the frame faceup on a mat-cutting board or bench, and use an X-Acto knife at a 45-degree angle to cut away the excess along the frame's edge. This is perhaps the fastest way, but it is also the riskiest way, as one little slip of the knife, and you could shave wood away from your frame.

A much safer way is to lay the frame face-down and crease the seal with your thumb along the outer edge of the frame. Then lay a straight-edge along one side of the frame, about 1/16 inch inside the edge, and cut along the straightedge with an X-Acto knife. Repeat the process along each edge until all excess paper has been trimmed away.

The easiest way to trim a dust seal is with a framer's border knife, which you can buy for about $5 or so. If you have much framing to do, I recommend the investment. The knife uses X-Acto and similar blades and makes trimming

A better way is to lay the frame facedown, and crease the paper along the rear edges of the frame.

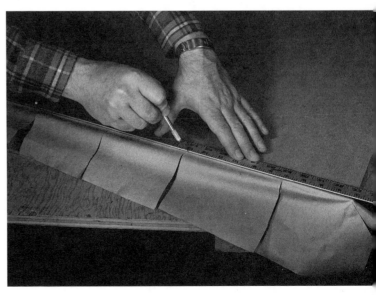

Then trim away excess with a straightedge and X-Acto knife.

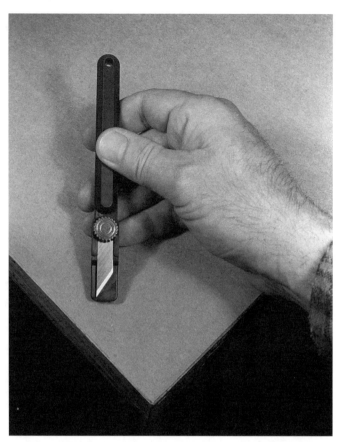

A framer's border knife makes trimming dust seals easy.

a dust seal a breeze. After creasing the seal along the edges of the frame, cut the excess away, with no need of a straightedge and no fear of cutting into the frame. The knife keeps the blade running about 1/16 inch from the frame's edge and makes trimming foolproof.

You can also attach dust seals with double-sided tape or adhesive transfer tape and the Scotch applicator. Some who use this method recommend cutting the kraft paper the same size as the frame and laying it on the taped rear edge of the frame, but this is risky. Better to cut the paper oversize, as with the wet method, skip the dampening with a sponge, lay the taped frame on the paper, turn it over, and trim the excess.

I have never been completely satisfied with my results using the dry method, but maybe that's just my lack of competence. I suggest you try both methods, and pick the one that works best for you.

INSTALLING OILS, ACRYLICS, BATIKS, AND THE LIKE

Although most of the works you frame will probably be installed in the manner we have just discussed, you might have occasion to frame oil paintings, acrylics, and other works that are not displayed behind glass. They require different treatment entirely. You won't find much in print on the techniques, perhaps because any method that securely holds a work in a frame without damaging it is sufficient. There are a few practices used by some framers and discussed in some of the framing literature, however, that I want to caution you against.

Before installing paintings on canvas boards, hardboard, or canvas and stretcher frames, stick a small self-adhesive felt cushion near each inside corner of the liner or frame to prevent any damage to the image area behind the molding lip. If the molding lip is too narrow for precut cushions, cut your own from a sheet of self-adhesive felt.

Works on canvas attached to stretcher frames are usually set inside liners and frames or frames without liners, depending on the framer's preference. Many framers nail the stretcher frame to the liner or frame, a practice I avoid, as it makes any later removal of the canvas and stretcher frame difficult and often leads to damage. What's more, nails will eventually rust and stain canvas edges, which might reduce the value of the work.

Some framers also seal the backs of such frames with cardboard or kraft paper, and this, too, is a practice you should avoid. Works on canvas and stretcher frames require free air circulation, which such seals inhibit.

I have heard it argued that these seals help protect canvases from damage when they're laid on sharp objects—presumably knives, swords, spikes, barbed wire, bungee sticks, machetes, saws, chisels, and the like. To my way of thinking, any dolt so careless with a valuable painting as to lay it on a sharp object deserves whatever happens. A painting spends most of its time hanging on a wall, where—barring brawls, gunfights, earthquakes, and tornadoes—it ought to reside in relative safety. If you must attach something protective to the rear of the frame, make it a piece of fiberglass screen, which will afford a modicum of protection while allowing air to circulate.

Use a straightedge and utility or X-Acto knife to trim the screen to the stretcher frame's outside dimensions. Then staple the screen to the back of the stretcher frame or attach it with small wire nails.

Liner and frame moldings come in various depths or thicknesses and accommodate stretcher frames differently. In a deep molding, a stretcher frame will fit with plenty of room for attaching hardware. In a shallow molding, the stretcher frame will protrude beyond the rear of the molding, calling for different installation techniques.

Some framers treat stretcher frames as they would mounted and matted works, and in a deep molding simply secure them with brads. In shallow moldings, they drive brads into the rear edge of the frame or liner molding, then bend the brads over to secure the stretcher frame.

At some frame shops and hardware stores, you will find brass or brass-plated hardware you can use to secure stretcher frames inside most moldings. Use offset clips with brass screws to secure stretcher frames that protrude beyond the frame or liner molding. You can also use offset clips on stretcher frames set in deep moldings, although there are other methods you might prefer.

Graphik Dimensions offers simple metal clips that just snap in place to hold canvases in frames with spring tension. They require no tools, and a set of four is only 50 cents. (See the Source Directory.)

Turn buttons and mending plates are some of the hardware you can use to secure canvases on stretcher frames inside picture frames.

Canvas clips from Graphik Dimensions, Ltd., make framing stretched canvas a snap. PHOTO COURTESY OF GRAPHIK DIMENSIONS, LTD.

Nylon-filament tape and heavy-duty staples at each corner can secure a stretcher frame inside a picture frame.

If there's sufficient room in a deep molding after the stretched canvas is set in place, you can simply secure it with tacking strips. Cut the strips from parting bead or lattice that you can rip to a 1/2-inch width. Tack them to the inside surfaces of the molding, just behind the stretcher frame with 1-inch brads or wire nails. Use only enough fasteners to hold the painting in place, and the job will be easily reversible, should you ever need to remove the painting from the frame. This is also the method I prefer to use with works done on canvas boards or on hardboard, both of which are considerably thinner than stretcher frames and allow for easy installation.

Other methods and materials work well too. If the rear of the stretcher frame is flush with the rear of the liner or frame molding, you can attach a small piece of mending plate at each corner to hold the stretcher frame in place. You can also use turn buttons attached with screws and even nylon webbing attached with staples.

As I said, any methods and materials are appropriate, as long as they secure a work in its frame without doing damage. On a trip to the Far East, I bought an original oil painting by

Roger San Miguel, an artist hailing from Manila. I later decided that shipping it in a frame might help protect it, so I had a rather massive frame made for the large painting in Okinawa, only to learn later that the two would have to be shipped separately.

When my painting arrived in the States some months later, it was in perfect shape, but the frame was broken. I repaired it and temporarily installed the painting in it with strips of nylon-filament (strapping) tape across each rear corner of the stretcher frame. I reinforced each strip of tape with two more strips, and drove staples through the tape into the frame molding. I hung the painting on a wall—the safest place to store it—until I could get around to building a new frame for it, or at least installing it with the proper hardware. That was more than thirty years ago, and since then that painting has hung in three apartments, a log cabin, and two houses. Those strips of filament tape are still holding the stretcher frame in place as well as any hardware might. So I now use this method regularly for similar installations.

INSTALLING HANGING HARDWARE

The most common way to prepare works for hanging is with screw eyes and picture-hanging wire, which is a lightweight braided cable. Keep an assortment of different-sized screw eyes on hand, and use the longer, heavier-gauge ones with large works and massive moldings.

To install hanging hardware, turn the frame facedown on a protected surface and measure about a third of the way down the rear edges of the left and right sides. Make a small pencil mark on each side in the center of the molding, and use a nail set or scratch awl to punch a screw-starter hole at each spot. Then drive a screw eye into each starter hole. Start the screw eyes by hand, and finish driving them with the nail set or awl for added leverage.

Wolfcraft makes a handy little tool called the Hook Driver that effortlessly drives screw eyes in seconds. It handles all but the smallest eyes and hangs from a pegboard hook when not in use. (See the Source Directory.)

Run several inches of picture-hanging wire through one screw eye, double the tag end back on the main length, and wrap it in a tight spiral. Secure the other end to the opposite screw eye the same way, so that when the wire is pulled toward the frame top, it will be from 1 to 6 inches from the top frame edge, depending on the size of the work and your own preferences. You'll do yourself a great favor by carefully measuring this wire-to-frame distance with a steel rule or with a picture-wire jig you can make. This is doubly important for any pictures you will hang in groups, as this makes precise hanging much easier.

Large and heavy frames require heavy-duty rigging. Install screw eyes as above, as well as two more on the bottom molding strip, about a third of the way in from each bottom corner. Attach the picture wire to one of the bottom screw eyes, thread it through the nearest side screw

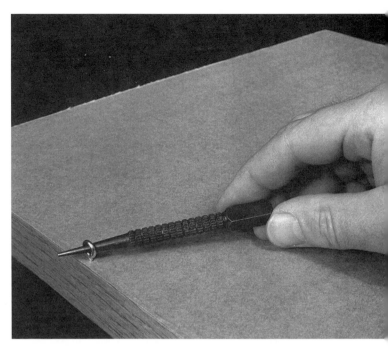

Installing screw eye with nail set.

The Hook Driver from Wolfcraft installs large screw eyes with ease.

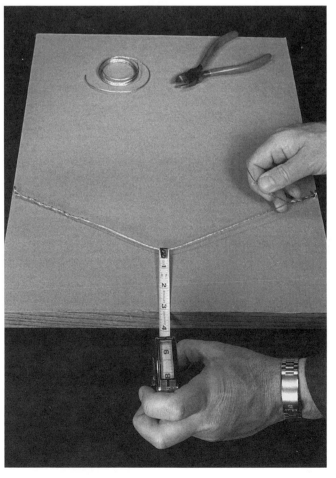

Attaching picture-hanging wire.

On heavy frames, install four screw eyes as shown.

Velcro has a number of uses in the framing craft. It comes in small kits and large rolls.

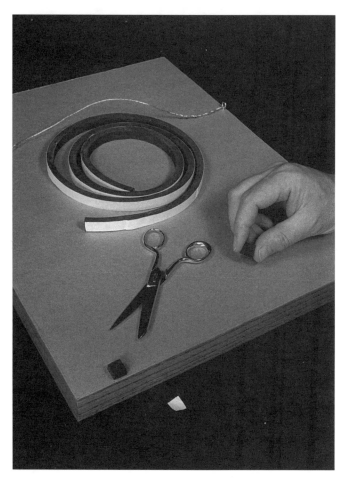

Attaching self-adhesive rubber pads.

eye, across to the opposite eye, and finally to the remaining bottom eye. Secure it by twisting, and use a steel tape rule or picture-wire jig to determine the frame-to-wire distance, as above.

Most professional framers attach small, self-adhesive felt cushions to the bottom corners of the frame to prevent dust from collecting and to allow air to flow freely around the frame back. I use the felt cushions on some small frames and where the screw eyes are attached inside the frame so the frame will hang flat against a wall, but then I use cushions on all four corners.

Normally, instead of the felt cushions, I make tiny rubber pads from 1/4 x 1/2-inch self-adhesive, high-density weather-seal tape. I stick a pad several inches inside each bottom rear corner. This not only allows air to flow around the frame and keeps dust from collecting, but it also makes frames hang parallel to the wall. Moreover, the rubber material clings to the wall, keeping pictures hanging straight.

Small, self-adhesive rubber pads and soft polyurethane bumpers also work well for such purposes. You'll find them at hardware and department stores, home-improvement centers, and frame shops, as well as in some mail-order catalogs.

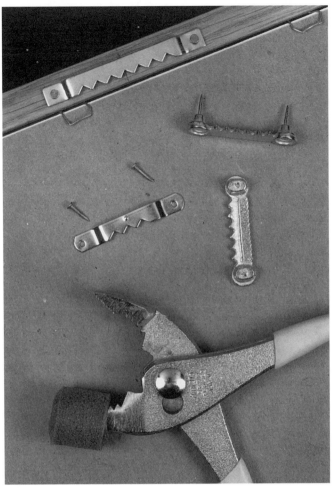

Sawtooth hangers come in several sizes and styles and can be installed with cushioned pliers.

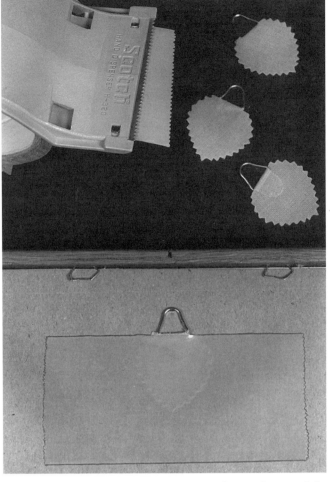

If you use gummed hangers, reinforce them with packaging tape.

On some commercial frames where I can't use my rubber pads, and in areas where heavy foot traffic keeps pictures dancing on the walls, I have found that Velcro works well. You can buy it in kits of self-adhesive hook-and-loop pieces, or do as I do and buy it by the roll. On small frames, put one piece bottom center on the rear of the frame, and its mate on the wall. On large frames, use two pieces on each frame, several inches inside the bottom rear corners, and mate them with two more on the wall. It takes a bit of adjusting to get each frame set just right on the wall, but once it's done you won't have to do it again.

Sawtooth hangers are useful with some frames, particularly those that are too narrow to accept even the smallest screw eyes. Some commercially made certificate frames are this small and require sawtooth hangers. To install them, it's best to position them in the rear center of the top frame section, and squeeze the nails in with pliers. The slip-joint pliers with cushioned jaws I described for driving brads work well for this.

There are gummed hangers available for lightweight frames. Although I can't heartily recommend their use, I must confess that I have used them on some commercially made frames. They work well with metal frames, for example, when attached to the backing board. I have never trusted the adhesive on them, so I always reinforce them with a strip of package-sealing tape or several strips of nylon-filament tape. Truth be known, they have worked well for me, so my reluctance to recommend them must be viewed as a personal prejudice.

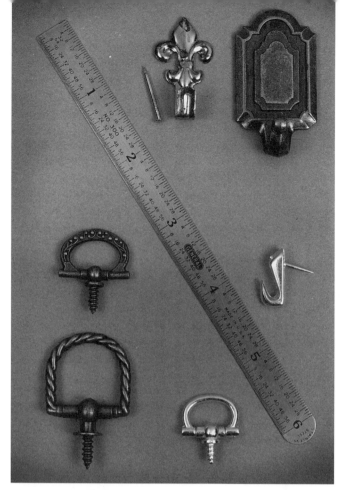

Decorative hooks and rings come in several sizes and styles.

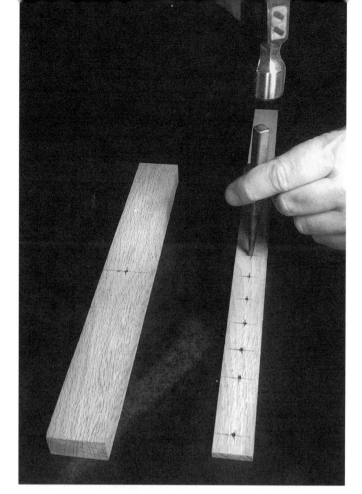

Picture-wire jig, Step 3.

Decorative rings are another alternative. On a small work, you can install one in the center of the top frame section. On larger works, install two in the top of the frame, each just inside a top corner.

Since decorative rings allow nails or hangers to show, I don't care much for them. So I rarely use them. There are some decorative hangers, however, that complement the rings and aren't half bad. I have used them from time to time, and while I haven't been enthralled by them, they haven't made me ill.

HOW TO MAKE AN ADJUSTABLE PICTURE-WIRE JIG

With a few scraps, several hardware store cheapies, and a little time in the shop, you can make an adjustable picture-wire jig that will make picture-hanging jobs foolproof.

Although you can make this jig with soft-wood scraps, hardwood is better. Even though I made mine from oak, you can use walnut,

maple, cherry, mahogany, or whatever you have on hand, and you can make it from two kinds of wood if you wish. And you can use hardwood plywood instead of the 1/4-inch Micro Wood.

All you need is a scrap of 1 x 2 at least 12 inches long, a scrap of 1/4-inch Micro Wood measuring at least 1 x 8 inches, a 1/4 x 1-inch brass flathead machine screw, a 1/4-inch brass wing nut, and a 3/16 x 3/4-inch copper rivet.

If you don't own a table saw, skip Steps 6 and 7, and use a 1/4 x 11/4-inch brass screw instead of the 1-inch screw called for. Here's how it all goes together.

Step 1. From a scrap of 1/4-inch oak Micro Wood (or plywood) at least 8 inches long, rip a 1-inch-wide strip. Then trim a scrap of oak 1 x 2 to 12 inches.

Step 2. Scribe a line across a broad surface of the 1 x 2 at 6 inches from each end, mark the center of the line, and center punch a drill-starter hole there.

Step 3. Scribe lines across a broad surface of the Micro Wood strip at 1/2, 21/4, 31/4, 41/4, 51/4, 61/4, and 71/4 inches from one end. Mark the center of each line, and center punch a drill-starter hole at each spot.

Step 4. Drill a 3/16-inch-diameter hole 1/2 inch from the end of the Micro Wood. Then drill a 9/32-inch-diameter hole at each of the remaining spots marked on the Micro Wood and through the center of the 1 x 2.

Step 5. Use a conical grinding attachment to countersink the 3/16-inch hole in the Micro Wood to accommodate a 3/16 x 3/4-inch copper rivet. Then countersink the hole in the 1 x 2 to accept the brass machine screw.

Step 6. Stand the 1 x 2 on a narrow edge, measure along the other narrow edge, and make marks 51/2 inches from each end. Then use a combination square to scribe guidelines across the narrow edge at those marks.

Step 7. Remove the blade guard from a table saw, and set the blade for a 1/4-inch depth. Lay the 1 x 2 on the saw table with the countersunk hole up. Then use the miter gauge to run the 1 x 2 over the blade repeatedly to remove the material be-

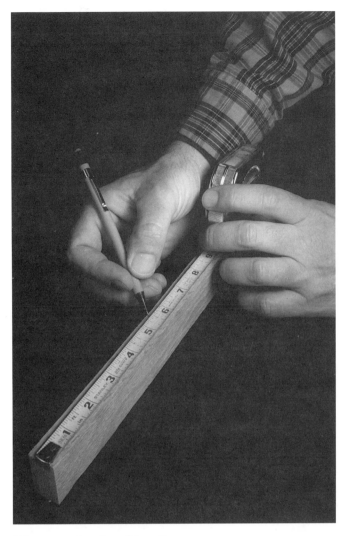

Picture-wire jig, Step 6.

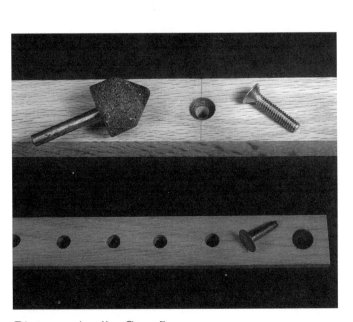

Picture-wire jig, Step 5.

Picture-wire jig, Step 7.

tween the guidelines, creating a 1/4-inch-deep, 1-inch-wide dado in a broad surface of the 1 x 2.

Step 8. Trim the Micro Wood strip to 8 inches. Then mix a small amount of five-minute epoxy cement, and apply it sparingly to the counter-sunk surface of the 3/16-inch hole in the Micro Wood. Push the rivet into the hole, and let stand until the cement sets.

To attach picture-hanging wire with the aid of your picture-wire jig, decide on what distance you want between the picture wire and the top edge of the frame, and set your jig for that distance. The holes in the Micro Wood strip are spaced at 1-inch increments from 1 to 6 inches from the rivet.

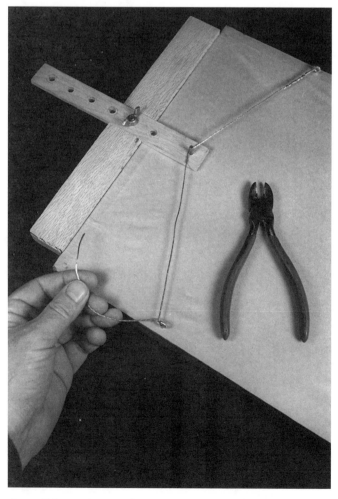

Attaching picture-hanging wire with the aid of the jig.

With the frame facedown and screw eyes installed, attach one end of the picture wire to one screw eye as you normally would. Then scribe a centered vertical line across the top frame section, and align the jig at the top of the frame by centering the guideline in the holes in the Micro Wood stem. Loop the picture wire over the rivet, and run it through the other screw eye. Pull the wire tight, and wrap the tag end around the wire as you normally would. The picture wire will now be a specified distance from the frame top. If you had the jig set at the third hole above the rivet, for example, the wire will be 3 inches from the frame top.

TIPS ON HANGING AND DISPLAYING

Something often said about a clumsy, inept person who has no mechanical aptitude or tool savvy is "He can't even hang a picture straight." The implication is that any dolt with five thumbs on each of his two left hands can hang a picture. Well it is easy, but there's more to it than pounding a nail into a wall and draping the picture wire over it.

In hanging and displaying pictures, so much depends on tastes, personal preferences, the requirements of the works being displayed, and the characteristics of the display environment that it's impossible to lay down laws or rigid rules. But a few general tips and suggestions might help you accomplish what you're setting out to do.

One of the first things to consider in hanging any work or collection of framed items is how high on the wall they should be. Of course, furnishings and fixtures in any room will influence such decisions, but there is a generality that at least provides a starting point. A common suggestion is to hang a picture at eye level. Whose eye level? I daresay, there's a difference between the eye level of the typical NBA star and the average jockey, just as there's a difference between the eye level of a 6'2" man and his 5'2" wife. And there's possibly a difference between what looks good to me and what looks good to you.

I suspect there's a tendency among tall folks to hang pictures too high. I know I had that tendency until I started paying close attention to

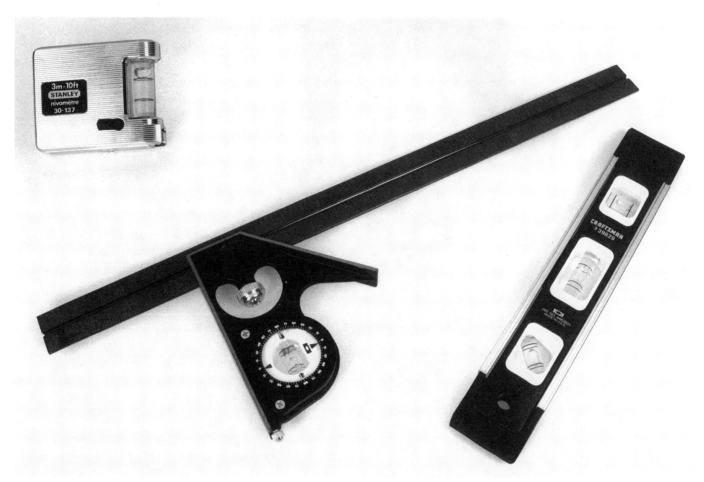

Keep a small spirit level handy for straightening framed works. This Stanley 10-foot steel tape measure (top) has an integral spirit level, as do most combination squares (center). Torpedo levels, such as this Craftsman model, are compact and just right for picture-hanging jobs.

such matters in museums, galleries, and even in others' homes and offices. I soon concluded that the pictures hanging a bit lower than I would have hung them were the ones that looked best. So I began hanging pictures lower.

I wish I could give you a convenient formula for this, but I can't. There is none. What I do now is find the visual point of impact in any framed item, which I try to hold at my eye level as I take my measurements from the floor or ceiling. Then I hang the item 8 inches lower, which is my wife's eye level. When I back off, it looks just right to me. We might surmise, then, that this would be too high for my wife, but I asked her and it seems just right to her, too.

In a typical room with an 8-foot ceiling, my pictures end up hanging slightly above an imag-inary horizontal centerline. And so do group-ings, which I consider as single entities, with each picture a part of the whole. But how high they hang depends on a number of variables. In our master bedroom, on a small stretch of other-wise bare wall hangs a large vertical oil paint-ing that's 41 inches high. The bottom of the frame is 30 inches from the floor, and the top is 25 inches from the ceiling. In another room are two vertical prints comparable in size to the oil painting, but they hang 10 inches higher, be-cause beneath them is a stereo cabinet that's 36 inches tall.

In rooms with vaulted ceilings and in open stairways with high ceilings, pictures can be po-sitioned higher. In such areas we can often take advantage of great expanses of wall space to cre-

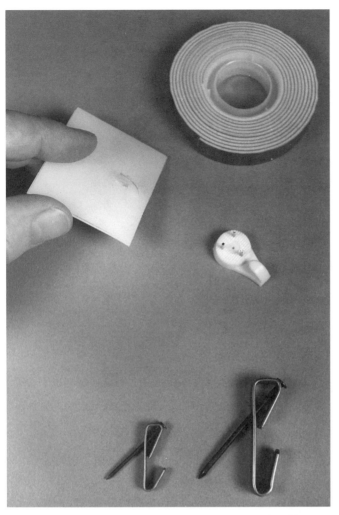

To hang pictures on hard walls, use self-adhesive foam mounting tape, self-adhesive plastic hangers, or plastic hardwall hangers. On other walls, use standard picture hangers (30-pound- and 100-pound-capacity hangers shown).

ate interesting displays, from low to high. In other areas we can sometimes take advantage of spaces that are confined horizontally or vertically by exploiting them with works that are strongly horizontal or vertical. A strong horizontal, for example, might work well displayed above sliding glass doors, while a strong vertical might fit best next to an entry door or on a wall at the end of a hallway.

Large pictures do well in areas where they can be viewed from a distance, such as at the end of a corridor or on a wall in a large room opposite the entrance. Small works that should be viewed at close range are best displayed where the viewer is forced into closer proximity, such as along a hallway, down a stairway, or in a small bathroom. In our house, a long, narrow hallway that has no furniture in it is where we have our family "rogues' gallery" hanging—portraits and snapshots of friends, relatives, reprobates, pets, kids, and assorted outcasts.

When we hang most items, we intend them to be seen by viewers who are either standing or walking by. Consider, though, that in some rooms occupants will be sitting most of the time. For that reason, in our dining room and in my office, I hung pictures several inches lower than I normally would have.

Some people have difficulty imagining what the visual effect of any picture or group of framed items will be on the viewer in a particular setting. My advice is to sketch out the wall in scale to get an idea of how everything will come together. You don't have to be a skilled artist to do this. I measure any furniture or other fixtures along a particular wall, and sketch them in, erasing and rearranging as necessary until I come up with a pleasing display. Then it's a simple matter to count off the squares on the graph paper and determine where my framed items will hang, relative to floor, ceiling, furnishings, and the like.

Groupings pose the biggest problem for most people. I find my 4-foot aluminum drywall square a big help in locating where my nails or picture hangers are to go. And I use a small spirit level to adjust pictures once they're up.

I hang nearly everything with standard picture hangers. Some books on framing and decoration recommend hanging each picture with two hangers to keep them hanging straight, but I have trouble getting two picture hangers nailed into the wall at precisely the same distance from the floor or ceiling. And if one is so much as a mere 1/16 inch off, the picture will hang noticeably crooked. I prefer to use one hanger of appropriate size for each framed item and keep it hanging straight the ways I discussed earlier. One exception is when I'm hanging unusually heavy items, in which case I use two 100-pound-capacity hangers side by side, which is overdoing it, but it makes me feel more confident.

Standard picture hangers do not work on such hard surfaces as brick, stone, concrete, and ceramic tile. For hanging pictures on most brick, concrete, and cinderblock walls, there are special hardwall hangers made of plastic, with three case-hardened steel pins that you hammer into the wall. For natural stone, ceramic tile, and other very hard materials, use special self-adhesive plastic hangers made for such purposes, or try the double-sided adhesive mounting tape made by the 3M Company.

Several years ago, I was framing a limited-edition print with which I had received a small sheet of paper telling a bit about the artist and his work. I wanted to keep the paper, but I knew once the print and paper were separated I would never find it again. So I attached it to the dust cover. I now do so routinely with any important papers I wish to keep with the artwork, including brief notes I make on what materials I used in mounting and matting. If I have elected to let the mats cover a signature and number on a limited-edition print, I note that as well. I attach single sheets or envelopes containing several sheets of information and notes with plastic mounting corners I buy from Light Impressions (see the Source Directory).

CHAPTER ELEVEN

Making Rustic Wood Frames

Rustic wood frames are among the most popular and, for many of us, the most attractive of frames. They fit any decor and can be used with the widest array of artworks, photographs, needlework, and three-dimensional items. Their rough finishes stand them in stark contrast to the neat, clean, and orderly contents they house.

If you are a fan of rustic wood frames, you're in luck, because rustic moldings are easy to make from some of the cheapest materials you'll find. Techniques for turning common stock into rustic moldings are easy and fun. What's more, if you remain alert for materials that will work as rustic frame moldings, you'll discover bargains frequently.

COMMERCIALLY MADE RUSTIC MOLDINGS

The rough-hewn and distressed looks are popular enough for frame-molding manufacturers to offer an assortment of commercial moldings. Some are ordinary moldings that have been artificially distressed, usually by mechanical or chemical means.

Rustic moldings are available at most frame shops and at some lumberyards, home-improvement centers, and department stores. Use any commercial molding that you find attractive or that meets your needs, but exercise some caution when you shop.

Moldings that are simply made of rough lumber are fine. Those that obviously have been sandblasted or wirebrushed for texture or stained to achieve a weathered look should be safe for

any framing job. Those that look like barn siding or driftwood, and others that appear naturally distressed, could pose problems that I will cover momentarily.

Of course, you can ask questions about such moldings and how they were made, and maybe you'll be fortunate enough to find somebody with answers. If your experiences coincide with mine, however, you will find that the people trying to sell you these moldings know little or nothing about them, except the price, which is always too high.

Notable exceptions include products offered by two companies listed in the Source Directory. Graphik Dimensions, Ltd., sells different styles of rustic picture frames that are entirely safe to use. XYLO, Inc., makes several sizes of barn-siding molding that you can use with confidence. Just be sure to seal any exposed wood surfaces as you would with any wood frame or molding.

UNSUITABLE WOODS

The rustic look is so popular that there are people who make good money roaming rural areas in search of old barns and other outbuildings they can buy, dismantle, and sell, board by board. And the price a farmer or rancher gets for such a building is usually enough for him to put up a new building and pocket a profit at the same time.

In coastal areas, driftwood is plentiful and free for the taking. Boards, limbs, and whole trees that have done sea duty and then washed up on beaches have that gray, weathered look that is so appealing and useful in many decorating and craft projects.

To be sure, some fine-looking frames have been made of moldings cut from barn siding, fence slats, driftwood, and other salvaged woods. But these are potentially some of the most damaging materials to use in any framing job. I recommend you steer clear of them entirely.

Most of these woods have been invaded and occupied by any number of wood-boring insects and larvae—critters that can continue to do damage to the wood even after it has been turned into a picture frame. They can also invade the frame's environment (your house) and damage the frame's contents.

Any lumberman might tell you that one sure way to kill these wood borers and prevent any further damage is to run the wood through a kiln. And he's right. During the kiln-drying process, any insects or larvae inhabiting wood are killed, as are various fungi that attack trees. But the average do-it-yourselfer doesn't have access to a kiln. And even if you could put your salvaged wood into a kiln long enough to kill the pests, you would still have to deal with the problems of chemicals, salts, and other contaminants.

All sorts of chemicals, such as various fertilizers and insecticides, are stored in farm and ranch buildings and used near them. Defoliants often get sprayed along rural roadsides, near fence lines and buildings. Driftwood absorbs salt and minerals from the water. So there's no telling what these woods have been subjected to and what sort of damage they might cause.

BEST WOODS FOR RUSTIC FRAMES

The best woods for rustic frames are often the worst woods for other woodworking projects. Look for the unfinished or partly finished woods, those that are partly or poorly surfaced, the rough-hewn woods, the flawed and blemished boards and strips, the kiln-dried lumber that was once inhabited by wood borers and attacked by fungi.

You can't make frames with rotten wood or any product that is badly warped, cupped, checked, or too damaged to make into a molding. The wood must be flat, kiln-dried, and free of any contaminants. Beyond those, there aren't many strict requirements. In short, you will be looking for woods that others reject. Consequently, you will usually find them at good prices, or you will get them marked down when you point out the imperfections.

Whenever it's possible, I like to use woods that are naturally colored and require no staining. This saves time and money and makes finishing a simple matter. Generally, the darker woods—such as redwood, walnut, and some cedars—are best for such use, although there is at least one exception.

For some time I had kept watch for a suitable substitute for barn siding that would be relatively inexpensive, easy and safe to work with, plentiful, and readily available, but every bit as handsome as barn siding in rustic frames. One day, my search ended as I walked through a warehouse at a local lumberyard. As I passed an area where kiln-dried pine leaned against a wall in lengths from 8 to 20 feet, I noticed a stack of 4-foot 1 x 4s off to one side. They had probably been trimmed from 12-footers and discarded for their shabby appearance.

Rather than the familiar pine blonde, these boards were the dull gray of barn siding, the result of having been invaded by a fungus that attacks pine trees in the forest. Worst of all for most buyers, but perfect for my purposes, the wood was full of borer holes of every imaginable size and shape from having been inhabited by wood-eating larvae. A few tight knots and pitch pockets here and there only added character to the wood. For the average woodworker, handyman, or professional builder, this stuff was junk. For me, it was a treasure.

As I scanned the great stacks of 1 x 4, I could see that beautiful shade of gray showing along the edge of one board every once in a while. I decided I should ask some questions about this wood before I began piling up a load for my pickup truck.

At the sales desk, I learned that it was indeed kiln-dried. It was graded No. 4 common pine, and the price was 10 cents a linear foot. Eureka!

That day, I loaded 244 feet of usable 1 x 4 into my truck and later turned it into 488 feet of

Pine 1 x 4 in the center is what most buyers want, but the gray boards full of borer holes are best for rustic picture frames.

1 x 2. So I ultimately ended up with 488 feet of rustic molding that cost me $24.40, or about what one small rustic frame would cost me at a frame shop.

I stop by that lumberyard regularly, and I always check the No. 4 common pine to see if it has been restocked recently. When a new shipment arrives, I sort through it and haul off another supply of framing material. At first, I looked only for the 1 x 4s grayed by long-dead fungi, but I noticed other colors that were striking in their own ways. Some were deep, rich brown; others were redder than Philippine mahogany. And all these were natural colors that penetrated the wood, which meant that moldings made from the material would not have to be stained.

Since that day of discovery, more than a dozen years ago, the price of No. 4 common pine 1 x 4 has risen to 25 cents a linear foot. So the 1 x 2 molding I make with it now costs me 12½ cents a linear foot—which is still a bargain by any standard.

I stay alert for any rough woods that I can easily turn into rustic moldings. I browse in the bargain sections of lumberyards and home-improvement centers where I frequently find small quantities of various species of wood that meet my needs. It's a kind of prospecting that is both profitable and enjoyable. Try it.

In addition to the rough woods and naturally distressed woods, some species are particularly suitable for making moldings that you can distress in the shop. The softwoods are best for this, and my favorites are incense cedar and pine, although I have worked with others to my satisfaction, such as redwood, fir, and hemlock.

I suggest you work with small quantities of inexpensive local softwoods to determine which of these are best. Start with pine and cedar, and try some scraps of local hardwoods, too.

CREATING RUSTIC EFFECTS

You needn't have immediate access to a supply of naturally distressed woods, because you can achieve rustic effects in your workshop that are hard to tell from the ravages of nature. In a few minutes, you can create ridges and valleys in the surface of a piece of wood that look identical to those nature took years to create with salt, sand, and sun. You can make holes in fractions of seconds that look like those it took whole populations of wood borers many generations to create. And you can have fun in the process.

You needn't be an artist, skilled technician, or master craftsman to make distressed picture frames. In fact, some of my favorite techniques are those I have discovered through my own klutziness. Perhaps that's one reason I find this sort of work so gratifying; it's as if I'm somehow getting even with those forces that cause a hammer to miss a nail and dent the surface of a fine piece of wood, or that cause the hammer to hit the nail but split the wood in the process, or that make screw threads strip, or that put gaps in miter joints.

Tools required are simple, and most are hand operated. In fact, you won't need power tools except to distress hardwoods. And you need no specific tools. Just look for anything that might work and try it. Chances are, you already have most or all the tools in your shop or somewhere nearby.

Some kind of hammer is good for denting. Any kind of hammer—claw, tack, upholsterer's—will do, but I particularly like the ball-peen for this work. The ball surface is ideal for making circular dents in the wood's surface—the harder the blow, the deeper the dent and larger the circle. With some moldings you might want to strike numerous surface dents of various sizes and depths, creating a sort of randomly textured surface. Then use the other striking surface of the hammer to put dents along the face corners of the frame or molding.

You can also use other objects that you strike with a hammer to create various interesting impressions in the wood. Put a paper clip on the wood, and strike one of the curved ends with a hammer to make a U-shaped dent. Bend a piece of wire in various ways, and strike it at random spots on the molding surface. Lay a screw on the molding surface, and strike its shank to make an impression of the threads. Try various sizes and kinds of screws. Use an awl, ice pick, and various sizes of nails to put scratches in the surface; then lightly sand the feathered edges of the scratches.

Use rasps, files, and scrapers to texture surfaces and round over sharp edges. Create texture by scraping the molding surface with a notched paint scraper, the tines of a fork, or the teeth of a coarse rasp.

I use 1 x 2 box and flat moldings for most of my rustic frames. I sometimes distress the moldings before making the frame; other times I distress the assembled frames. Usually, if it is a technique or combination of techniques I can accomplish quickly, I distress the molding. If it's a slower, more tedious process, I work on the assembled frame.

To create the weathered look of driftwood or barn siding with a 1 x 2 flat molding, for example, I start with a coarse wood rasp at one end of the molding, and I scrape the surface with the end teeth of the rasp, following the grain for the length of the molding. This creates a wavy pattern of shallow grooves, running with the grain. Then I use a scratch awl to add deeper grooves—fewer in number and looser in pattern—for the length of the molding. I use a rasp to coarsely

round over the front corners of the molding and to roughen the outside edge. Finally, I use a scratch awl or ice pick to punch holes of various sizes into the entire surface of the molding to simulate borer holes. I punch some holes straight in and others diagonally, as in nature. And I vary the force of the thrust to change the diameter and depth of the holes.

I get best results using these techniques on incense cedar, with pine running a close second. You can achieve similar effects with hardwoods, but you will probably want to use power tools then. Professional carvers use industrial grinders, which are high-speed router-type tools, with various round and pointed bits. You can use the same or similar bits in an electric drill or a Dremel Moto-Tool.

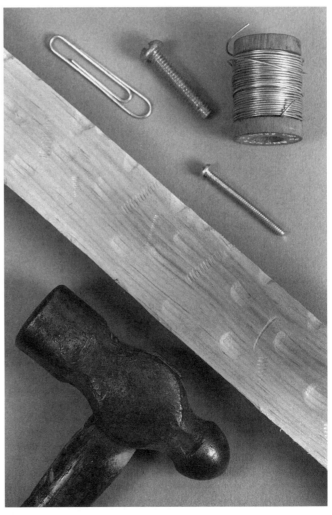

Some of the tools for distressing wood moldings.

Various scrapers, rasps, and awls are good for creating the appearance of naturally distressed wood.

With a wood-burning tool you can create texture and color in a frame.

You can also use heat to achieve some stunning effects. For example, with a propane torch, you can scorch the surface of pine flat molding until it is uniformly blackened. Then use a wire brush to scrape with the grain to remove the blackened wood, leaving behind a deeply textured surface ready for staining and finishing. With pine already naturally colored, you can skip the stain.

Build a frame of pine, cedar, or another softwood, and use a wood-burning tool to create both texture and color in the frame's surface. Start at one corner miter, and work with the grain toward the center of that frame section. Then work from the miter at the opposite corner toward the center of the frame section. Do all sections the same way, and vary your techniques as

you see fit. Start with a loose pattern of fairly deep wavy impressions running with the grain. Then fill in between with lighter and shallower strokes. The effect is stunning.

THE ROUGH-EDGE BOX FRAME

Often, the hardwoods I use in various woodworking projects come in boards that are surfaced (finished to a smooth surface) only on their broad surfaces, usually referred to as "surfaced two sides" or "S2S." I resaw these boards to the various lengths and widths that I need, and for years I treated the unsurfaced edge strips as scraps for the kindling pile. When it dawned on me, however, that these rough edges would make attractive rustic faces on box-style frames, I started turning those scraps into molding.

I usually rip the strips from the board with my table saw or bandsaw to a width of 1½ inches to make my standard 1 x 2 box molding. I sometimes rip only 1 inch from the rough edges to leave more usable hardwood on the boards for other projects and to create a narrower box molding.

Making molding is a simple matter of cutting a rabbet into the strip with my table saw or routing the rabbet with my router and router table. Often, I accumulate scraps of this rough-edged material in random lengths, and when the mood strikes me, I turn it into frame molding. Then I build the frames at my leisure, or whenever I need one for a specific job.

THE WANE FRAME

As far as lumber quality and grading go, a wane is a defect that occurs in the edge of a board that has been cut from the outer portion of a log. It is the appearance of bark or the absence of wood along a board's edge. It usually takes the shape of an irregular bevel and is caused by the curvature of the log. Such boards are usually downgraded and sold cheap. But a few always manage to get by the grader and will be found with the higher grades of lumber.

Keep watch for such boards. When you can buy them cheaply, do so. If you find them with expensive lumber, let a salesman know and ask that they be downgraded and reduced in price. You should know, though, that some hardwoods are sold in slabs with wanes on one or both narrow edges, and these won't be marked down.

Like most people, for years I sorted out and culled such defective boards whenever I shopped for wood. And when I brought home a load of lumber and found a waned board later, I cursed the grader who let it slip by and questioned his ancestry.

On one such occasion, I pulled a badly waned board from a stack of pine and was ready to cut it into kindling when it dawned on me that I could make frame molding from it that might not look half bad. So I ripped the wane from the board and stacked the strip with other 1 x 2 waiting to become molding. I found another

Rough-edge box frame and molding.

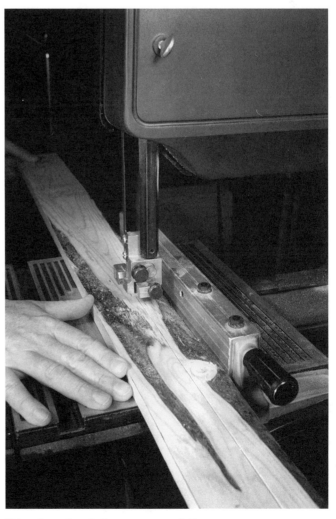

Ripping 1 x 2 for wane molding.

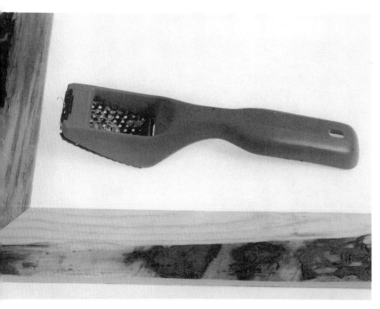

Use a wood rasp or scraper to shape pieces at corners.

piece of pine with a large pitch pocket in it that matched the dark color of the wane in the other board, and later used these pieces in a large frame I made.

My wane frame got favorable comments from many who saw it, and I have since kept a sharp eye out for good buys on such lumber. Most of my wane frames are made of 1 x 2 flat molding. At the outside corners, where adjoining pieces don't usually match because of the uneven bevel of the wanes, I use a small scraper or rasp to form and match the pieces.

If the wanes and pitch pockets in the woods you use are attractively colored, you might not want to stain the frame at all, or you might wish to only lightly stain it. With some wane frames, you might also want to try combining some of the distressing techniques mentioned earlier.

Finished wane frame.

Making rustic Style #1 frame.

Frame Style #1.

Frame Style #1.

RUSTIC SYSTEM FRAMES

I have developed a system for using my basic box and flat moldings and matching 1 x 2 stock to create a variety of frame configurations. I think you will find the system useful in your own framing. You can also use this same system with finer, smooth-surfaced woods, but my own preference leans toward the rustic appearance.

Consider Frame Style #1 to be the simple box frame, made from 1 x 2 according to directions in chapter 8. This frame is suitable for framing any work requiring a narrow molding.

Frame Style #2 is ideal for subjects requiring a wider molding. Start by constructing the basic Style #1 frame. Then clamp a piece of matching 1 x 2 broad side down in a miter box, and cut one end at a 45-degree angle. Use the basic frame as a guide to mark the 1 x 2 for the second cut; the inside edge of the 1 x 2 should match the outside edge of the corresponding piece in the basic frame.

After making the second cut, attach the 1 x 2 with glue and 1¼-inch brads, flush with the frame's rear edge. Attach miter-cut 1 x 2s to the remaining three sides of the frame, applying glue to the joints as well as to the inside edges of the 1 x 2s. Finally, drive and countersink a brad at each corner to secure the joints. When the glue sets, your Style #2 frame is ready for final finish.

Although only ½ inch wider than the Style #2 molding, Style #3 molding appears more massive and complex, yet requires only one more strip of molding. It's a good choice for dynamic or dramatic artworks that will be prominently displayed.

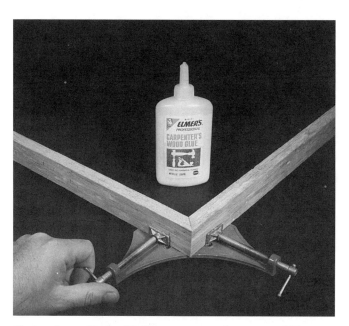

To make a Style #2 frame, start by assembling a Style #1 frame.

Start by building a Style #2 frame. Then miter cut a piece of Style #1 molding to fit one outer edge of the 1 x 2, apply glue to the inside of the molding, and attach it to the 1 x 2 with 1¼-inch brads. Continue attaching molding to the remaining three sides, applying glue to the joints as you proceed. Countersink the brads, and when the glue sets, your Style #3 frame is ready for finishing.

These are the three basic molding styles, but this system allows you to make other combinations as well. Make a flat molding from 1 x 2 stock, for example, and consider that Style #4. Now build a basic Style #4 frame and add the Style #1 molding to its edges for a completely new effect. Call that Style #5.

Attach strips of matching, miter-cut 1 x 2 to the outer edges of the Style #5 frame, and you have a Style #6 frame.

This is a versatile and useful system that should serve you well on many framing jobs. In your spare time, play around with some scraps of Style #1 and Style #4 moldings and scraps of matching 1 x 2 and discover some of your own designs.

FINISHING RUSTIC FRAMES
Rustic frames usually require minimal finishing. You might need to do a little sanding to shape a piece or make two adjoining pieces match. If

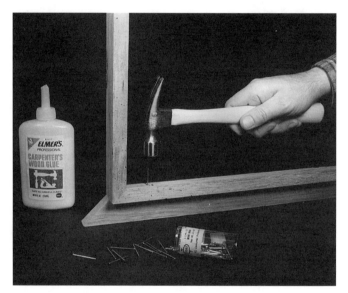

Attaching miter-cut 1 x 2s to Style #1 frame to make a Style #2 frame.

Frame Style #2.

Making rustic Style #3 frame.

Frame Style #3.

you're using a wood that has been inhabited by wood borers, use an awl and various sizes of nails and brads to pick clogged dust out of the holes. And clean frames thoroughly before staining or applying final finish.

Most rustic frames can be finished without staining, particularly those that are already naturally colored. But others will need to be stained. As with any other frames, experiment with various stains on scraps of the same wood the frame moldings were made of.

Stains that have black pigment in them work well if you're trying to simulate the weathered look of barn siding or driftwood. Depending on the type of wood you're using, try Watco English Oak Danish Oil Finish straight or diluted with Watco Natural. Try oil-base ebony stains, straight or diluted with mineral spirits or paint thinner.

Seal frames with a coat of shellac; then apply the final coat of your choice. You will probably find a dull matte or satin sheen polyurethane works best.

CHAPTER TWELVE

Making Floater Fixtures and Frames

Pictures that seem to float off the wall with no visible means of suspension, and those that seem to float as mysteriously inside their frames, are popular illusions. The effects are easy to achieve with simple but deceptive techniques.

Photographs are probably the most popular items to be displayed in such ways, although you might occasionally see paintings on Masonite and some mounted three-dimensional items or carvings floated off a wall or in floater frames. Sometimes whole arrangements are floated at different distances from the wall to form floating collages.

Although commercially made floater or "California floater" frames and floater-frame moldings are on the market, they aren't widely available. So you will either have to do some searching or resort to more reliable and less expensive alternatives: making your own floater fixtures and frames. By now, you should know what my recommendation will be.

HOW TO MAKE FLOATER FIXTURES

Photographs are often mounted and displayed without mats, glass, or even frames. One attractive way to display flush-mounted or border-mounted prints is with the aid of floater fixtures that are easy to make and install.

If you plan to display pictures this way, you must, of course, mount them first. Although you can use conventional mount boards made of mat board or chipboard, it's best to use something more rigid and durable, such as Gatorfoam, codaFoam, or Masonite.

Mount your photographs to the appropriate material, according to directions in chapter 4. Depending on the photographs and your intentions, you might wish to coat the edges of the mount board in some way to make them less conspicuous. Most of the prints I display this way are flush mounted, and I use a permanent felt marker to blacken the edges.

To make floater fixtures, cut scraps of 3/4-square stock or 1 x 2 to lengths of 3 inches. (You'll need two for each print.) Sand the ends to remove any splinters left by the saw, and use a combination square set at 1 1/2 inches to scribe a center line across each.

To keep pictures hanging parallel to the wall, you will need to mount two fixtures to the back of each mount board. For pictures 8 x 10 inches or larger, use either 3/4-square or 1 x 2 fixtures, and mount one fixture 2 inches from the top edge of the mount board and another 2 inches from the bottom edge. For pictures smaller than 8 x 10 inches, use only the 3/4-square fixtures, and mount them 1 inch inside top and bottom edges.

To attach fixtures, first scribe a vertical center line on the back of the mount board. Then, depending on the size of the picture, scribe horizontal guidelines across the mount-board back 1 or 2 inches from the top and bottom edges. Mix a small amount of five-minute epoxy cement, apply it to one surface of the fixtures, and press them in place, using the guidelines to center them on the mount-board back, 1 or 2 inches from the top and bottom edges.

There are several ways to hang these pictures. If you are going to hang them on plaster walls or any other wall that might be damaged by adhesives, use a screw eye and nail to hang each one. Before attaching the two fixtures to the back of any mounted picture, install a small screw eye in the center of the top edge of the top fixture. When fixtures have been attached, use a small wire nail to hang each picture.

On hard walls or wherever you can hang your pictures without concern for any damage adhesives might do, there are two excellent ways to "float" your pictures. After attaching the floater fixtures, apply a strip of double-sided foam mounting tape to each fixture, and mount the pictures directly to the wall. Another way—

Top fixture with screw eye attached for hanging.

Attaching 3/4-square fixtures with epoxy cement.

Velcro on fixtures.

Floater frame, Step 1.

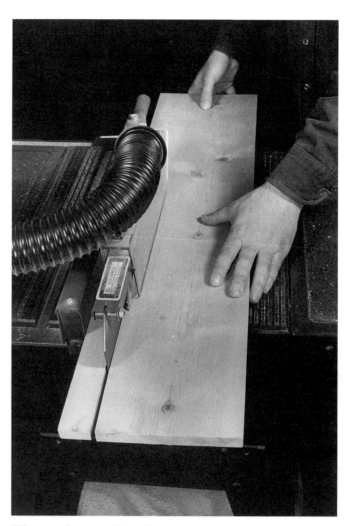

Floater frame, Step 2.

and the one I prefer—is to attach self-adhesive Velcro tape to the fixtures and to the wall. Pictures mounted with Velcro are easy to adjust, and they can be removed and replaced by other similarly mounted pictures.

You can make fixtures out of other materials, too, and you will want to do so if you wish to display them at different distances from the wall. With fixtures made of screen molding, for example, pictures will hang 1/4 inch from the wall (not including the thickness of the mounting medium). Parting-bead fixtures will float them 1/2 inch from the wall. Fixtures made of 2 x 2 allow 1 1/2 inches distance.

A coat of flat black paint on the fixtures will keep them from being visible in the shadows behind the pictures.

HOW TO MAKE FLOATER FRAMES

What gives the impression of a picture floating inside a frame is the frame's slightly larger dimensions and its black interior. The dark space around the edges of the mounted picture, between the picture and the frame molding, not only creates the illusion, but also functions the way a mat or liner does to separate a work from its frame.

Making floater frames from scratch is easy. For the molding, you can use any wood that is suitable for picture molding, and you can stain and finish it any way you wish.

For the frame illustrated, I used pine 1 x 2 that I ripped from 1 x 10 stock. When the frame was assembled, I stained it with a half-and-half mixture of Fuller O'Brien Pen-Chrome #640-06

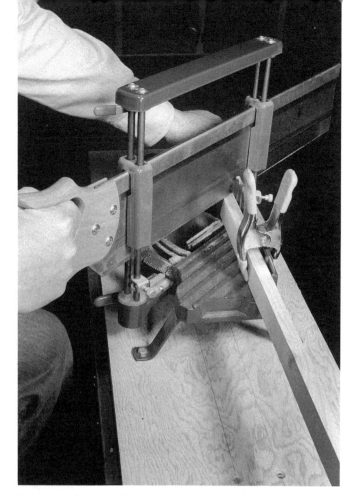

Floater frame, Step 3.

Floater frame, Step 4.

Flemish Black and #640-13 Platinum stains to give the frame an overall grayish tint, suggestive of the foggy scene being framed.

You also have a choice of the amount of space you want around the picture, or between the picture edges and the frame molding. You probably won't want this distance to be more than 1/2 inch or less than 1/8 inch.

Once you have made decisions on such variables, follow these easy steps to build your floater frame.

Step 1. After mounting your picture to a suitable mount board (Masonite in this case), use a permanent felt marker to carefully blacken the edges. Then measure the height and width of the mounted picture. Double-check the measurements, and record these dimensions on a note pad.

Step 2. Set the table-saw fence 1 1/2 inches from the near teeth of the blade, and rip 1 x 2s from available stock.

Step 3. Set the fence 1 1/2 inches from the far teeth of the blade and the blade for a 1/4-inch depth. Lay each 1 x 2 on a broad side, with a narrow edge against the saw fence, and cut a 1/8 x 1/4-inch rabbet into the other narrow edge.

Step 4. With a miter box and backsaw set at 45 degrees, cut a vertical frame section 1 inch

Rabbeted molding next to a 1 x 2.

Floater frame, Step 5.

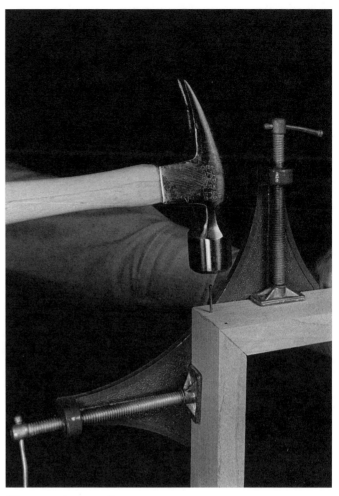

Floater frame, Step 7.

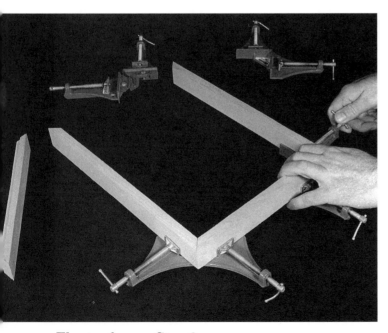

Floater frame, Step 6.

longer (inside measurement) than the height of the mounted picture, and a horizontal section 1 inch longer than the width of the picture. (This will result in a 1/2-inch space around the picture; for a 1/4-inch space, cut sections 1/2 inch longer than picture dimensions.)

Step 5. Cut one end off two pieces of molding at a 45-degree angle. Then use the sections cut in Step 4 to mark the molding strips for second 45-degree cuts, creating two more sections.

Step 6. Assemble a basic frame with glue and corner clamps. (If necessary, review frame-building procedures in chapter 7.)

Step 7. Drive two 1¼-inch brads at each corner, and countersink them.

Floater frame, Step 8.

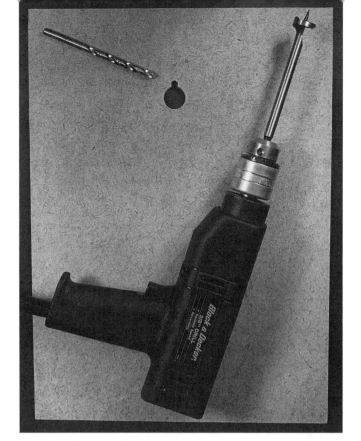

Floater frame, Step 11.

Step 8. Use a wood filler to fill the brad holes, and let the frame stand with clamps in place until the glue and filler set.

Step 9. Sand the frame with a pad sander and 120-grit and 220-grit sandpaper, rounding over outside corners and edges as you sand. Then clean the frame, apply the stain of your choice, and let it dry.

Step 10. Lay the frame facedown, and measure the height and width of the frame inside the rabbets. Then cut a piece of 1/8-inch tempered hardboard 1/16 inch smaller in height and width.

Step 11. Lay the hardboard smooth side up, and scribe a vertical center line on it. Measure down from the top and make marks at 25/8 inches and 25/16 inches. Then drill a 1/4-inch hole at the top-most spot and a 3/4-inch hole at the other spot.

Step 12. Run a narrow bead of glue along the rabbet in the rear of the frame, lay the hardboard

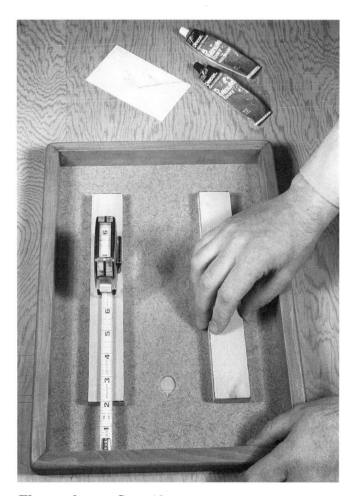

Floater frame, Step 13.

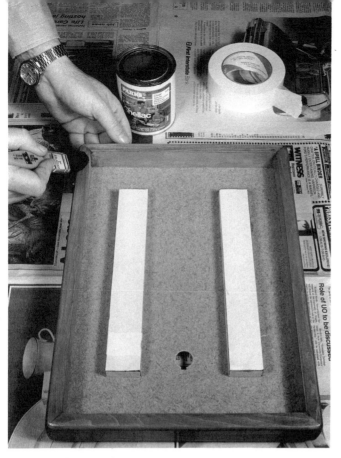

Floater frame, Step 14.

Floater frame, Step 16.

Floater frame, Step 15.

Floater frame, Step 17.

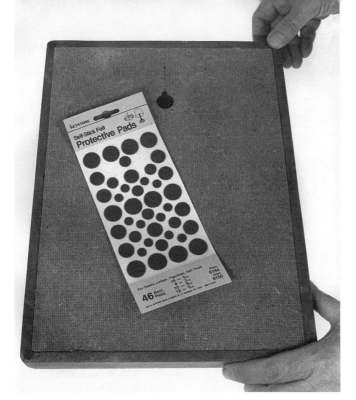

Floater frame, Step 18.

Finished floater frame.

in place in the rabbet, and put a can of paint or other heavy object on it until the glue sets.

Step 13. Cut two 1 x 2 glue blocks 4 inches shorter than the inside height of the frame. Mix a small amount of five-minute epoxy cement, and apply it to a broad surface of each piece of 1 x 2. Attach one glue block 2 inches from the top, bottom, and right inside edges of the frame and the other block 2 inches from the top, bottom, and left inside edges.

Step 14. Apply an even coat of shellac to the frame molding, and let it dry completely. Then apply the finish coat of your choice to the face and sides of the molding (satin sheen polyurethane, semigloss lacquer, etc.).

Step 15. Attach painters' masking tape to the broad faces of the 1 x 2 glue blocks. Then attach tape to the face of the frame molding, leaving the inside surface of the molding exposed.

Step 16. Apply two coats of flat black enamel to all interior surfaces of the frame and let dry. Then carefully remove the masking tape.

Step 17. Mix a small amount of five-minute epoxy cement, and coat the broad surfaces of the

glue blocks. Lay the mounted picture on the glue blocks, position it carefully with the aid of a steel tape rule, and lay a tissue-paper-covered book on it until the cement cures.

Step 18. Stick a 1/4-inch self-adhesive felt protective pad just inside each rear corner of the frame, and your picture is ready to hang with a small wire nail.

You can make floater frames from stock other than 1 x 2 molding, but this is a good size to start with. For a narrower molding, use bull-nose stop with the rounded edge as the face of the frame. For an even narrower, slat-type molding, use lattice. With either of these, follow the same directions as above, except in Step 3. Instead of setting the blade for a 1/4-inch depth, set it for a 1/8-inch depth, which will create a 1/8 x 1/8-inch rabbet in this thinner material.

CHAPTER THIRTEEN

Framing without Miters

Although the miter joint is the customary joint to use in building picture frames, there's no law that says all frames must be made the same way. Not long ago, I did some experimenting in an attempt to come up with some simple but attractive alternatives to the miter-joined frame. I ended up with two styles of frames that are not only pleasing to look at but also offer a few other advantages.

I still make the great majority of my frames with miter joints and will continue to do so. But when the mood strikes me to do something a little different, I like knowing I have the option.

All of the frame designs described and illustrated here call for my old standby 1 x 2s, but feel free to use narrower, wider, or thicker stock, either hardwood or softwood. Finishes are matters of builder's choice, and the frames can be used with any work that would work as well in any mitered frame made with flat molding.

So when you're in the mood for a change of pace, build one of my butt-joint or lap-joint frames.

HOW TO BUILD BUTT-JOINT FRAMES

To build a simple butt-joint frame, start by cutting two vertical sections 1/8 inch longer than the vertical measurement of the mounted artwork, mats, and glass. Double the width of the molding material, add that to the horizontal dimension of the work, plus 1/8 inch, and cut two horizontal sections to that length.

To make a 1 x 2 frame for an 11 x 14-inch vertical subject, for example, you would cut two vertical sections of 1 x 2 to 14 1/8 inches. The horizontal sections would be 11 1/8 inches plus twice the width of the 1 x 2 (2 x 1 1/2″ = 3″), or 14 1/8 inches.

Similarly, a 1 x 2 frame for a 16 x 20-inch horizontal subject would require two vertical sections at 16 1/8 inches and two horizontal sections at 23 1/8 inches (20 1/8″ + 3″ = 23 1/8″).

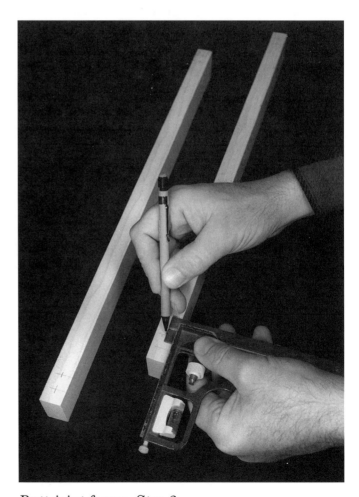

Butt-joint frame, Step 2.

For purposes of illustration, let's assemble a 16 x 20-inch butt-joint frame for a vertical subject. Here's how.

Step 1. With a miter box and backsaw set at zero degrees, cut two horizontal pieces of 1 x 2 to 19$\frac{1}{8}$ inches and two vertical pieces to 20$\frac{1}{8}$ inches.

Step 2. Stand the two short sections on their narrow edges. Set a combination square at 1 inch, and scribe a line across the top narrow edge of each piece, 1 inch from each end. Reset the square at $\frac{1}{2}$ inch, and scribe lines across the ends. Set the square at $\frac{3}{8}$ inch, and mark the center of each line.

Step 3. Centerpunch a drill-starter hole and drill a pilot hole at each spot marked, using a $\frac{7}{64}$-inch bit in an electric drill.

Butt-joint frame, Step 4.

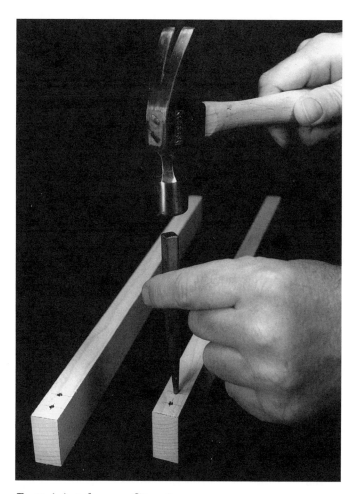

Butt-joint frame, Step 3.

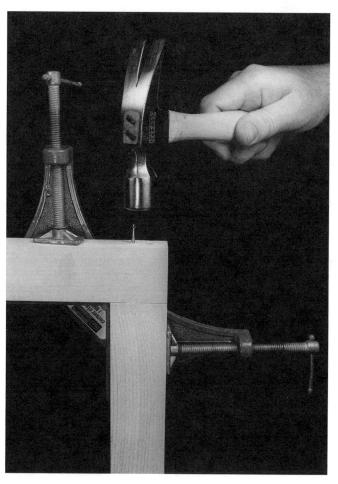

Butt-joint frame, Step 5.

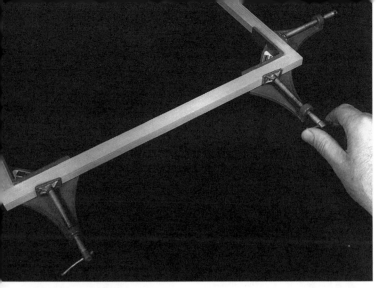

Butt-joint frame, Step 7.

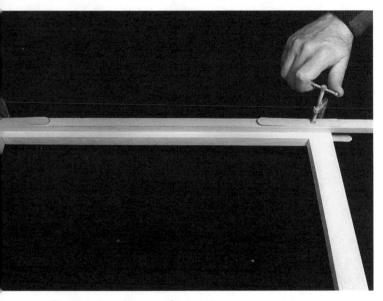

Butt-joint frame, Step 10.

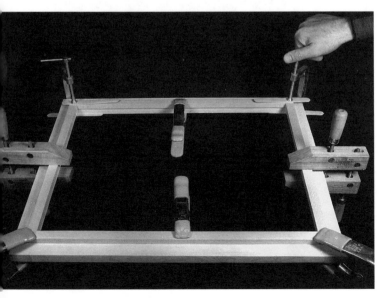

Butt-joint frame, Step 11.

Step 4. Apply glue to the end of a vertical section, butt it to one end of a horizontal section at a right angle, and clamp the two pieces with a corner clamp. Attach another vertical section to the opposite end of the horizontal. Then glue and clamp the other horizontal to the opposite ends of the verticals.

Step 5. Drive a 6d finishing nail through each hole in each vertical, and countersink the nails. Then fill the nail holes and let the frame stand until the glue and filler set.

Step 6. With a miter box and backsaw set at zero degrees, cut two horizontal pieces of parting bead to 17⅛ inches and two vertical pieces to 19⅝ inches.

Step 7. Apply glue to the end of a vertical section, butt it to one end of a horizontal section, and clamp it with a corner clamp. Continue assembling the frame with glue and clamps, as in Step 4.

Step 8. Drive a 1-inch brad near each end of each horizontal into the vertical sections. Countersink the brads, fill the holes, and let the frame stand until the glue and filler set.

Step 9. Sand all surfaces of both frames with a pad sander and 120-grit and 220-grit sandpaper.

Step 10. Lay the large frame faceup. Measure in 1 inch from the top and bottom left corners, and make light pencil marks near the top and bottom frame edges. Align a strip of wood with the two marks, and clamp it to the frame with two C-clamps.

Step 11. Run a narrow bead of glue along the front edge of the frame window. Lay the small frame atop the large frame, against the wood strip and 1 inch from the top, bottom, and right edges. Clamp the small frame to the large frame at each corner and elsewhere as necessary. Then let it stand until the glue sets.

Step 12. When the glue has set, sand the frame, as required, with a pad sander and 220-grit sandpaper, slightly rounding over front edges and corners as you sand.

Step 13. Brush and vacuum the frame to remove all dust. Apply the stain of your choice and let it stand overnight. Then apply a coat of shellac and finish coat of your choice.

Of course, there are other ways to finish your butt-joint frames. They can be painted with frame colors matching colors in the work being framed. You might also stain the frame, then paint only the smaller frame in a color matching the predominant color in the work. Another option is to build the wide frame with one type of wood (pine, fir, oak, or maple) and the narrow frame with a similar species but contrasting color (redwood, red cedar, walnut, or mahogany).

HOW TO MAKE A LAP-JOINT FRAME

The lap-joint frame is a bit more complex than the butt-joint frame. The required cuts can be made with a table saw, even a small benchtop model. Joinery requires simple C-clamps or spring clamps, rather than the usual corner clamps. And the glued lap joints make one of the strongest of frames.

Butt-joint frame ready for stain and final finish.

LAP-JOINT FRAME DIMENSIONS

Glass and Mat Outside Dimensions (in inches)	Lap-Joint Frame Inside Dimensions (in inches)	Lap-Joint Frame Outside Dimensions (in inches)
5 x 7	5 1/8 x 7 1/8	7 3/8 x 9 3/8
8 x 10	8 1/8 x 10 1/8	10 3/8 x 12 3/8
9 x 12	9 1/8 x 12 1/8	11 3/8 x 14 3/8
11 x 14	11 1/8 x 14 1/8	13 3/8 x 16 3/8
12 x 16	12 1/8 x 16 1/8	14 3/8 x 18 3/8
14 x 18	14 1/8 x 18 1/8	16 3/8 x 20 3/8
16 x 20	16 1/8 x 20 1/8	18 3/8 x 22 3/8
18 x 24	18 1/8 x 24 1/8	20 3/8 x 26 3/8
20 x 24	20 1/8 x 24 1/8	22 3/8 x 26 3/8
24 x 30	24 1/8 x 30 1/8	26 3/8 x 32 3/8
24 x 36	24 1/8 x 36 1/8	26 3/8 x 38 3/8

Cutting a lengthwise groove in a narrow edge with a table saw.

Making the second cut to create a rabbet.

The inside dimensions of your lap-joint frame should be 1/8 inch greater than the outside dimensions of the mounted work, mats, and glass, as with any conventional frame. For standard sizes, refer to the accompanying chart to determine the right length for the 1 x 2 sections of the miterless frame. For odd sizes or frames larger or smaller than those listed, there is a simple formula. After determining the frame's inside dimensions, add 2 1/4 inches to the length of each frame section.

To turn the 1 x 2 into frame molding, you'll need to cut a 3/8 x 3/8-inch rabbet along one edge of each piece. After removing the table saw's blade guard, set the blade for a 3/8-inch-deep cut, and position the rip fence 3/8 inch from the far teeth of the blade.

With a frame section resting on a narrow face, and with a broad face against the fence, use push blocks to run it through the saw, creating a lengthwise groove. Lay the piece broad side down, and run it through the saw again, creating the rabbet. Do the same with the other pieces. (*Caution:* The sliver being removed from each piece will shoot right out of the saw. So stand to one side, as you always should when op-

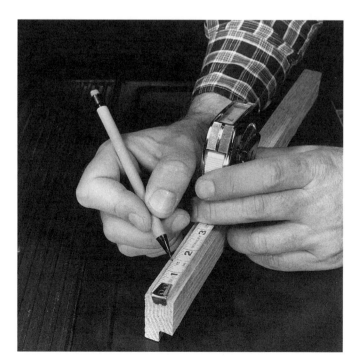

Making guide marks 1 1/2 inches inside each end of each short piece.

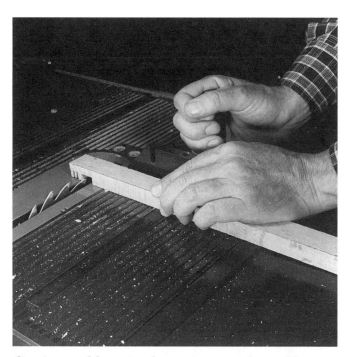

Cutting end laps in short pieces with a table saw.

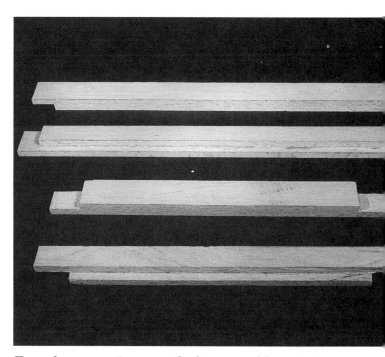

Four frame sections, ready for assembly.

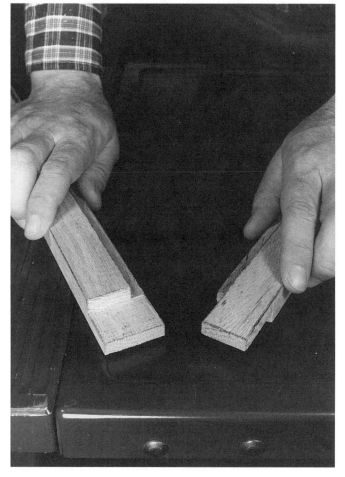

Mating pieces are shown here facedown.

Assembling the frame with glue and clamps.

Closeup of the lap-joint corner.

Finished lap-joint frame.

erating a table saw, and make sure no one else is in the path of the blade.)

Whether you're framing a horizontal or vertical picture, cut the laps into the frame-piece ends the same way. Remove 1½ inches of material to a depth of 3/8 inch at each end of the face side of the short pieces, and 1⅛ inches of material from each end of the back side of the long pieces.

To accomplish this, remove the saw's rip fence and set the miter gauge at zero. Measure 1½ inches inside each end of each short piece, and make a guide mark. Lay the piece facedown on the saw table, against the miter gauge, and position it so the saw will make the first 3/8-inch-deep cut 1½ inches from the end. After making the cut, continue making passes over the blade until the material from the mark to the end has been removed. Do likewise at the opposite end of the piece.

Do the same on the long pieces, except lay them faceup, and mark for laps 1⅛ inches from the ends. Check joints for fit, and carefully rasp away any excess material.

Apply an ample and even coat of wood glue to the end laps, and join the verticals to the horizontals. Clamp each corner with a C-clamp and clamp cushions or a spring clamp with cushioned jaws.

When the glue has set, sand the frame with a pad sander and 120-grit and 220-grit sandpaper, carefully rounding over corners and edges as you sand. Clean the dust away, and your frame is ready for finishing.

To the red-oak frame shown, I applied a coat of Fuller O'Brien Pen-Chrome #640-11 English Oak Stain, let it penetrate fifteen minutes, wiped the frame dry with paper towels, and let it stand overnight. The next day, I gave it a coat of sanding sealer and a coat of satin sheen polyurethane and burnished lightly between coats with 400-grit waterproof sandpaper.

Everything else was standard procedure. I stacked the glass, matted work, and backing in the frame, secured everything with glazier's points, and attached a dust seal. I installed hanging hardware, and my framed work—in this case a color photograph of a Labrador retriever—was ready for display.

CHAPTER FOURTEEN

Framing without Frames

It's possible to display some framable items without frames, and should you wish to do so, there are several methods and an assortment of products and materials you ought to know about.

We touched on the idea of frameless display in chapters 4 and 12 in discussing photographs and posters, which are the items most often displayed without frames. Of course, it is possible to display other items using the techniques that follow, but keep in mind that these are not archivally safe procedures. So I cannot recommend their use on anything of significant value.

Most of the frameless display methods offer easy changeability, which is another reason they appeal to photographers, who often produce more photographs than there is room to display at one time.

Similarly, when children discover the joys of drawing and coloring, they often produce more works than can ever be taped to the refrigerator door. Give them special treatment with some of the quick-change methods and means that follow.

Mainly, this is an idea chapter, something to get your creative juices flowing. Here I will introduce you to some of the various commercial products available and a few of the items you can make yourself. But as I have done before, I'm going to recommend that you browse at the frame shops, photo-supply outlets, and in the frame departments of department stores to see what's available there.

Although there are some products that will be around for a long time to come, this is a changeable area, and the only way to keep abreast of what's in and what's out is to browse.

PASSE-PARTOUT'S PASSÉ

Some people use vinyl tape or linen tape to sandwich photographs, posters, or inexpensive reproductions between glass or acrylic and backing material. The vinyl tape comes in black, white, and a few bright colors and sometimes can be matched with a color in the work being displayed. This so-called passe-partout method of displaying a work was more popular before the development of quicker and easier alternatives. Those who still favor it argue that it is a better method because the tape keeps dust from collecting behind the glass. Frankly, I would rather use one of the other methods and take my chances with the dust, which I can always remove later if I wish. Remember, we're not talking about displaying valuable artworks here. And the fact is, I have never had a dust problem with any of the alternative methods.

You can use glass or acrylic in this method; each has its advantages and disadvantages. Glass is sharp-edged, so you must be extremely careful when you tape the edges. But glass is more rigid and does not tend to bow as acrylic might. Acrylic is lighter, but it scratches easily and attracts dust and lint.

Both glass and acrylic are difficult to keep clean during the taping process, because you must handle the material so much. Glass will provide sufficient rigidity for any mount-board material, but if you use acrylic, you should make

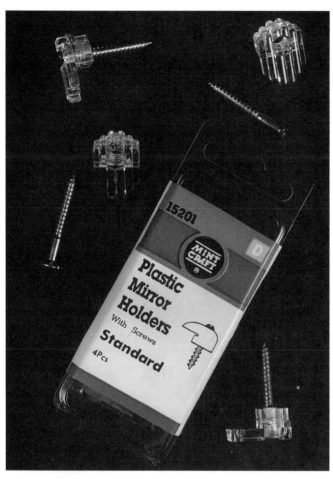

Mirror holders.

Intercraft Frameless Frames, available in standard sizes.

sure that your mount board or backing is sufficiently rigid. For that reason, such products as Gatorfoam, codaFoam, and hardboard work best with large items sandwiched behind acrylic.

My major objection to this old-fashioned technique is that it is tedious and time-consuming, and the results don't justify the expenditure of energy and time. What's more, there are products on the market now that make displaying without frames quick, easy, and enjoyable.

FRAMELESS DISPLAY AIDS

I have already mentioned using Velcro hook-and-loop tape for "floating" pictures off walls and for keeping framed works hanging straight. You can also use it for frameless display of any mounted photograph or poster. It's especially valuable for its quick changeability, and for that reason is also good for displaying children's art.

For most mounted works up to 11 x 14 inches, you can usually get by with two 1-inch pieces of Velcro attached to the back of the mount board in the center and an inch from top and bottom edges. With prints and posters 16 x 20 inches or larger, put a 1-inch piece of Velcro about an inch inside each corner of the mounting board. Then attach the mating pieces to the wall, and you will be able to switch like-sized works anytime you wish.

At the hardware store, home-improvement center, or the hardware department of any department store you will find plastic mirror holders that come four to a package, with screws, for about $1. You can use these little clear-plastic brackets to display mounted photos and posters of any size on walls and solid-core doors. Always attach the bottom two brackets first. Then use the mounted work as a guide for mounting the top two brackets. Allow 1/8 inch extra room for expansion and to make display changing easy.

Intercraft manufactures a large variety of frames and related items that you will find in the frame departments of department and discount stores. One of its products is called the Frameless Frame, and it comes in all the usual standard sizes. It consists of 1/8-inch hardboard backing material, a matching piece of nonglare acrylic, and four spring clips.

To use one of the Frameless Frames, first disassemble it by pressing each clip inward and lifting it out of the groove in the back of the hardboard. Then separate the acrylic and hardboard, remove the protective film from the acrylic, and clean the acrylic to remove fingerprints and other smudges. Sandwich the framable item between the acrylic and hardboard, attach the four clips, and your work is ready for display.

The clips on the Frameless Frame serve two purposes other than holding everything together. Each also functions as a hanger for vertical or horizontal placement, and all four keep the work hanging parallel to the wall.

Another Intercraft product I like is even simpler to use. It's a clear acrylic box with a white cardboard box that fits snugly inside. These units come in standard sizes. Remove the cardboard box, clean the acrylic as necessary, lay your photograph or other framable item in the acrylic box, and press the cardboard box back in place. Punch out the appropriate hole in the back of the cardboard box, and hang your work vertically or horizontally.

THE UNI-FRAME

There are several products available that provide suitable alternatives to the passe-partout technique. At frame shops and some mail-order suppliers you will find various metal and plastic clips, brackets, and systems designed for sandwiching photographs, posters, and other works between glass and backing.

Eubank Frame, Inc., makes several such products, and my favorite is the Uni-Frame, which comes in two sizes. One is for works with outside dimensions up to 20 x 20 inches and sells for about $7. The larger model will handle prints and posters from 16 x 16 inches to 40 x 40 inches and is the one I use for most of my posters. It costs about $9.

With the Uni-Frame you can sandwich material up to 1/4 inch thick, which includes glass, mat, picture or poster, and mount board or backing. I recommend foamboard for mounting or

Spring-clip hangers on Intercraft Frameless Frames snap into grooves in hardboard back to sandwich work behind acrylic.

Intercraft acrylic boxes, available in standard sizes.

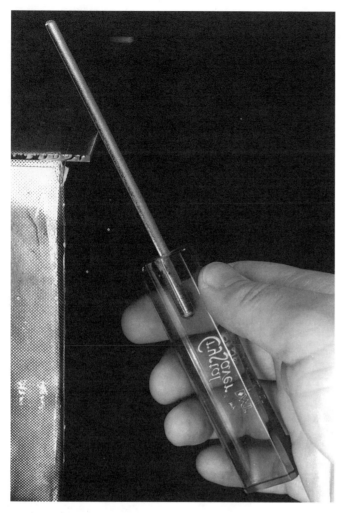

You can lightly smooth over the sharp edges of glass with a diamond file, such as the DMT Crystal Saver.

backing, and you can use it in either 1/8-inch or 3/16-inch thicknesses, depending on how thick the rest of the sandwich is. I use the 3/16-inch board, because I don't normally use mats with posters.

Use glass with the Uni-Frame, not acrylic, because glass is rigid and will not bow as acrylic will. The glass edges will be exposed in this arrangement, so you might want to have the edges seamed (beveled) at the glass shop, or you can lightly smooth them over with a fine diamond hone or diamond file, such as the DMT Diamond Whetstone or DMT Crystal Saver, available at cutlery shops from Diamond Machining Technology, Inc. (See the Source Directory at the back of this book.)

It's difficult to make any poster and glass match perfectly in size. Invariably, one will be a tiny fraction of an inch larger than the other. So it's important to check the glass and the poster before assembling the Uni-Frame.

I always lay a poster facedown on my matting bench and lay the glass atop it. If the poster is slightly larger, I trim it with an X-Acto knife, using the glass edge as a guide. If the poster is slightly smaller, there's nothing to do but let the backing disguise the fact. If the poster has white borders, the white of the foamboard conceals the size discrepancy. If the poster has black borders, I don't want white foamboard showing, so I make a black border on the foamboard face with

Uni-Frame, Step 2.

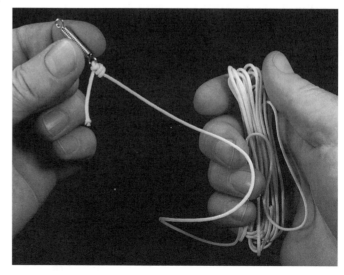

Uni-Frame, Step 3.

a permanent felt marker. I also blacken the edges of the foamboard.

Foamboard and glass, of course, should be cut to identical dimensions. Whether or not the poster should be mounted depends upon its condition. If it has been carefully stored flat and has no dents or dings, you can simply sandwich it between glass and foamboard. If it is curled, wrinkled, or otherwise damaged, mount it or have it mounted.

The Uni-Frame couldn't be simpler. It consists of only four corner clamps, a tension spring, and a length of cord that pulls everything together. Here's how it works.

Step 1. Adjust the four clamps to fit the size and format of the work you're sandwiching, according to the manufacturer's directions.

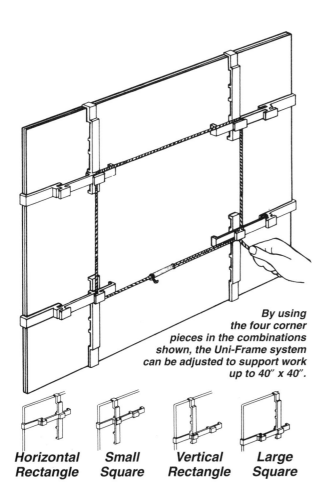

By using the four corner pieces in the combinations shown, the Uni-Frame system can be adjusted to support work up to 40″ x 40″.

Horizontal Rectangle **Small Square** **Vertical Rectangle** **Large Square**

Uni-Frame assembly.

Step 2. Lay the glass, mat, poster or other work, and foamboard on a work surface in that order. Then position a clamp at each corner.

Step 3. Securely tie one end of the cord to one end of the tension spring with a double knot or clinch knot.

Step 4. Facing the bottom of the foamboard, position the spring between the bottom two clamps, with the cord end on the left. Run the cord clock-

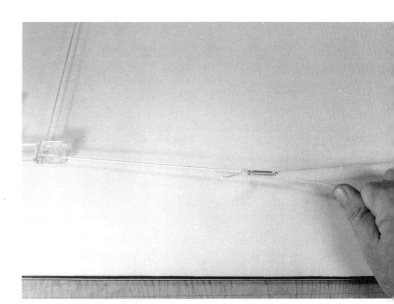

Uni-Frame, Step 4.

Uni-Frame, Step 5.

Don McMichael poster in a Uni-Frame.

wise around all four cleats, and put it through the remaining ring on the spring.

Step 5. Pull the cord tight enough to slightly tense the spring, loop it around the cleat on the bottom right clamp, and pull it tight to secure it.

That's all there is to it. Use a standard picture hanger, and drape the top horizontal length of cord over the hanger. The plastic corner clamps will then keep the work hanging parallel to the wall.

The whole process takes only minutes and couldn't be easier. What's more, the results are mighty pleasing to look at.

The very day I used a Uni-Frame to sandwich a killer whale poster by popular West Coast artist Don McMichael, I was at a local shopping mall and walked past a gallery displaying that very poster in a Uni-Frame. When I saw the $95 price tag, I walked out laughing.

These posters are on sale at various outlets up and down the coast for $20, unframed. I paid $22.50 for the glass, Uni-Frame, and foamboard backing, or $42.50 for everything. The whole job couldn't have taken me more than fifteen minutes, including the time it took to clean the glass and trim one edge of the poster. Yet my labor turned out to be worth $52.50 on this job. That's $210 an hour!

I never cease to be amazed by the amount of money people can save by doing their own framing and related chores.

MAKE YOUR OWN FRAMELESS DISPLAY BRACKETS

You can make brackets and strips for displaying mounted works without frames that allow for quick and easy changeability. You will find a variety of readily available materials—even scraps—that are suitable for making them, and some require only the simplest of tools. A pair of brackets will display a single item, and two strips will display several.

All such brackets and strips are similar in that the one designated as the bottom piece has a lip or groove for the mounted work to stand in, and the top piece is identical, but with the lip or groove facing downward to act as a retainer.

The only difference between the brackets and strips is length. Brackets are short; strips are long. You can make the brackets to exactly match the width of the item being displayed, or you can cut them shorter or longer. For example, if you're making a pair to display an 8 x 10-inch horizontal photograph, you can make your brackets as short as 3 inches, exactly 10 inches, or slightly over 10 inches. I prefer them slightly oversized.

No matter whether you're making brackets or strips, and regardless of their size, their lips or grooves should be at least 1/8 inch wide to accommodate mounted works with single mats and to allow easy switching of pictures. If you want to display items with multiple mats, make the grooves or lips wider.

You might make a pair or several pairs of strips to span a few feet or the full length of a long wall. Longer strips should be securely anchored to the wall. Either mount them with screws attached to the studs, or use toggle bolts in hollow sections of the wall.

If you own a table saw, you can make the simplest of brackets and strips by merely cutting a centered groove into the narrow edges of lengths of 1 x 2. Remove the blade guard and splitter, set the blade for a 1/4-inch depth and the fence 5/16 inch from the near teeth of the blade. Then stand a 1 x 2 on a narrow edge, with a broad face against the fence, and use push blocks to run it over the blade, creating a centered groove 1/8 inch wide and 1/4 inch deep for the entire length. Then turn the piece over and groove the opposite edge. Do likewise with the matching bracket or strip.

You can rout the edges of such brackets and strips, sand them, and apply the finish of your choice. They can be stained and varnished or painted. You can attach the brackets to the wall with adhesive foam mounting tape or screws. Use screws to attach the strips. If the screws will show, use oval-headed screws with finish washers. Or you can counterbore the screw holes and conceal screw heads with button plugs. (See directions on page 215 for "Decorative 1 x 2 Brackets.")

If you don't own a table saw, the simplest brackets and strips are those made with lengths of 1 x 2 and 3/4 x 3/4-inch outside corner molding. You'll need some small scraps of 1/8-inch Micro Wood, hardboard, or foamboard to use as spacers. Cut 1 x 2 to whatever length you deem appropriate for brackets or strips; then cut a piece of corner molding for each to the same length. Prenail one side of each piece of corner molding with 1-inch brads spaced about 6 inches apart. Run a thin bead of glue along the inside surface of the nailed side of the molding. Then press the molding in place on a matching piece of 1 x 2 with the glued edge against a narrow edge of the 1 x 2. Use spacers between the broad surface of the 1 x 2 and the other side of the molding to create a lip 1/8 inch wide, and drive the brads into the 1 x 2. Countersink the brads, and fill the holes with wood filler.

When the filler dries, sand the brackets or strips, as required, with 120-grit and 220-grit sandpaper, and they're ready for finishing and attaching to the wall.

You can make similar brackets and strips by substituting 1/2 x 1/2-inch (inside dimension) aluminum corner molding for the outside corner molding. Stain or paint the 1 x 2 before attaching the aluminum molding. Then use a hacksaw to cut the aluminum to the same length as the 1 x 2 and sand the ends to remove burrs. Drill screw holes in one side of the aluminum, and attach it to the 1 x 2 with 1/2 x #4 aluminum roundhead screws.

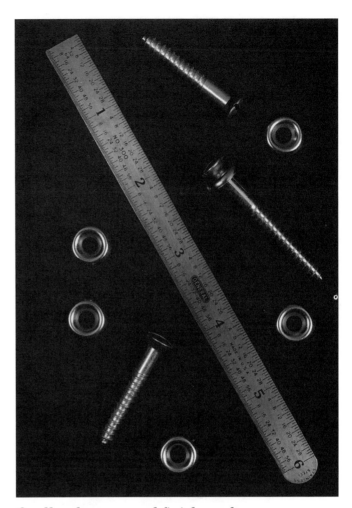

Ovalhead screws and finish washers.

Micro Wood Brackets

If you own a router and router table and some kind of bench-type or stationary power saw, you can make simple, attractive, and functional brackets from scraps of Micro Wood. Just follow these easy steps.

Step 1. With a table saw, radial-arm saw, or bandsaw, rip 1/4-inch Micro Wood into 1-inch-wide strips.

Step 2. Insert a 1/2-inch straight bit into a router collet. With router attached to a router table, adjust the bit for a 1/4-inch-wide, 3/16-inch-deep rabbet, and run each strip through the router table.

Step 3. Trim each bracket to a length slightly greater than the width of the item to be displayed.

Micro Wood brackets, Step 1.

Micro Wood brackets, Step 2.

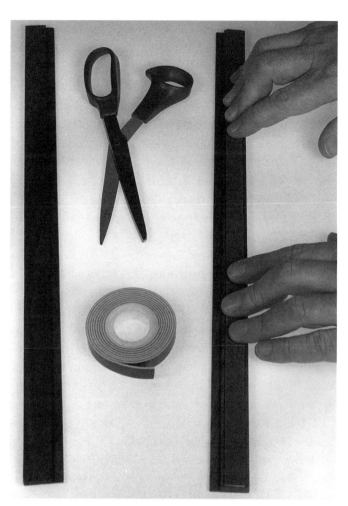

Micro Wood brackets, Step 3.

Then attach two or more pieces of double-adhesive foam mounting tape to the rear of each bracket.

Step 4. Peel the release paper from the foam tape on one bracket, and use a spirit level to position it on the wall—with the rabbet up—where you want the bottom of the work to be.

Step 5. Put the mounted work on the attached bracket, and use it as a guide to mark light pencil lines at the top corners of the mount board. Then make marks 1/8 inch above those, and erase the first marks.

Step 6. Peel the release paper from the foam tape on the remaining bracket. Align it with the guide marks made in Step 5, and press it in place with the rabbet facing down.

A bas-relief print of a caribou stands with vinyl-covered mat in Micro Wood brackets.

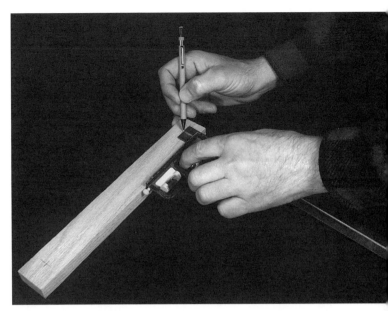

Decorative 1 x 2 brackets, Step 2.

Your Micro Wood brackets are now ready to display your mounted work. Simply slide the work behind the brackets' retaining lips, and change your display instantly, any time you wish to do so.

Decorative 1 x 2 Brackets

These brackets are a bit fancier than the others we've discussed, but they're still easy to make. What's more, they have one design improvement over most others: they have rabbets at the top and bottom, so they can be used in multiple displays, and in such use, fewer brackets are required. For example, you can display two mounted prints with only three brackets, or four prints with six brackets, and so on.

The brackets are made of 1 x 2. Use your favorite hardwood—oak, walnut, maple, cherry, birch—and buy some matching 3/8-inch button plugs (you'll need two per bracket). Apply the stain and finish of your choice, and don't forget to finish the button plugs the same way.

Here's how you can make these attractive brackets.

Step 1. Cut two pieces of hardwood 1 x 2 slightly longer than the width of the work you plan to display.

Decorative 1 x 2 brackets, Step 3.

Decorative 1 x 2 brackets, Step 4.

Decorative 1 x 2 brackets, Step 6.

Decorative 1 x 2 brackets, Step 5.

Step 2. Set a combination square at 1 inch, and scribe pencil lines across each piece, 1 inch from each end. Reset the square at 3/4 inch, and mark the center of each line.

Step 3. Centerpunch a drill-starter hole at each spot marked on the 1 x 2s. Then use a 3/8-inch brad-point bit to drill a 3/8-inch-deep hole at each spot, and drill through the center of each hole with a 3/16-inch bit.

Step 4. With a 1/2-inch straight bit in a router and the router attached to a router table, adjust the unit to cut a rabbet 1/4 inch wide and 1/8 inch deep. Then lay each 1 x 2 on the table with large holes up, and cut a rabbet along one inside edge. Turn each piece around, and cut a rabbet into the opposite edge.

Finished 1 x 2 brackets.

Step 5. Replace the straight bit in the router with a 3/8-inch-radius cove bit, and set it for a 1/8-inch depth. Lay a strip of 1 x 2 on the table with rabbets up and one end against the fence. Then run each end of each piece over the bit.

Step 6. Now lay a 1 x 2 on the table with rabbets up and a long edge against the fence. Run it over the bit, turn it around, and run the other edge over the bit. Then do likewise with the other piece to cut coves along all four sides of each piece. (If you want deeper coves, reset the router, and repeat Steps 5 and 6.)

Step 7. Sand brackets, as required, with a pad sander and 120-grit and 220-grit sandpaper. Then apply stain and finish of your choice to them and to four 3/8-inch button plugs.

Step 8. Install the brackets on a wall with #8 wood screws or toggle bolts (in hollow walls). Mount the bottom bracket first, using a spirit level to position it. Use the mounted work to mark guidelines for the top bracket, and position that one allowing an extra 1/8 inch.

CHAPTER FIFTEEN

Framing Calendars

Calendars seem to be everywhere. Offices and businesses always display them, and I think it's safe to assume they are in most homes. In fact, calendars often show up in several rooms of a house. We have one hanging in the kitchen, and I keep one in my office, another in my studio, and one in the shop. And I'm not even counting the digital calendars and the ones on our watch faces.

As useful, even necessary, as calendars are, and as decorative as so many calendar publishers try to make them, I have never considered them particularly attractive in any environment. To me, a calendar looks like an open magazine nailed to a wall sideways.

In some places this doesn't matter much, if at all. The besmudged calendar hanging on the grimy wall of my mechanic's garage could look much worse, but needn't look any better. The calendar in my workshop is just there to remind me of what day it is, not as a comment on proper shop decor. But in my cedar-walled studio and office, and certainly in our highly visible kitchen, I think calendars should blend with the room's decor.

If you have photographs displayed with thumbtacks, and posters taped to the wall, fine. Then go on and nail a calendar right up there with them. But chances are, you have photographs, posters, and artworks tastefully framed and carefully displayed. Perhaps you'll want to give calendars similar attention.

The plans that follow offer two ways to give any calendar special treatment. Inside dimensions of the calendar frame are 14 x 22 inches; the calendar case is 13 x 22 inches. These will accommodate many calendars. If you're accustomed to using larger calendars, you need only alter the dimensions to fit your needs.

In both the frame and case, calendars hang from small decorative hooks or hangers that come in various sizes and configurations. Some are self-adhesive; others attach with nails; still others have nail shafts attached to them. Take your pick, but if you use the last, clip off the nail shaft with wire cutters.

Incidentally, calendars are popular Christmas gifts. Consider what a fine gift a calendar would be inside one of these beautiful frames or cases.

MAKE A CALENDAR FRAME

This simple, attractive calendar frame offers you several options. Instead of the outside corner molding the directions call for, you can substitute any frame molding you like. Or you can skip the molding altogether and let the 1 x 2 frame your calendar unadorned, which was my intention in my original design of this frame.

Although the directions call for decorative rings as hanging hardware, you can attach the frame directly to the wall, if you prefer, with screws into the studs or toggle bolts in any hollow section of the wall. If that's what you want to do, after Step 6 below, before sanding the back panel, drill two 7/32-inch-diameter holes, vertically centered 4 inches from the top and bottom of the back panel. Then skip Steps 13 and 14.

You won't need much in the way of materials for this frame. In fact, you might be able to make do with scraps left over from other wood-

Calendar frame, Step 2.

Calendar frame, Step 3.

working projects. You'll need a 7-foot piece of oak 1 x 2, or two pieces at least 24 inches long and two at least 16 inches long. If you use the 3/4 x 3/4-inch oak corner molding or similarly narrow frame molding, you can squeak by with a 7-foot strip, but should probably buy an 8-footer. Or you can round up four pieces at least as long as the 1 x 2 sections. The back panel is 1/4-inch oak plywood, and you'll need a scrap at least 14 1/2 x 22 1/2 inches.

You will need glue, 3/4-inch brads, and wood filler. For hardware, buy a pair of decorative hanging rings or ring pulls, a small decorative picture hanger or hook, and a pair of decorative hangers to mount on the wall.

Here's how this one goes together.

Step 1. From a 7-foot strip or suitable scraps of oak 1 x 2, cut two pieces to 24 inches and two to 16 inches.

Step 2. Tighten a 1/2-inch straight bit in your router's collet, and adjust the router and table for a 1/4-inch-deep, 1/4-inch-wide rabbet. Then stand each oak strip on a narrow edge on the router table, and rout a 1/4-inch x 1/4-inch rabbet along one edge of each piece.

Step 3. Keeping the rabbet on the rear edge, cut off one end of each piece at a 45-degree angle with a miter box and backsaw or power miter saw.

Step 4. Align one end of a yardstick with the inside edge of the miter on each piece, and mark two pieces for cuts at 22 inches and the other two at 14 inches. Then make the second 45-degree cut on each piece.

Step 5. Apply wood glue to the mitered ends of the frame sections, and assemble the frame with four corner clamps. Let stand until the glue sets.

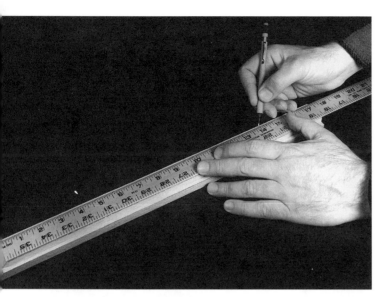

Calendar frame, Step 4.

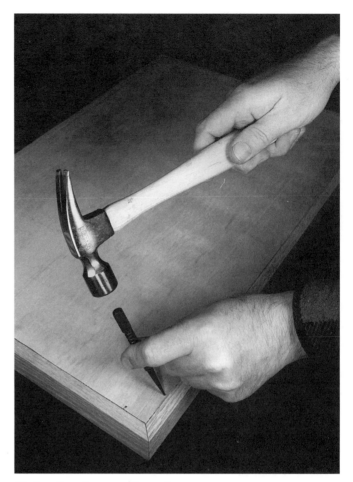

Calendar frame, Step 7.

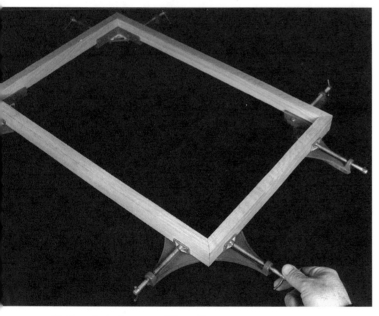

Calendar frame, Step 5.

3/4-inch brads through the back panel into the frame sections, and countersink the brads.

Step 8. Use a pad sander and 120-grit sandpaper to sand the face and sides of the 1 x 2 sections. Then use the sander to round over the inside front edges and rear edges of the sections.

Step 6. Lay the frame facedown and measure the height and width inside the rabbets. Then cut a piece of 1/4-inch oak plywood to 1/16 inch under those dimensions.

Step 7. Lightly sand the good face of the plywood with 120-grit and 220-grit sandpaper. Run a narrow bead of glue along the inside corner of the rabbet in all sections of the 1 x 2 frame, and lay the plywood panel into the rabbets. Toenail

Step 9. Cut a piece of 3/4 x 3/4-inch (outside dimension) oak outside corner molding with 45-degree angles at the ends, to fit one long edge of the frame. Mix a small amount of five-minute epoxy cement, and apply it to the inside corner of the molding. Clamp the molding to the frame with two or three spring clamps, and let it stand until the cement cures.

Step 10. Miter cut a piece of corner molding to fit one of the short frame sections; then cement

Calendar frame, Step 10.

Calendar frame, Step 13.

and clamp it in place. Continue cutting and cementing molding until the face of the calendar frame has been framed with corner molding.

Step 11. Sand the molding, as required, with 120-grit and 220-grit sandpaper, rounding over corners as you sand. Clean the frame to remove dust, wipe it with a tack cloth, and apply the stain and finish of your choice. The frame shown was finished with Watco Medium Walnut Danish Oil Finish.

Step 12. Unless you're using a self-adhesive hook or hanger for the calendar, mix a small amount of five-minute epoxy cement, and apply it to the back of a decorative hook. Then attach it near the top in the center of the back-panel face.

Step 13. Measure in 2 inches from each top corner, and make marks on the 1 x 2 frame 1/2 inch from the rear edge. Punch a pilot hole with a hammer and nail set or a scratch awl at each spot, and install a pair of decorative rings.

Step 14. Lay the frame facedown on a protected surface, and attach a 1/4-inch self-adhesive felt cushion just inside each rear corner.

Finished calendar frame.

Calendar case, Step 2.

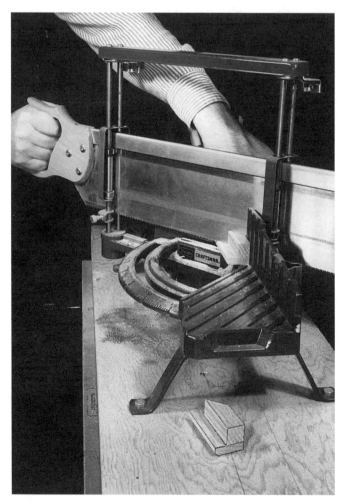

Calendar case, Step 3.

BUILD A CALENDAR CASE

You can build a fine-looking calendar case with little effort and a few scraps of oak 1 x 2, 3/4-square, bullnose stop, and 1/4-inch plywood. If you don't have suitable scraps on hand, buy one 7-foot piece each of oak 1 x 2, oak 3/4-square, and oak 3/8 x 1 1/4-inch bullnose stop. You will also need a scrap of 1/4-inch oak plywood, 13 1/2 x 22 1/2 inches or larger. And that's all the wood you'll need.

For hardware, you'll need two small brass hook-and-strap closures, two brass flat hinges, two 2 x #10 ovalhead wood screws, two #10 finish washers, a small brass knob, a small decorative hook or hanger, glazier's points, and 1-inch brads. If you will be mounting the case on a hollow section of wall instead of directly to the studs, substitute toggle bolts for the ovalhead screws.

You'll find numerous hinges that will work. Make sure the ones you pick are substantial enough to support the weight of the door and to hold up under use, but they should be no wider than 2 inches. The ones I chose are antique brass, and they're 1 1/2 x 3 1/2 inches.

At the glass shop, have a piece of window glass—not picture glass—cut to 12 15/16 x 21 15/16 inches.

When you have gathered these few materials together, you're ready to begin. Here's how.

Step 1. From suitable scraps or the 7-footers you bought, cut two pieces of oak 3/4-square to 24 inches and two to 15 inches. Do likewise with the oak bullnose stop.

Step 2. Coat one surface of each strip of 3/4-square with glue, and clamp a matching piece of bullnose stop to it with four C-clamps and clamp cushions to form strips of door molding with a beveled lip. Wipe away seeping glue with a damp sponge, and let stand until the glue sets.

Step 3. With a miter box and backsaw set at 45 degrees, cut two pieces of the door molding to 23 1/2 inches and two to 14 1/2 inches, each mitered at both ends. Then stand the oak 1 x 2 on a narrow edge in the miter box, and cut four pieces the same size as the door molding.

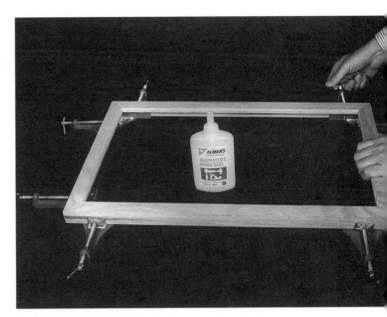

Calendar case, Step 6.

Calendar case, Step 4.

Step 4. Set the table-saw fence 1¼ inches from the near teeth of the blade and the blade for a ¼-inch depth. Lay a piece of the mitered 1 x 2 inside broad surface down on the saw table, with a narrow edge against the fence. Then use push blocks to run the piece over the blade. Do likewise with the other three pieces.

Step 5. Move the saw fence to 1⅜ inches from the near teeth of the blade, and run each piece of 1 x 2 over the blade again to create a ¼ x ¼-inch rabbet in the rear edge of each.

Step 6. Apply glue to the ends of the door molding, and assemble a simple frame with four corner clamps. Wipe seeping glue away with a damp sponge, and let the frame stand until the glue sets.

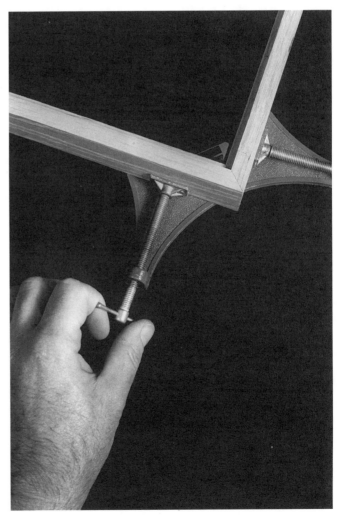

Calendar case, Step 7.

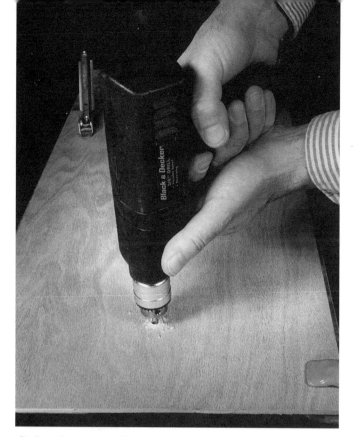

Calendar case, Step 10.

Calendar case, Step 11.

Step 7. Similarly, apply glue to the ends of the 1 x 2, and assemble a frame with corner clamps. Wipe excess glue, and let stand until glue sets.

Step 8. When frames are completed, sand them with a pad sander and 120-grit and 220-grit sandpaper, slightly rounding over the front edges of the door frame as you sand. Then clamp the two frames together with C-clamps and clamp cushions, and round over the corners with the pad sander so they will match.

Step 9. Lay the 1 x 2 frame facedown, and measure the height and width inside the rabbets. (It should be about 13½ x 22½ inches.) Cut a back panel of ¼-inch oak plywood about 1/16 inch smaller.

Step 10. Scribe a vertical center line down the rear surface of the back panel, and mark for screw holes at 4 inches from the top and bottom edges. Centerpunch a starter hole and drill a 7/32-inch-diameter hole at each spot.

Step 11. Sand the face of the back panel with a pad sander and 120-grit and 220-grit sandpaper. Run a narrow bead of glue along the rabbets in the 1 x 2 frame, lay the back panel in place, toenail 1-inch brads through the plywood into the 1 x 2, and countersink the brads.

Step 12. Thoroughly clean the partly assembled case to remove all dust, and wipe with a tack cloth. The unit is now ready for the finish of your choice.

Step 13. To duplicate the finish of the case shown, liberally apply Fuller O'Brien Pen-Chrome #640-11 English Oak Stain with a brush. Let it penetrate fifteen minutes, wipe it dry with paper towels, and let stand overnight. Then apply a coat of sanding sealer and two coats of satin sheen polyurethane, burnishing lightly between coats with 400-grit waterproof sandpaper.

Step 14. When the finish has thoroughly dried, clamp the two components together at the top and at the bottom with C-clamps and clamp

Calendar case, Step 14.

Calendar case, Step 17.

Calendar case, Step 15.

Finished calendar case.

cushions. Stand the unit on a narrow edge, and position the hinges 2 inches from the top and bottom corners. Use the hinges as guides to mark for screw holes. Punch the pilot holes with a hammer and nail set or scratch awl, and attach the hinges with the screws that were provided with them.

Step 15. Turn the unit over, and position the hook-and-strap closures 2 inches from the top and bottom corners. Then make marks for and punch the pilot holes, and attach closures with the screws provided.

Step 16. Lay the unit faceup. Measure down the door frame on the opening side, and make a mark 11¾ inches from the top edge and ½ inch from the outside edge. Centerpunch a starter hole, and drill a ½-inch-deep pilot hole slightly smaller in diameter than the knob screw. Then attach the knob.

Step 17. Clean the glass. Open the door, and lay the glass in place. Then secure the glass with equally spaced glazier's points—three each in top and bottom sections, and five each in the side sections.

Step 18. Unless you're using a self-adhesive hook or hanger, mix a small amount of five-minute epoxy cement, and apply it to the back of a decorative hanger. Then attach it near the top in the center of the back-panel face.

Your calendar case is now ready to hang on the wall with screws or toggle bolts. Attach the top screw first, and use a spirit level to make sure the case hangs evenly.

CHAPTER SIXTEEN

Framing Pegboard

Perforated hardboard, more commonly known as perfboard or pegboard, is one of the most useful products there is for various storage and organization projects. It's available at lumberyards, home-improvement centers, and at many discount or department stores. Primarily, it is a functional material, but it can be made attractive. And it's useful anywhere you might want to put it. Most often, it shows up in workshops, garages, basements, kitchens, sewing rooms, hobby rooms, and children's rooms. It is inexpensive but easy to work with, so homeowners find many applications for it.

When we built the house we currently live in, I covered one 24-foot wall of the garage with pegboard and have since covered nearly every square inch of it with tools, implements, camping gear, cordage, boating equipment, and anything else that will hang from a peg or hook. There, I first put up furring strips and attached the pegboard to the strips to allow the necessary space behind the pegboard for the hooks and pegs. Elsewhere in the house, though, I have taken a different approach.

By building pegboard units that I frame and hang like pictures, I have made the material more attractive, versatile, and useful in other rooms. The method and materials I use allow me to put up pegboard and move it later, if I wish. In this way, I can take a board down if I'm painting a room. Or if a unit has outlived its usefulness in one room, I can put it to work in another. And if we move to another house, we can take our pegboard units with us.

One of the first boards I built was a 36 x 48-inch vertical unit for the kitchen that houses all sorts of utensils that used to clutter the kitchen cabinets and drawers. On the pegboard, they're always within easy reach. The pegboard not only keeps all these items organized and easy to find, but it looks good too.

There's a 48 x 60-inch board hanging horizontally above a large work table in my studio. I call it my framing project board, and on it I keep mat and frame corner samples, drafting tools, matting and framing tools, and all sorts of other framing paraphernalia. My framing project board keeps me from wasting time looking for items that might get stacked here or there or would be tossed into a desk drawer with a hundred other things.

In my darkroom, I installed a board identical to the kitchen unit, except that this one hangs horizontally. I have two safelights wired into it, and I hang all sorts of photographic gadgets and gizmos on it.

Two narrow vertical units hang on the ends of kitchen cabinets. These small, light-duty boards make use of otherwise wasted space and hold an assortment of small kitchen utensils that normally get lost in a drawer.

No matter where you might need one of these organizing boards, you'll find the materials readily available and the building techniques simple.

HOOKS AND FIXTURES

Wherever pegboard is sold, you'll find numerous sizes and shapes of hooks, tool holders, and other fixtures and hangers. You can buy them individually or in kits of several different sizes and types. They come in sizes to fit 1/8-inch and 1/4-inch pegboard. For starters, buy a kit with a large assortment. Then determine which of these you need more of, and buy them. Be sure to keep extras on hand, as you will gradually find other items to hang until you have completely covered any board.

For small boards, you can usually make a list of the items you plan to hang and take the list when you go shopping for hooks and fixtures. In any event, shop around at several stores to find what's available and what might work best for you.

There are both metal and plastic fixtures. Some are designed to hold tiny objects, others will hold large and heavy items, some hold items under tension, and still others will hold sets or collections of like items. There are also protective plastic tips that fit over the ends of metal hooks to protect any finely finished items you might hang.

No matter what kind of hooks and fixtures you end up buying, I suggest you look for those that are self-stabilizing or buy a packet of little wire clips that you can use with standard hooks and hangers to secure them to the board. Otherwise, you will frequently knock the various hooks and hangers out of their holes, which is definitely a nuisance.

BUYING PEGBOARD AND FRAMING MATERIALS

The standard size for pegboard is a 48 x 96-inch sheet, the same as plywood, paneling, and other sheet stock. At some home-improvement centers and department stores, it is available in smaller sizes, usually 24 x 48 inches and 48 x 48 inches. If you plan to make more than one board, you might need a full sheet or even more, and you will surely find uses for any leftovers.

Pegboard comes in 1/8-inch and 1/4-inch thicknesses, either tempered or untempered. Although the 1/8-inch board is suitable for a variety of applications, I prefer the 1/4-inch tempered board for most jobs. The thicker board is more rigid and less susceptible to warping. Tempered

board is also more warp-resistant than nontempered, is less affected by temperature and humidity fluctuations, looks good when left unfinished, and is the better choice for any board that is to be painted.

For small units, you can use any kind of picture-frame molding that suits you. So you need buy only enough molding to fit the boards you're planning. Or you can make your own table-saw, router, or glued molding.

For larger, heavier-duty units, you will need different materials. Once you have decided how large a piece of pegboard you want to hang, buy enough kiln-dried 1 x 2 common pine or fir (or rip your own) to make a rear framework and an equal amount of 1-inch outside corner molding. For example, for framing a 36 x 48-inch piece of pegboard, you'll need two 8-foot 1 x 2s and the same amount of corner molding.

For small, light-duty boards, you will need only the usual frame-assembly materials and hanging hardware: glue, brads or glazier's points, small screw eyes, picture-hanging wire, and picture hangers. I also put a 1/4-inch self-adhesive felt cushion inside each rear corner of the frame on each small board.

For larger, heavy-duty boards, you will need glue and brads, wood filler or spackling paste, and heavy-duty hanging hardware. Use four 1-inch screw eyes—two in the bottom section and one in each side section—for the picture wire, as you would with a large painting. For most boards, standard picture wire will suffice, but if you are building a board larger than 48 x 48 inches and will hang some fairly heavy items on it, use stronger wire. And for safety's sake, hang each heavy-duty board with two 100-pound-capacity picture hangers.

FRAMING LIGHT-DUTY BOARDS

The small, light-duty boards are the easiest to make, as they go together just like a picture. For that reason, they are simpler to finish, because you can apply the finish to the frame and pegboard separately, any way you wish. If you want, you can stain and polyurethane or lacquer the frame, and leave the pegboard natural. You can paint the pegboard. You can paint the frame and leave the pegboard natural. Or you can paint everything one color or paint the frame one color and the pegboard another. Do whatever suits you and fits the room's decor.

With these small boards, you can take advantage of any usable space that is going to waste, and if you carefully plan the way to display the items you will store on them, the boards will become attractive additions to any room.

The secret to success with the small boards is to think little. Don't think that you have to hang two dozen items on a board to make it a worthwhile project. If you can fit three, four, or a half-dozen items on one, fine. In the case of small items, you'll not only be able to hang more, but you'll also be organizing the things that are most likely to disappear in a drawer or cabinet.

Also, when you think little, you will begin finding places for these small boards that you never even considered before. If you have a spot where an 11 x 14-inch picture would fit but might look out of place or would be hidden from view, consider an 11 x 14-inch piece of pegboard, attractively framed and storing a few useful items.

When I planned to make the small boards to hang on the ends of our kitchen cabinets, I decided on 1/8-inch pegboard, because I wanted to use the smaller-gauge hooks and fixtures. I also wanted to use the narrowest of moldings, and the 1/8-inch board assured me the proper clearance for the hooks.

I shopped around for a suitable commercial molding, but I found nothing that I liked or would work in the confined spaces where I planned to hang these boards. Ultimately, I decided to make my own molding from oak 3/4-square, and this turned out to be an ideal molding for small boards. So I'm sure I will be using more of it in the future.

Of course, you will want to make some boards to fit in specific places, so the dimensions that follow won't work in every case. But these boards fit in many tight areas, and they work beautifully with standard kitchen cabinets.

For a pair of these boards, you will need a 24 x 24-inch sheet of 1/8-inch pegboard, two 7-foot strips of oak 3/4-square, glue, glazier's points or brads, self-adhesive felt cushions, the usual hanging hardware, and the finishes of your choice. Here's how they go together.

Step 1. Cut the pegboard in half to yield two 12 x 24-inch pieces. Then evenly trim the long edges of each piece to a width of 10 inches (10 x 24 inches overall).

Step 2. Tighten a 5/8-inch straight bit in a router collet, and set the router and table to rout a 5/16-inch-wide, 1/8-inch-deep rabbet. Run the 3/4-square over the bit. Reset the router for a

Light-duty board, Step 2.

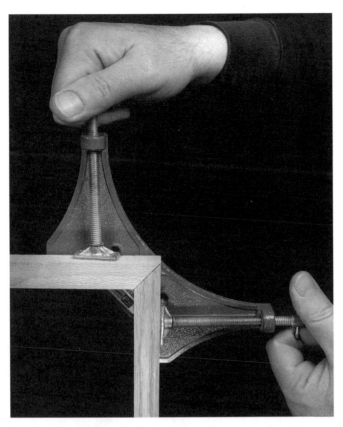

Light-duty board, Step 4.

Light-duty board, Step 9.

1/4-inch depth, and make another pass. Reset the router to take off an additional 1/8 inch, and make the final pass, leaving a 1/8-inch-thick lip on the molding.

Step 3. With a miter box and backsaw set at 45 degrees, cut four pieces of the 3/4-square molding to 24 1/8 inches inside the rabbets, and four more pieces to 10 1/8 inches. Lightly sand the cuts with 120-grit sandpaper to remove any splinters.

Step 4. Apply glue to the ends of the molding, and use corner clamps to assemble two frames, each measuring 10 1/8 x 24 1/8 inches. Wipe seeping glue away with a damp sponge, and let frames stand for several hours or overnight.

Step 5. Use a pad sander and 120-grit and 220-grit sandpaper to sand the outside surfaces of the frames, slightly rounding over outside edges and corners as you proceed. Clean frames and boards, and they're ready for finishing.

Step 6. To duplicate the finish of the boards shown, apply a coat of shellac to the pegboard pieces if they are not tempered. Lightly burnish the shellac with 400-grit sandpaper, clean the boards to remove dust, and apply two coats of flat or semigloss latex paint to match the room's decor.

Step 7. Brush a liberal coat of Fuller O'Brien Pen-Chrome #640-11 English Oak Stain onto the frames, let penetrate for fifteen minutes, and wipe dry with paper towels. Then let the frames stand overnight.

Step 8. When stain has dried, apply three coats of Deft Semi-Gloss Clear Wood Finish to all surfaces of the frames, and let dry.

Step 9. Lay frames facedown on a protected surface. Lay boards in place inside the frames. Then secure the boards with brads or glazier's points.

Step 10. Install screw eyes in the inside surface of the frame molding so the units will hang flush against the wall or cabinets, and attach picture

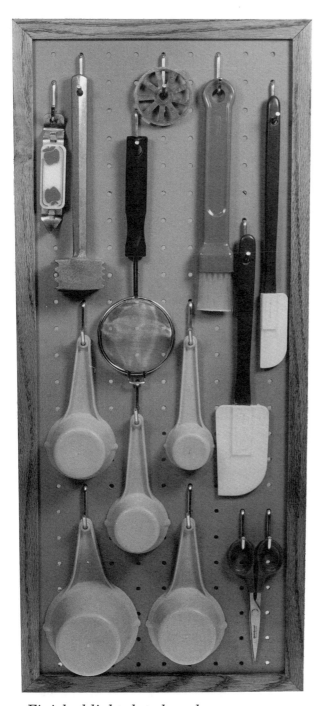

Finished light-duty board.

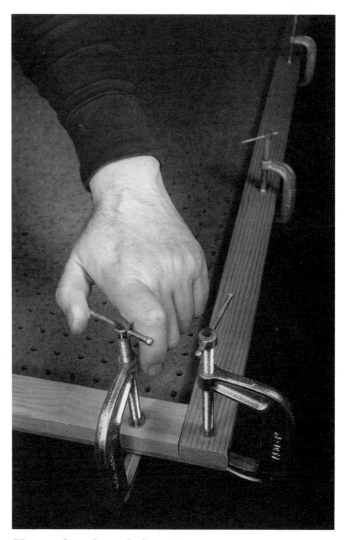

Heavy-duty board, Step 2.

wire. Then stick a ¼-inch self-adhesive felt pad just inside each rear corner of each frame.

Step 11. Lay boards faceup, and arrange the items each will store until you have an eye-pleasing arrangement. Then install the proper hooks and fixtures and hang the boards.

FRAMING HEAVY-DUTY BOARDS

Pegboard can be affected by temperature and humidity, so large boards require sturdier construction than any of the lightweight, light-duty boards. The rear framework and face frame keep the board from warping. The directions that follow are for any large board.

Step 1. Once your board is cut to size, lay it facedown (smooth side down) on a flat working surface. Then use a miter box and backsaw to cut two 1 x 2s the same length as the longest edges of the pegboard.

Step 2. Run a wavy bead of glue along the back of the pegboard near each long edge, lay a 1 x 2

Masking a board before painting.

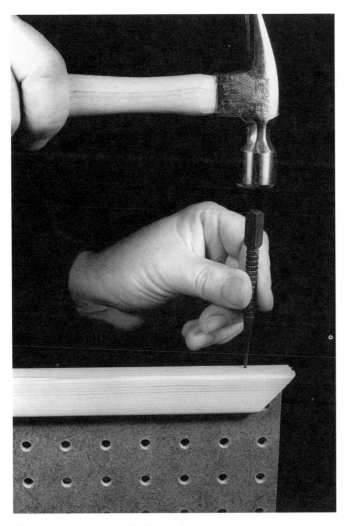

Heavy-duty board, Step 4.

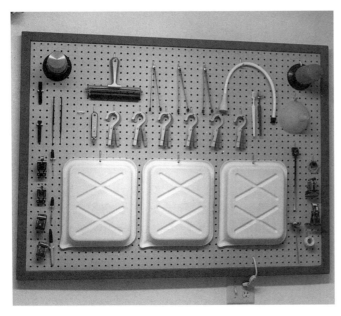

Author's darkroom board.

on the glue and flush with the edge, and clamp each strip to the pegboard with C-clamps spaced about 12 inches apart.

Step 3. Measure the distance along the short edges of the pegboard between the 1 x 2 strips, and cut two 1 x 2s to fit. Glue and clamp them to the pegboard, and let stand with clamps in place until the glue sets.

Step 4. With a miter box and backsaw set at 45 degrees, cut one end off a piece of corner molding. Lay the molding along one edge of the board, and mark the molding for the second cut. Miter cut the opposite end, apply glue to the inside of the molding, and press it in place on the face of the board. Drive 1-inch brads through the molding into the side edges of the rear frame, and countersink the brads.

Step 5. Miter cut one end of another piece of molding, fit it to an adjacent edge of the board face, and mark it for the second cut. Miter cut the opposite end, and attach the piece as you did the first one. Continue cutting molding and attaching it the same way to the remaining two sides.

Step 6. Fill brad holes with spackling paste if you plan to paint the board or wood filler if you plan to stain and polyurethane or lacquer the board. Let the filler dry; then sand with 120-grit and 220-grit sandpaper. Vacuum the board to remove dust, wipe it down with a tack cloth, and it's ready for installation of hanging hardware and the finish of your choice.

These large boards look best painted, and you can paint the board face one color and frame another, if you wish. Try to coordinate the colors with those of the room where the board will be used. To keep from marring the finish, install screw eyes and hanging hardware before you paint the board.

To give you an idea of how you can coordinate or contrast colors when painting, the board in my studio is painted charcoal black, and the molding is light olive. These colors match the colors of filing cabinets, a desk, and other furnishings in my studio. My darkroom board is gray with blue trim, which matches the primary colors of my darkroom, even my enlarger.

Nontempered pegboard will absorb water from latex paints. So if you use this material, apply a coat of shellac to the board face before painting. Then lightly burnish it with 400-grit waterproof sandpaper before painting, and wipe it with a clean tack cloth.

With tempered board, you can skip the shellac seal. But if you plan to use two colors, run a strip of wide painters' masking tape around the pegboard where it meets the frame. Apply two coats of paint to the frame, remove the tape, and apply two coats of paint to the face. You also have the option of leaving the pegboard face natural.

CHAPTER SEVENTEEN

Framing Bulletin Boards

Bulletin boards, like pegboard organizers, are utilitarian objects, but they can also be attractive adjuncts to a room's decor. You can make them any size you want from a variety of suitable and readily available materials. You can hang them anywhere, but you will probably want to give first consideration to the kitchen, workshop, and home office or den. Hang a small one wherever there's a phone. Use several small ones for decorative purposes.

Any bulletin board consists mainly of an underlayment, a covering material, and a frame. The choice of underlayment depends on the design of the board and what it will be covered with. For years, corrugated containerboard has been a popular lightweight underlayment, but I find foamboard a much better choice. For covering materials requiring a rigid underlayment, plywood and hardboard are best.

Burlap and cork are probably the most popular covering materials. With burlap, you have a choice among several colors or natural beige. Cork is available in dark brown, light brown, and a composite of both. It comes in rolls, sheets, and 12 x 12-inch squares, some of which are self-adhesive.

Burlap is a coarse, broad-weave fabric. Although many kinds of adhesives will make burlap stick to an underlayment, some cause the material to become hard and brittle, and others seep through the weave and stain it. You can use fabric adhesives, but those I have checked are comparatively expensive. I prefer general-purpose aerosol adhesives, such as those made by 3M, which are fast, clean, and efficient adhesives for burlap.

Some glues and cements do not work at all with cork. Of the various ones I have tried over the years, several have worked well. Panel adhesive and all-purpose construction adhesive—both of which come in cans or in tubes you use with a caulking gun—are good, relatively inexpensive products. Some epoxy cements work with cork, but be sure to read the labels to make certain before buying any. Again, though, I have come to prefer the aerosol adhesives I mentioned above, because they are so easy to work with, and they do a good job.

Of course, you can also use self-adhesive mount boards available from various sources. You can attach burlap to self-adhesive foamboards and mount cork to self-adhesive Masonite, Gatorfoam, and codaFoam boards.

MAKE A BURLAP BULLETIN BOARD

Lightweight burlap boards can be used anywhere you need a bulletin board. You can frame them with any commercial molding, or with molding you have made. You can hang these boards with conventional hanging hardware, but because of their light weight, you can also put them up with adhesive foam mounting tape, which makes them ideal for use on hard walls, hollow doors, and anywhere else standard hangers don't work.

Here's how to build a 24 x 36-inch board.

Step 1. Use a straightedge and an X-Acto knife to trim a piece of 3/16-inch foamboard to 24 x 36 inches. Then cut a piece of burlap slightly larger.

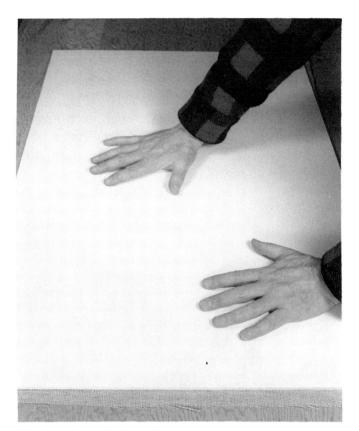

Burlap board, Step 3.

Burlap board, Step 2.

Step 2. Lay newspapers on your work surface and the foamboard on the newspapers. Then spray an even coat of all-purpose adhesive, such as 3M Super 77, over the entire surface of the foamboard.

Step 3. Carefully set the foamboard aside and remove the newspapers. Spread the burlap on the work surface. Then lay the foamboard on the burlap, adhesive side down, and press the board to the burlap. Turn the board over, and use a roller to press the burlap to the board.

Step 4. Use scissors to carefully trim away excess burlap from the edges of the board. Then let stand until the adhesive cures.

Step 5. With a miter box and backsaw, cut two pieces of frame molding to 24¹/₈ inches (inside the rabbets) and two more pieces of 36¹/₈ inches.

Burlap board, Step 3.

Step 6. Apply glue to one end of a long molding strip, and attach it to a short strip with a corner clamp. Continue connecting strips with glue and corner clamps until the frame is assembled.

Step 7. Drive a 1-inch brad through each corner, and countersink the brads. Fill brad holes with wood filler, and let frame stand with clamps in place until glue and filler cure.

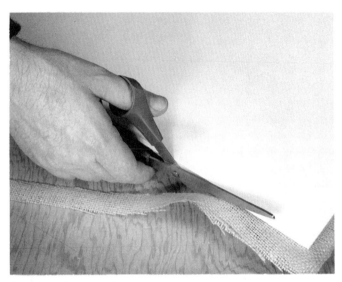

Burlap board, Step 4.

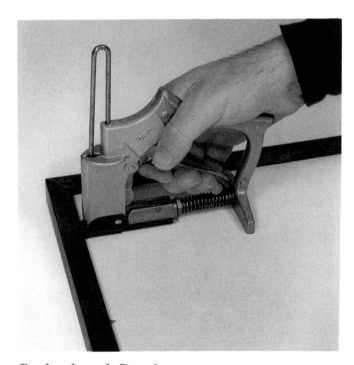

Burlap board, Step 9.

Step 8. Sand the frame, as required, with a pad sander and 120-grit and 220-grit sandpaper. Then apply the stain and finish of your choice.

Step 9. With the frame facedown, lay the burlap-covered board in place, and secure it with brads or glazier's points.

Step 10. Install two small screw eyes in opposite frame sections, attach picture-hanging wire to them, and the burlap bulletin board is ready to hang.

MAKE MINIATURE CORK BOARDS

The fastest and easiest way to make a cork bulletin board is with self-adhesive cork squares. Of course you can use this material to make boards of any size, but I find them particularly handy

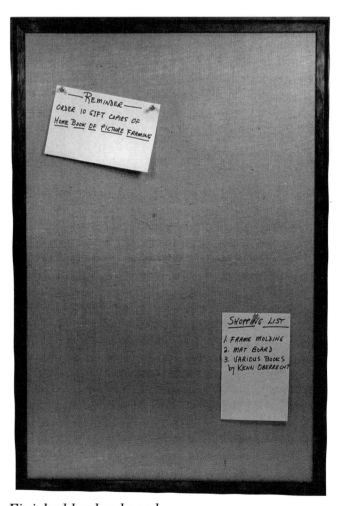

Finished burlap board.

for small boards that I put near phones and wherever else they might prove convenient.

Since the squares are 12 x 12 inches, it's best to make underlayments with dimensions divisible by 12: 12 x 24 inches, 24 x 24 inches, 12 x 36 inches, and so on. You can cut cork, if you must, but it's much easier and neater to make the underlayment fit the cork than vice versa.

The miniature boards can be displayed alone or in eye-catching groupings. For example, instead of one large bulletin board, you might prefer to hang an arrangement of small boards.

For underlayment you can use any suitably rigid material, such as tempered 1/4-inch hardboard and 1/4-inch or 1/2-inch plywood. For small boards, 1/4-inch plywood will work, but you must make sure the material is flat. I prefer 1/2-inch plywood for these boards, no matter the size, as it provides a rigid foundation, and I needn't worry about it warping later.

To make the 12 x 24-inch board shown, you will need a scrap of 1/2-inch plywood that size or larger, an 8-foot clear fir 1 x 2 (or suitable scraps), two 12 x 12-inch self-adhesive squares, glue, brads, wood filler, hanging hardware, and the finish of your choice. When you've gathered your materials, follow these simple construction steps.

Miniature cork board, Step 2.

Step 1. Trim a piece of 1/2-inch plywood to 12 x 24 inches. Lightly sand the edges with 120-grit sandpaper to remove any splinters left by the saw blade.

Step 2. Clean the board to remove dust, and wipe it down with a tack cloth. Peel the release paper from two cork squares, and press them to the plywood board. Use a roller to firmly seat the cork squares.

Step 3. Use a radial-arm saw, table saw, or router and router table to turn the 1 x 2 into a simple box molding (see chapter 8).

Step 4. With a miter box and backsaw set at 45 degrees, cut two frame sections from the box molding to 12 1/8 inches and two to 24 1/8 inches.

Miniature cork board, Step 6.

Finished miniature cork board.

Big cork board, Step 1.

Step 5. Apply glue to the frame-section ends, and use four corner clamps to assemble a frame that's 12¹⁄₈ inches by 24¹⁄₈ inches (inside dimensions).

Step 6. Drive two 1¹⁄₄-inch brads at each corner of the frame, and countersink the brads. Fill the holes with wood filler, and let the frame stand with clamps in place until glue and filler set.

Step 7. Sand the frame with a pad sander and 120-grit and 220-grit sandpaper, slightly rounding over sharp edges and corners as you proceed. Clean the frame, wipe it with a tack cloth, and it's ready for the finish of your choice.

Step 8. When the finish dries, lay the frame facedown on a protected surface. Then lay the cork board in place in the frame, and secure it with brads or glazier's points.

Step 9. You can hang the board vertically or horizontally. So install two small screw eyes on the inside surface of the appropriate frame sections, and attach picture-hanging wire.

Step 10. With the board facedown, attach a ¹⁄₄-inch self-adhesive felt cushion just inside each rear corner of the frame. Then hang the board with a standard picture hanger.

BUILD A BIG CORK BOARD

The board shown here is the heavy-duty one I built to hang in my shop. I made it mostly from scraps left over from other projects, but had to buy the cork.

For the rear frame you will need two 6-foot 1 x 2s or suitable scraps: two 3-footers and three 2-footers. You will also need a 24 x 36-inch piece of ¹⁄₄-inch plywood, cork to cover it, and two 6-foot pieces of 1-inch outside corner molding. Glue, brads, wood filler, and hanging wire complete the list.

Follow these construction steps to build an identical board for your shop or elsewhere.

Step 1. Trim a piece of ¹⁄₄-inch plywood to 24 x 36 inches with a table saw or circular saw and guide. Then use a straightedge and X-Acto knife to trim a sheet of cork to the same dimensions.

Step 2. Cut two strips of 1 x 2 to 36 inches each. (If you aren't using scraps, cut one piece from each of two 6-footers.) Stand them on their narrow edges, and run a bead of glue down the top edge of each. Lay the plywood on them, attach it with 1-inch brads, and countersink the brads.

Step 3. Measure the distance between the 1 x 2s (should be about 22½ inches), and cut three pieces of 1 x 2 to fit.

Step 4. With plywood faceup, measure down each long edge, and make marks at 18 inches. Then align a yardstick with these marks, and scribe a pencil line across the plywood.

Step 5. Run a bead of glue along one narrow edge and both ends of a piece of 1 x 2, and press it in place between the two attached strips at one end of the assembly. Drive two 1½-inch brads through each of the attached strips into the ends of the 22½-inch strip. Secure the plywood to it with 1-inch brads, and countersink the brads. Attach another strip the same way at the opposite end of the plywood.

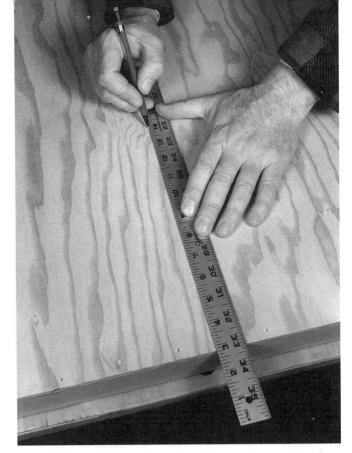

Big cork board, Step 4.

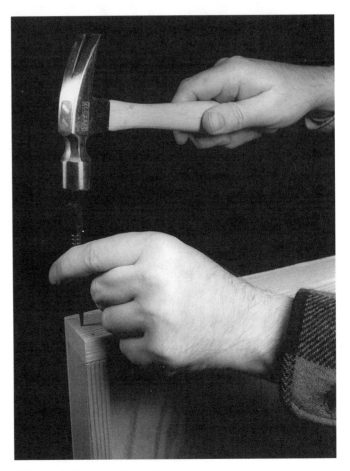

Big cork board, Step 2.

Big cork board, Step 5.

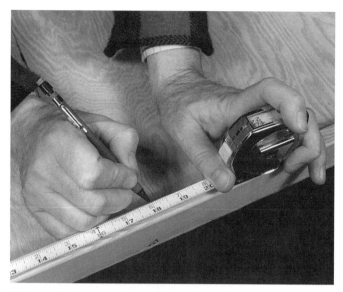

Big cork board, Step 6.

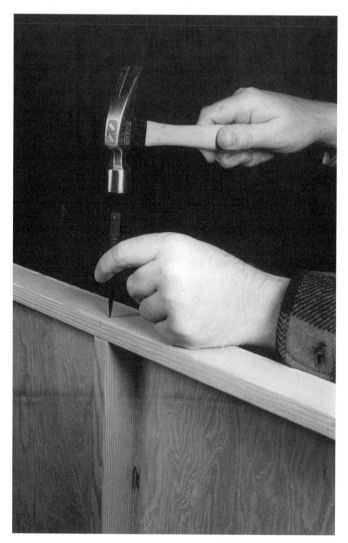

Big cork board, Step 6.

Step 6. Lay the assembly facedown, and make guide marks at the center of each long strip of 1 x 2. Apply glue to the remaining piece of 1 x 2, align it with the guide marks, and drive 1½-inch brads into the ends. Lay the assembly faceup, drive 1-inch brads along the guideline scribed in Step 4, and countersink the brads.

Step 7. Cover the sides of the assembly with masking tape. Lay the unit faceup on newspapers, and apply a liberal coat of an all-purpose aerosol adhesive, such as 3M Super 77.

Step 8. Lay the cork sheet atop the plywood, align it with the edges, and firmly press it in place. Then use a roller to set the cork in the adhesive, and let stand until the adhesive cures.

Step 9. After removing the masking tape, use a miter box and backsaw to cut a piece of 1-inch outside corner molding, with 45-degree miters at

Big cork board, Step 7.

each end, to fit each edge of the unit. Run a bead of glue along the inside corner of each piece of molding, and attach it with 1-inch brads, driven through the sides into the 1 x 2 strips. Countersink the brads.

Step 10. Fill all brad holes with wood filler. When the filler dries, lightly sand it, as required, with a pad sander and 120-grit and 220-grit sandpaper.

Step 11. This board was designed to hang vertically. Lay it facedown, measure 12 inches down each vertical 1 x 2, and attach screw eyes on the inside surface of the 1 x 2s. Attach picture-hanging wire to them.

Step 12. Attach a 1/2-inch self-adhesive cork or felt cushion just inside each rear corner of the 1 x 2 framework, and your bulletin board is ready to hang.

Big cork board, Step 9.

Big cork board, Step 8.

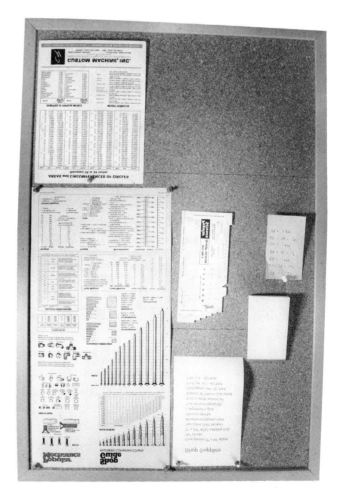

Finished big cork board, hanging in author's workshop.

CHAPTER EIGHTEEN

Framing Three-Dimensional Objects

Three-dimensional objects pose some problems for the framer, most of which are easily solved by the use of shadow-box frames. Commercially manufactured shadow-box frames are available through some retail outlets, but many are meant for two-dimensional pictures and require modification before you can display three-dimensional objects in them. And those I have seen aren't the best quality.

I have done some shopping around for shadow-box frames and moldings at local outlets and haven't found anything useful. Although some commercially made moldings can be adapted for use in making shadow boxes, they require more work than I can justify; it's as easy to make my own moldings from scratch.

Commercially made shadow-box moldings are time-savers, but they're often difficult to find at the usual local outlets. The best source I know of is XYLO, Inc. This company offers a good selection of shadow-box moldings and extensions at reasonable prices. (See the Source Directory.)

Shadow-box frames offer aesthetic and practical advantages. The deep frame walls add a subtle visual appeal to the subject by casting shadows that change with the viewer's position—hence, the name *shadow box*. The frame walls also provide the extra depth that three-dimensional objects require.

The variety of items suitable for display inside shadow-box frames is endless. You might want to give such treatment to certain carvings, ceramics, needlework, and any deep-relief art-work. You can use shadow boxes to frame medals, ribbons, and other awards. Use them for artifacts and collections of all kinds.

There aren't any rules when it comes to framing three-dimensional objects. I have seen them attached to plaques and simple slabs of wood and displayed against backgrounds of every imaginable material.

The use of glass is a matter of personal choice. Its main function is to keep dust off the object being framed. So if what you're framing might be harmed by dust (some fabrics, for example) or simply might be a nuisance to keep clean (anything intricate), then you'll probably want to frame it behind glass.

MOUNTING THREE-DIMENSIONAL OBJECTS

Before you build a shadow-box frame for any three-dimensional object or collection of objects, you need to give some thought to how the items should be mounted. In fact, you will probably want to see to any necessary matting and mounting before you build the frame.

Some objects should be wired to mount boards or background boards or attached with monofilament fishing line, but most can be attached with some kind of adhesive. Epoxy cement is an excellent mounting adhesive, because it will work with so many different kinds of materials. You will find two-part (resin and hardener) epoxy kits that cure in several hours or overnight and others that will set in four or five minutes. Take your pick.

Epoxy cement should be considered a permanent adhesive. If you are mounting anything of value or potential value and want to use a reversible adhesive, use silicone glue and seal, which cures to a rubbery consistency and can be peeled off with some effort.

You can mount most items directly to mat board or to mat board, hardboard, foamboard, or plywood that has been covered with any appropriate material. Some popular coverings are burlap, linen, vinyl, leather, acrylic, cork, plastic sheeting, and wallpaper. Naturally, heavy objects should be mounted to a substantial board, and if the board is covered, the covering material should be durable and permanent.

SHADOW-BOX FRAME WITH GLASS

To make a shadow-box frame for displaying items behind glass, I designed a frame molding that goes together as simply as any frame and requires none of the usual inserts commonly used with box molding to make shadow-box frames. The molding looks simple but is a bit more complicated than some. Nevertheless, it's easy to make if you just take your time and follow the directions.

When this molding is made from 1 x 2, as the directions stipulate, there will be a 1-inch clearance between the frame lip and the rear rabbet. Allowing for the thickness of the glass and mat, you can display items up to 3/4 inch thick. If you want to display thicker items, use stock wider than 1 x 2, and adjust saw-blade settings as necessary.

Use picture glass with this frame, not nonglare glass, which would distort the items being framed because of the distance between the glass and the mount board.

Unlike other frames in which your glass, mats, and mount board are all cut to identical dimensions, with this frame, your mount board and backing will be larger than the glass and mats. In an 8 x 10-inch frame, such as the one shown, the dimensions inside the rear rabbets are 8½ x 10½ inches. So for this frame, I cut the mount board and hardboard backing to 8⅜ inches x 10⅜ inches.

To make an 8 x 10-inch frame, you'll need a 4-foot 1 x 2 (I used oak for the frame shown), a scrap

of ⅛-inch hardboard, glue, glass, and the usual hanging hardware. Here's how it goes together.

Step 1. Set the table-saw fence ¼ inch from the *near* teeth of the blade and the blade for a ¼-inch depth. Lay a 1 x 2 broad side down on the saw table with a narrow side against the fence, and run it over the blade.

Step 2. Stand the 1 x 2 on the narrow side farthest from the groove cut in Step 1, with the ungrooved broad surface against the fence. Then run the piece over the blade to create a groove in a narrow side.

Step 3. Set the fence ¼ inch from the *far* teeth of the blade and the blade for a ½-inch depth. Then lay the 1 x 2, grooved broad side down, on the saw table with the grooved narrow side against the fence, and run the piece over the

Shadow-box frame, Step 2.

Shadow-box frame, Step 3.

Shadow-box frame, Step 4.

blade to create a 1/4 x 1/2-inch rabbet in one narrow side of the piece.

Step 4. Reset the blade for a 1 1/4-inch depth. Stand the 1 x 2 molding on the saw table with the rabbeted edge down and the grooved broad side against the fence. Now run the piece over the blade to create a rabbet in the broad side with a 1/4-inch lip at the face edge of the molding. This completes the shadow-box molding.

Step 5. To make an 8 x 10-inch shadow-box frame, use a miter box and backsaw set at 45 degrees to cut two sections to 8 1/8 inches and two to 10 1/8 inches inside the miters. Sand the inside surfaces between the front lip and rear rabbet with 120-grit sandpaper to remove saw-blade marks. Then assemble the frame with glue and corner clamps, and let the frame stand until the glue sets.

Step 6. Sand the frame with a pad sander and 120-grit and 220-grit sandpaper, slightly rounding over the front outside edges and corners as you proceed. Clean the frame to remove dust, and wipe it with a tack cloth. The frame is now ready for the finish of your choice.

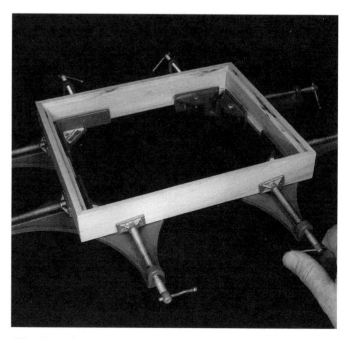

Shadow-box frame, Step 5.

Step 7. To duplicate the finish of the frame shown, apply a coat of Fuller O'Brien Pen-Chrome #640-11 English Oak Stain, let penetrate for ten to fifteen minutes, and wipe dry with paper towels. Let stand overnight, and apply three coats of Deft Semi-Gloss Clear Wood Finish.

Step 8. Lay the frame facedown on a protected surface. Clean the glass, and lay it in place on the lip of the frame. Next, lay the mat or mats against the glass, and secure everything with glazier's points.

Step 9. Check the rear dimensions of the frame, and cut the mount board slightly undersize to fit. Mount the three-dimensional object on the mount board with epoxy cement or silicone glue and seal. (Let the latter stand for twenty-four hours before proceeding.)

Step 10. Cut a piece of 1/8-inch hardboard the same size as the mount board to fit the rear of the frame. Lay the mounted work in place in the rabbet at the rear of the frame. Then run a narrow bead of silicone glue and seal around the rear edge of the frame, press the hardboard in place, apply more silicone if necessary, and let stand for twenty-four hours.

Step 11. Attach a sawtooth hanger to the rear of the frame near the top center. Attach self-adhesive felt or foam weather-stripping cushions near the bottom corners, and the framed work is ready for hanging.

GLASSLESS SHADOW-BOX FRAME

In designing the molding for a glassless shadow box, I came up with one that has proved to be a favorite and one I will be using on many projects in the future, for both three-dimensional and two-dimensional works. It's an easy molding to make, and the frames made from it are quite attractive.

To make the 8 x 10-inch frame shown, all you need is a 4-foot strip of oak 1 x 2, a 4-foot strip of oak 3/4 x 3/4-inch cove molding, glue, and hanging hardware.

Shadow-box frame, Step 9.

Finished shadow-box frame.

My original plan was to make a box molding, glue the cove molding to it, and make my frames from this. Then I decided to experiment with my router and router table, and I routed a cove into the outside corner of the molding, and that's what turned a simple, handsome molding into an elegant one. You might want to experiment with other bits to see what effects you can achieve. Try ogee and beading bits for starters.

With this frame, cut mats and mount boards to identical outside dimensions, as you would with most frames.

To build the frame, follow these steps.

Step 1. Set the table-saw fence 1¼ inches from the *far* teeth of the blade and the blade for a ¼-inch depth. Lay a 1 x 2 broad side down on the saw table and run it over the blade.

Step 2. Reset the fence ¼ inch from the *far* teeth of the blade and the blade for a 1¼-inch

Glassless shadow-box frame, Step 4.

depth. Then stand the 1 x 2 on a narrow edge on the saw table with the grooved surface against the fence, and run the piece over the blade to create a basic box molding.

Step 3. Cut ¾ x ¾-inch cove molding the same length as the 1 x 2. Mix enough five-minute epoxy cement to coat one flat edge of the cove molding, and apply a thin coat to it. Press it in place behind the lip of the box molding, and secure it with spring clamps. (If you don't have enough clamps, tightly wrap masking tape around the molding about every 12 inches.) Let stand until the cement cures.

Step 4. Tighten a ⅜-inch-radius cove bit in the router collet. Set the router and table for a ⅛-inch depth. Then lay the molding facedown on the router table and rout a cove into the outside corner. Make as many more passes as necessary to achieve effects you like. Two passes at ⅛-inch increments sufficed for the molding shown.

Step 5. To make an 8 x 10-inch frame, use a miter box and backsaw to cut a piece of molding to 10⅛ inches and another to 8⅛ inches, inside the rabbet. Use those pieces to mark two more

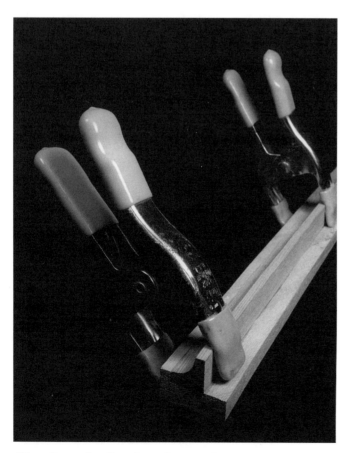

Glassless shadow-box frame, Step 3.

Glassless shadow-box frame, Step 5.

Finished glassless shadow-box frame proves ideal for this fish fossil.

sections, and cut them. Then assemble the frame with glue and corner clamps, and let stand until the glue sets.

Step 6. The frame should require little sanding. Use a pad sander on flat surfaces and an abrasive sponge on areas difficult to sand. Clean the frame, wipe it with a tack cloth, and it's ready for the finish of your choice.

Step 7. To duplicate the finish of the frame shown, brush on a coat of Fuller O'Brien Pen-Chrome #640-11 English Oak Stain, let it penetrate ten to fifteen minutes, wipe dry with paper towels, and let stand overnight. Then apply three coats of Deft Semi-Gloss Clear Wood Finish.

Step 8. Lay the frame facedown on a protected surface, and lay the mounted and matted piece on the frame. Secure it with brads or glazier's points.

Step 9. Install two small screw eyes on the inside surfaces of the left and right frame sections so the frame will hang flat against the wall, and attach picture-hanging wire. Then stick a 1/4-inch self-adhesive felt cushion just inside each rear corner of the frame.

MAKING SHADOW-BOX MOUNTS AND MATS

Many three-dimensional objects, including collectibles and carvings, are particularly suited to display inside shadow-box mounts and mats that are as easy to make as they are pleasing to view. In such displays, the mount boards are visible and serve as backgrounds in the finished products, so they're normally made of mat board, although you can certainly use other materials to suit your needs and tastes. For example, you might find some objects look best against a background of 1/4-inch hardwood plywood, nicely stained and varnished. Or you might try 1/4-inch tempered hardboard covered with an attractive fabric or other material. Use your imagination.

Shadow-box mount and mat, Step 3.

Shadow-box mount and mat, Step 4.

If you decide on mat board for both mount and mat, you can use contrasting colors or matching boards. You can pick white, black, or colored cores.

The mount and mat are attached with an intermediate spacer material, the thickness of which is determined by the depth of the object or items being framed. Any number of materials are suitable for such purposes, including strips of mat board, foamboard, and wood. If there's any chance that the spacer material might be visible from an angle, as is often the case with objects of considerable depth, paint the strips with flat-black spray enamel to make them effectively invisible.

Among the wood products useful for shadow-box mounts and mats are 1/2 x 3/4-inch parting bead, 3/4 x 3/4-inch stock, and 1 x 1-inch stock, all available in the molding section of lumberyards and home-improvement centers. Nominal 1 x 2

and larger strips and boards are also useful and can be ripped to any width you might need.

Use any suitable adhesive to glue up the shadow box. Dots of five-minute epoxy cement every few inches will work, as will dots of hot-melt glue, but with the latter you must work fast. You can also use wood glue or white glue, but you'll need to clamp the shadow box or lay something heavy on it until the glue dries. Double-sided tape and adhesive transfer tape also work well. If you need to paint spacer material, avoid getting paint on the surfaces where you'll apply adhesives.

For the decoy carving by artist Royal Cook in the accompanying photographs, I decided on a mount board and mat of matching blue mat board with a black core. The depth of the carving is 1 1/2 inches, so I used nominal 1 x 2, which is 1 1/2 inches wide, for spacer material. And I put everything together with my handy-dandy Scotch 752 ATG tape gun.

The carving is about 7$\frac{1}{2}$ inches long by 4$\frac{1}{4}$ inches high, so I decided on mount and mat boards of 11 x 14 inches. A mat border width of 2$\frac{1}{4}$ inches on all sides left a mat window of 6$\frac{1}{2}$ x 9$\frac{1}{2}$ inches. To make a similar shadow-box mount and mat, here's how it all goes together. Just alter dimensions to fit your needs.

Step 1. Cut a mount board and mat to identical dimensions. Then use a mat cutter and guide to cut a mat window to appropriate size.

Step 2. Use a miter box and backsaw to cut two strips of 1 x 2 or other stock the length of the mount and mat side edges. Cut two more pieces to fit flush along the top and bottom edges of the mount and mat boards, between the side pieces.

Step 3. Lightly sand the ends of the wood strips, wipe them free of dust, and wrap a strip of $\frac{1}{2}$-inch masking tape around the narrow edges of each. Spread newspapers on a work surface, and apply an even coat of flat-black spray enamel to one or both broad surfaces of each strip. (Both broad surfaces were painted for illustration purposes and later framing options.)

Step 4. Butt the ends of two long strips to the opposite inside surfaces of one short strip, and secure with two corner clamps. Then drive and

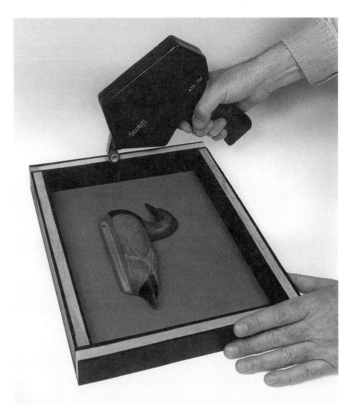

Shadow-box mount and mat, Step 7.

countersink two 1$\frac{1}{2}$-inch brads at each corner. Remove the clamps, and clamp the other short piece to the opposite ends of the long pieces the same way. Then attach with brads to complete the spacer frame.

Step 5. Lay the spacer frame on a work surface and position the backboard on it. Then use a staple gun to attach the backboard to the spacer frame with staples every few inches.

Step 6. Lay the assembly faceup, carefully position the object to be mounted, and mark the position with small pieces of wood. Put several dots of hot-melt glue on the backside of the object, and glue it in place.

Step 7. Lay down a continuous line of transfer adhesive (or apply any appropriate glue or cement) along the face of the spacer frame. Then position the mat atop the frame, and press it onto the adhesive. The shadow-box mount and mat are now ready for framing.

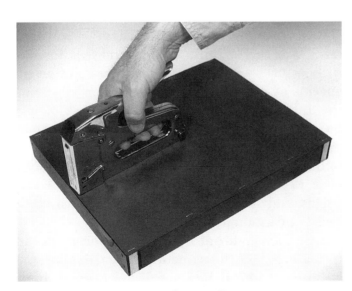

Shadow-box mount and mat, Step 5.

CHAPTER NINETEEN

Building Collector Frames

If you or someone in your household is a collector, you will probably want to build frames to house and display your collections. You can make such frames in a variety of sizes and designs to accommodate all sorts of collectible items: carvings, models, dolls, shells, bottles, china and glassware, ceramics, tools, and various antiques.

You needn't be an avid collector, however, to find uses for collector frames. In children's rooms such frames are useful for storing toys in an attractive way. A large frame will hold potted plants. Use one to display a chess set, or in a kitchen you can fill one with spice jars. Simple, unadorned collector frames are useful in workshops and hobby rooms for holding containers of hardware and small parts.

The two frames featured in this chapter can be put to use in a number of ways, and by building them you will learn the basics of collector-frame construction. But the most useful frames will be the ones you design yourself for specific uses and collections.

DESIGNING COLLECTOR FRAMES

The first step in designing any collector frame is to assemble all the items you plan to store in it. Lay them out on the floor and arrange them as you might in a collector frame to get an idea of how much wall space you will need. Once you have decided on rough dimensions, you might find it helpful to cut a scrap of cardboard, mat board, or foamboard to size, and lay that on the floor with your collection arranged on it.

When you have achieved a pleasing arrangement, sketch it roughly on a sheet of paper. Then rearrange the items to find other possibilities, and sketch them. Try horizontal and vertical displays. If your collection is large, you might want to house it in several frames.

The widest item in your collection will determine the width that all shelves must be. Objects of similar height can be put on a shelf together. Anything taller than the other items might look best in a compartment by itself. If you have two or three such items, make a single space for them, or design separate spaces. Try it both ways, and pick the design that looks best.

There are several materials you will find useful for shelves and partitions. In the smallest frames, you can use 1/4-inch-thick lattice. Micro Wood, which comes in 3 x 24-inch strips of 1/8-inch and 1/4-inch hardwood, can be ripped into shelves and partitions of various sizes. For larger units, you should look for 1/2-inch stock available in several different species at many lumber outlets. For example, the lumber company where I do most of my business stocks clear fir in 8-foot strips that measure 1/2 x 31/2 inches, which is what I used to build a large collector frame that covers just over 12 square feet of wall and holds all the spices and many other items that once cluttered our kitchen cabinets.

Another material I plan to use for a similar frame is oak of the same dimensions as the fir, but this material has one beveled edge. It is used for splashboard on oak counters and is ideal as shelving for large oak collector frames.

Plywood is the best and most useful material for back panels. You can also use plywood for the top, bottom, sides, shelves, and partitions if you take measures to conceal the laminations in the front edges of the material. If you will be painting the unit, you can use a putty knife to spread spackling paste on the plywood edges; then sand it smooth when it dries. With hardwood plywood, you can use edging tape or various moldings that fit.

Another useful material to keep in mind for collector frames of all sizes is 1/4-inch plate glass. This excellent shelving material slides into 1/4-inch dadoes and needs no gluing. Find a glass shop that reclaims plate glass from damaged store windows, as this salvaged glass is much cheaper than new glass. Once you've settled on a design for any frame, determine the number and dimensions of the glass shelves you will need, order them cut to those dimensions, and ask to have one long edge of each shelf seamed or beveled. This will take the sharp edges off. Use the seamed edges as the fronts of your shelves.

Once you have decided on the dimensions and chosen your materials, it's a good idea to make a scale drawing on graph paper. This will enable you to determine how much of each ma-terial you will need, and it will also be an aid in the shop when you're building your frame.

MINIATURE COLLECTOR FRAME

Here's a little frame that is easy to build and goes together quickly with a few inexpensive materials. It can hold a collection of small items. Several will hold a larger collection. Use it in a kid's room for Matchbox cars, or put one in the kitchen to hold spice containers, or make one to display chessmen.

Of course, you can alter dimensions to fit your needs. But to make the frame shown, you will need a 3-foot pine or fir 1 x 4, a 5-foot piece of 1/4 x 15/16-inch lattice, a scrap of 1/4-inch plywood at least 12 x 141/2 inches, glue, brads, and hanging hardware.

To make the frame a bit fancier, you can attach screen molding, corner molding, decorative molding, or frame molding to the front edges. If that's your preference, you'll need a 6-foot strip.

Here's how to put this one together.

Step 1. With a miter box and backsaw set at zero degrees, cut a piece of 1 x 4 to 15 inches.

Step 2. Set the table-saw blade for a 1/4-inch depth. Set the fence 31/4 inches from the *near* teeth of the blade. Lay the 1 x 4 broad side down

Miniature collector frame, Step 2.

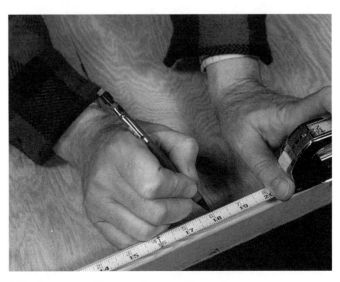

Miniature collector frame, Step 5.

Miniature collector frame, Step 6.

on the saw table, and cut a 1/4-inch-deep dado in it 3 1/4 inches from one end. Move the fence to 3 1/2 inches from the *far* teeth of the blade, and widen the dado to 1/4 inch.

Step 3. Set the fence 6 inches from the *near* teeth of the blade, and run the 1 x 4 over the blade again. Reset the fence at 6 1/4 inches from the *far* teeth of the blade, and run the piece through the saw again to create a second dado 2 1/2 inches from the first.

Step 4. Set the fence 8 3/4 inches from the *near* teeth of the blade, and start another dado. Reset the fence at 9 inches from the *far* teeth, and widen that dado to 1/4 inch.

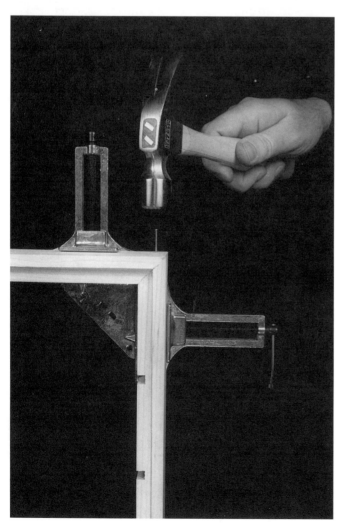

Miniature collector frame, Step 9.

Miniature collector frame, Step 10.

Step 5. To cut the last dado, set the fence 11½ inches from the *near* teeth for the first pass and 11¾ inches from the *far* teeth for the second pass.

Step 6. Set the blade for a ½-inch depth and the fence 3½ inches from the *far* teeth. Lay the 1 x 4 dadoed side down on the saw table with one narrow side against the fence, and run it over the blade to create a ⅛-inch-wide, ½-inch-deep rabbet. Rotate the piece, and cut a rabbet into the opposite edge. Do the same with a scrap of 1 x 4 that's at least 13 inches long. Reset the fence 3¼ inches from the *near* teeth, and widen the rabbets in each piece to ¼ inch.

Step 7. Install the blade guard on the saw. Set the fence 1⁹⁄₁₆ inches from the *near* teeth of the blade. Lay the dadoed 1 x 4 broad side down on the saw table with a narrow side against the fence, and rip a strip from the piece. Rotate the piece and rip another strip from the opposite edge. Then rip two strips from the other 1 x 4 the same way.

Step 8. With a miter box and backsaw set at 45 degrees, cut the ends off the dadoed pieces for an overall outside length of 15 inches. From the other strips, miter cut two 13-inch pieces.

Step 9. Use glue and corner clamps to assemble a 13 x 15-inch frame from these four sections. Drive two 1-inch brads at each corner, and countersink the brads. Let the frame stand with clamps in place until the glue sets.

Step 10. Measure the height and width inside the rabbets in the rear of the frame, and cut a piece of ¼-inch plywood slightly smaller to fit. Sand the face of the plywood with a pad sander and 120-grit and 220-grit sandpaper. Run a narrow bead of glue along the corner of the rabbet on all four sides of the frame. Lay the rear panel in place, secure it with toe-nailed ¾-inch brads, and countersink the brads.

Step 11. Carefully measure the distance between each pair of dadoes, and use a miter box

Miniature collector frame, Step 12.

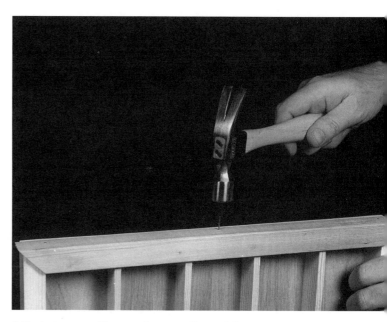

Miniature collector frame, Step 14.

Finished miniature collector frame.

side corner molding to fit the frame face. Then attach the molding with glue and 3/4-inch brads. If you're using decorative molding or an intricate frame molding, you might prefer attaching it with five-minute epoxy cement and clamps.

Step 15. Vacuum the frame to remove dust, and wipe all surfaces with a tack cloth. The frame is now ready for the finish of your choice. Although you should be able to brush on a stain without any trouble, make sure your final coat—lacquer, polyurethane, enamel—is an aerosol, which will enable you to coat all surfaces neatly.

Step 16. When the unit is finished, install two sawtooth hangers inside the top rear corners, or two decorative rings in the top of the frame, 2 inches from the corners and 1/2 inch from the rear edge. If you use sawtooth hangers, attach two 1/4-inch-thick foam weather-stripping pads inside the bottom rear corners. With decorative rings, use 1/4-inch-wide self-adhesive felt cushions inside all four rear corners.

OAK COLLECTOR FRAME

Here's a frame that can hold a variety of objects and will look good in any room. By building this one, you will also learn some techniques that will serve you well when you design your own collector frames.

You will need a 7-foot piece of oak 1 x 4, a 7-foot strip of oak screen molding, a 7-foot strip of oak panel molding, two 1/4 x 3 x 24-inch strips sof oak Micro Wood, a 15 x 19-inch piece of 1/4-inch oak plywood, glue, brads, and the usual hanging hardware.

To build this attractive frame, just follow these easy steps.

Step 1. Set the table saw or bandsaw fence 2 3/4 inches from the *near* teeth of the blade, and rip the oak 1 x 4 to that width. Reset the fence 2 1/2 inches from the *near* teeth, and rip the oak Micro Wood to that width.

Step 2. With a miter box and backsaw set at 45 degrees, cut two vertical frame sections from the

and backsaw set at zero degrees to cut four strips of lattice to fit. Cut these for a snug fit. If you own a belt-and-disc sander, cut the strips about 1/16 inch longer than you need, and gradually sand the ends until they fit perfectly.

Step 12. Mix a small amount of five-minute epoxy cement, and apply a tiny bit to the inside of each dado. Then slide lattice shelves into the dadoes, and let stand until the cement cures.

Step 13. Fill brad holes and any other holes or imperfections with wood filler (if unit will be finished naturally) or spackling paste (if unit will be painted), and let stand until filler sets. Then sand face and sides with a pad sander and 120-grit and 220-grit sandpaper. (If you plan to add molding to the face, you can skip the 220-grit sanding there.)

Step 14. Use a miter box and backsaw set at 45 degrees to cut four pieces of screen molding, decorative molding, frame molding, or 1-inch out-

ripped 1 x 4 to a length of 18 inches inside the miters (19½ inches overall) and two horizontal sections to 14 inches inside the miters (15½ inches overall).

Step 3. Remove the blade guard from the table saw. Set the fence 2¾ inches from the *far* teeth of the blade and the blade for a ½-inch depth. Lay one of the frame sections inside surface down on the saw table, with the face surface against the fence. Run the piece over the blade to cut a ⅛-inch-deep, ½-inch-wide rabbet in the rear edge. Do the same with the remaining three frame sections. Then reset the fence 2½ inches from the *near* teeth, and run each piece over the blade again to create a ¼-inch-deep, ½-inch-wide rabbet in each piece.

Step 4. Use a pencil to mark the four frame sections: *top, bottom, left,* and *right.* Lay the bottom section inside surface up. Measure from the left inside edge of the miter, and make marks at 4 and 4¼ inches. Then use a combination square to scribe parallel lines across the piece at those marks. Turn the piece so it stands on its rear edge, and scribe identical lines across the face surface.

Step 5. Lay the vertical side sections inside surface up. Measure down each from the inside edges of the top miters, and make marks at 5¼ and 5½ inches. On the right vertical only, make marks 6¼ and 6½ inches from the inside edge of the bottom miter. Then use a combination square to scribe parallel lines at these marks across the inside and face surfaces of the vertical sections.

Step 6. Set the table-saw blade for a ¼-inch depth. Lay the bottom frame section inside surface down on the saw table, and use the miter gauge to move it over the blade to remove the material between the parallel lines scribed in Step 4, creating a ¼-inch-wide, ¼-inch-deep dado in the piece. Do the same on the inside surfaces of the left and right vertical sections.

Step 7. Apply glue to the ends of the frame sections, and construct a 15½ x 19½-inch frame

Oak collector frame, Step 3.

Oak collector frame, Step 5.

Oak collector frame, Step 6.

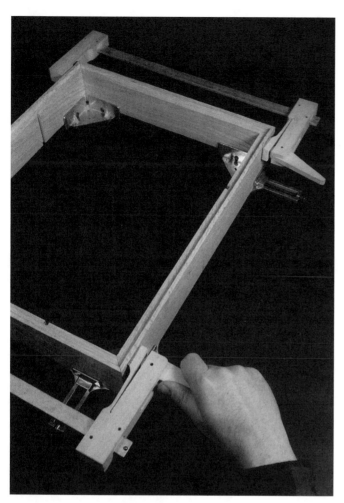

Oak collector frame, Step 7.

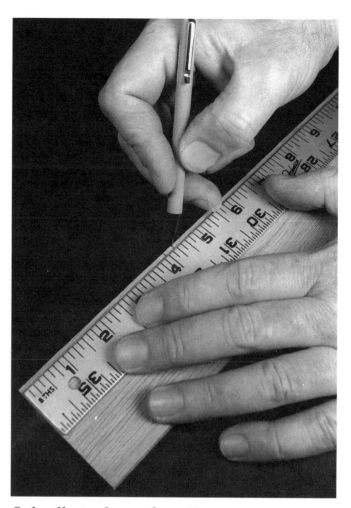

Oak collector frame, Step 11.

with four corner clamps. If necessary, draw the miter joints together at the rear edges of the frame with a pair of bar clamps. Then let the frame stand until the glue dries.

Step 8. Check the height and width of the rear of the frame, inside the rabbets. Then cut a piece of 1/4-inch oak plywood 1/16 inch smaller. Sand the face of the plywood back panel and the inside surfaces of the frame with a pad sander and 120-grit and 220-grit sandpaper.

Step 9. Mix a small amount of five-minute epoxy cement and apply it sparingly to the rear of the frame, being careful to avoid the inside edge of the frame. Lay the back panel in place in the rabbets, and clamp with four bar clamps, or place a heavy object on it until the cement cures.

Step 10. Measure the distance between the top dadoes in the frame side sections (should be about 14 1/2 inches). Use a miter box and backsaw set at zero degrees to cut the top shelf from a piece of 2 1/2-inch-wide oak Micro Wood to fit.

Step 11. Lay the shelf top side down, measure from the left, and make marks on the underside at 4 1/4 and 4 1/2 inches. Use the marks as guides to scribe two parallel lines with a combination square. Then mark the face surface of the shelf the same way.

Step 12. Set the table-saw blade for a 1/8-inch depth. Lay the self faceup on the saw table, and use the miter gauge to move it over the blade, as in previous steps, to cut a 1/4-inch-wide, 1/8-inch-deep dado.

Step 13. Measure the distance between the dado in the shelf underside and the dado in the frame bottom section. Then cut a Micro Wood partition to fit.

Step 14. Measure from the bottom of the Micro Wood partition and make marks on the right broad surface at 6½ and 6¾ inches. Using the marks as guides, scribe parallel lines across the right and face surfaces with a combination square. Then cut a ¼-inch-wide, ⅛-inch-deep dado between the lines.

Step 15. Slide the Micro Wood partition into the appropriate dadoes, and measure the distance between the dado in the Micro Wood and the one in the right frame section. Then cut a piece of Micro Wood to fit.

Step 16. After checking for fit, remove all the Micro Wood pieces from the frame, and sand them with a pad sander and 120-grit and 220-grit sandpaper. Mix a small amount of five-minute epoxy cement, and apply a tiny amount to the inside of each dado with the tip of a tooth-pick. Then put small tacking spots of cement along the back edge of each piece, and slide them into place, starting with the top shelf.

Step 17. Sand the face of the frame with a pad sander and 120-grit sandpaper. Then vacuum the frame to remove dust.

Step 18. With a miter box and backsaw, cut one end off of a strip of screen molding at a 45-degree angle. Lay the strip along one face edge of the frame, and use the frame as a guide to mark the strip for the second cut. Cut the piece to fit, and dry clamp it to the frame with two bar clamps. Cut the pieces to fit the other three edges, and dry clamp them to check for fit. Mark the pieces *left, right, top,* and *bottom.*

Step 19. Mix a small amount of five-minute epoxy cement, and apply a thin coat to the right face surface of the frame, near the outside edge. (Keep cement about ¼ inch away from the in-

Oak collector frame, Step 16.

Oak collector frame, Step 18.

Oak collector frame, Step 19.

Finished oak collector frame.

side edge so it won't seep there. Seepage along the outside edge won't matter.) Clamp the right strip of screen molding to the glued right face with two bar clamps or edge clamps. Attach the left piece the same way. Then apply cement to the top and bottom face edges, and press the remaining strips of screen molding in place. Let the frame stand until the cement cures.

Step 20. When the cement dries, remove clamps and use a sharp knife to trim away the cement that seeped from the screen molding. Then sand left, right, top, and bottom surfaces of the frame with a pad sander and 120-grit and 220-grit sandpaper.

Step 21. Use the miter box and backsaw to cut four pieces of panel molding to fit the four sides of the frame. Mix a small amount of five-minute epoxy cement, and attach the molding, one strip at a time, with cement and two spring clamps per piece. (When applying the cement, avoid the front edge to prevent seepage onto the frame face.) Let the frame stand with clamps in place until the cement sets.

Step 22. Do any necessary sanding with 120-grit and 220-grit sandpaper. Vacuum the frame, and

wipe all surfaces with a tack cloth, and the frame is ready for the finish of your choice.

Step 23. To duplicate the finish of the frame shown, brush on a coat of Fuller O'Brien Pen-Chrome #640-11 English Oak Stain, let penetrate for ten to fifteen minutes, and wipe dry with paper towels. Let the frame stand overnight, and apply three coats of Deft Semi-Gloss Clear Wood Finish.

Step 24. Lay the frame facedown on a protected surface, and attach a sawtooth hanger inside each top rear corner. Then attach a 1-inch piece of 1/4-inch-thick foam weather-stripping tape inside each bottom rear corner. Use two wire nails to hang the unit.

CHAPTER TWENTY

Framing as a Business

By now, you certainly must realize that doing your own mounting, matting, and framing can save you a tremendous amount of money and will keep saving you money in the years to come. If you have entertained the notion of getting into framing as a business, perhaps you should think more seriously about it and start making plans and moving in that direction. Framing is a relatively easy business to get into and one that requires little in the way of overhead.

What's more, framing is a business you can approach gradually and on one or more of several levels. You can keep it a hobby. You can turn enough of a profit on your hobby to pay for your materials and tools. You can work at framing as a part-time job, or you can make it a full-time business. You can specialize or generalize. You can work in a garage or basement workshop, or set up business in a commercial building. The choices are yours.

It's probably best to start out slowly. After all, you might find a particular niche you don't want to go beyond. By moving toward your goals gradually, you should be able to avoid the pitfalls and risks that often cause small-business failure.

In the beginning, you might want only to do framing jobs for friends and others on a limited part-time basis. Then, as you gain confidence in your skills and realize that you can, indeed, make substantial profits, you can seek more business.

THINK DEDUCTIBLE
Taxes are necessary nuisances in every business. You will probably have to register your business with some state or local bureaucracy to get a license to work, which usually means a license for the bureaucracy to take a portion of your earnings. And, of course, the feds will want their cut. There's no getting around it, but by being aware of what you will face you can take advantage of all the deductions that are rightfully due you.

Think deductible. From the very beginning, think deductible. In every aspect of your business, think deductible. When you go shopping, think deductible. When you travel on business, think deductible. When you buy a tool for mounting, matting, or framing, and when you buy framing materials, think deductible. When you have letterhead stationery and business cards printed, think deductible. When you buy $1,000 worth of oak that you will turn into molding for resale, and when you pay 49 cents for a container of brads you will use making frames for customers, think deductible.

Practically everything you buy and every service you pay for that is related to your framing business is deductible in some way. But you must be able to prove that you did indeed pay for an item or service before you can take the deduction. So, from the start, keep receipts on everything.

You will undoubtedly use a vehicle in your business. You will haul wood from lumberyards, and you will transport glass, mat boards, and other materials. You might deliver mats and moldings to various customers. You will drive to the office-supply store, the print shop, and the post office in connection with your business. And you will no doubt use your vehicle in a number of other business-related ways.

The IRS allows deductions for such uses of a vehicle, but you must be able to prove how much you used the family flivver in your business. So put a notebook in your car, and call it your *Business Mileage Log*. The first time you use the vehicle for business purposes, record the date and the odometer reading. Then, for every business trip you take—whether it's to a frame shop two blocks away or a lumber mill two states away—list the date, destination, starting odometer reading, ending odometer reading, and total miles. It's then an easy matter at the end of the year to determine the total miles driven and the portion of the total that was for business.

Support Your Local Artists

I'm a great fan of art of all kinds and the talented folks who create it. Most artists I've met are intelligent, witty, thinking, multidimensional individuals I've enjoyed knowing, but that's not why I'm suggesting that you get to know the artists in your vicinity. The reason is much shallower and crassly commercial, but mutually beneficial: the relationship could pocket you some bucks.

Matting and framing works for local artists isn't the only way to make money by acquainting yourself with the local art community. These days many artists are engaged in turning out work on a volume basis for the vast majority of interested and potential buyers who might not be able to afford high-priced original works. They're producing a broad assortment of lower-priced works, ranging from inexpensive miniatures, posters, cartoons, and unlimited prints to moderately priced, signed, and numbered limited-edition prints, many of which increase in value with time.

These are products you can buy at good prices, then mount, mat, and frame, and sell at a tidy profit. If you're planning to open a frame shop, you can decorate it with the works of local artists that you also offer for sale. If yours is a home-based business, you can still take advantage of such opportunities by including the framed works of local artists at the arts-and-crafts fairs where you rent booth space to sell your framing products and services.

Attending art exhibits is an excellent way to meet artists and learn about the works they have for sale. And you needn't restrict your interest to local artists, because others elsewhere may well have reasonably priced works available that you can turn a profit on. Meanwhile, I'm going to introduce you to four of my local artists and recommend that you contact them for their lists of available works.

I've known Jim Snook for more than twenty years. He's a former high-school art teacher who has been earning his living as a full-time artist for almost as long as I've known him. Although he's a highly talented western and wildlife artist, he's a very funny guy who turns out hilarious cartoons and posters suitable for framing.

I met Don McMichael shortly after he retired from the Coast Guard and moved to the town where I live. I'm a longtime fan of scrimshaw and was delighted to find Don's work showing up at local shops and galleries. Then he began painting whales and within a few years he was known internationally for his whale art. His great whale posters and limited-edition prints are available by mail.

The next local artist I got to know is a terrifically talented wood carver by the name of Royal Cook. I couldn't help meeting him, seeing as my wife and I built a house next

Whether you prepare your own tax return or have a professional prepare it for you, good records are essential. So you must keep track of every financial transaction. In addition to the receipts you must keep as a record of how much you have spent on your business, you must also keep accurate records of your income. One of the best ways is with a simple invoice system. You will find two-part invoice forms at any local office-supply outlet, or you can order them from Quill Corporation (see Source Directory). Whenever you sell anything to anyone, make out an invoice. If you sell two dozen mats to the One Stop Photo Shop, make out an invoice. If you sell 120 feet of molding to the Fancy Frame Shop, make out an invoice. When your neighbor hands

Framable cartoon by Jim Snook.

door to his. Royal turns out a great variety of wildlife, western, American Indian, and other carvings, many of which are suitable for framing and resale.

I met Dutch Mostert several years ago at a local art exhibit when my wife grabbed me by the arm, pointed to one of Dutch's exquisite waterfront scenes, and said, "I want that." We bought that one and another for our house and several more since. He paints highly detailed waterfront scenes like none other I've ever seen, and he sells limited-edition lithographs of them.

You'll find addresses and numbers for these four fine artists in the Source Directory. I think you'll find supporting my local artists as interesting and profitable as supporting your own.

you a $5 check for a framing job you did, make out an invoice. Give your customer the original invoice, and keep the copy for your records.

It's also a good idea to become familiar with the way small businesses are taxed. There are tax guides available at any bookstore, and you would do well to buy and read one. Also, the Internal Revenue Service will send you, on request, a copy of Publication 334, *Tax Guide for Small Business.*

GETTING YOUR NAME KNOWN

Well before you're ready to open your own framing shop you will need to consider advertising and allied activities as a way of getting your name established. The first step in that direction is to think up a name for your service or company and get letterhead stationery and business cards made. You might want to design some sort of logo, in which case a competent printer or graphic artist can be of tremendous help.

Next, contact your local phone company and get the name and number of the person you should talk to about a listing in the Yellow Pages. This is an inexpensive bit of advertising that will last a year and could shove a lot of business your way.

Go to every local art exhibit and craft show, and pass out business cards to all who will take them. You might even want to rent booth space for a display of your mats, moldings, and frames, as well as prints, posters, photographs, and other works you've framed for resale.

Get in touch with the local chapters of major fund-raising organizations, such as Ducks Unlimited, that stage annual banquets and auctions. Artworks of all sorts are popular at such events, and often these organizations have difficulty getting donated works matted, mounted, and framed in time for their festivities. Talk to the chapter chairman about doing some framing for them. You can offer your work at reduced prices, or you might even consider framing several items for the cost of the materials and donating your labor in exchange for the publicity you can gain.

Make no mistake: people are going to see your work. But you must make sure that as often as possible when they see your work they will also see your name, address, and phone number.

SUPPLIER ACCOUNTS

As soon as the ink dries on your business card, visit local businesses that might supply you with the various materials you need to run your business. Use the Yellow Pages to help you make a list of office-supply outlets, frame shops, lumber companies, glass shops, and any other suppliers you might buy from.

Talk to the sales managers or owners of these companies, and ask to set up accounts with them. Also inquire about professional discounts of 10 to 30 percent or more, which can go a long way toward keeping your costs down.

Once you are established with these various suppliers and they get to know you and your work, they will often refer potential customers to you.

MARKETING YOUR PRODUCTS AND SERVICES

You can build your business without risking capital, taking out a second mortgage, or hocking your watch. You can make mats, mount photographs, sell frames, manufacture moldings, do custom framing, or all of the above and then some.

You can let leftovers from various mounting and matting jobs accumulate in oddball sizes of mat board, or you can do as I do now and turn most of these scraps into standard-sized mats and mount boards. These standard-sized boards are much easier to store and to sell. When you have built up your stock of them, start looking for customers.

You can try the frame shops, but chances are, the folks there are already turning their scraps into standard mats and selling them. However, if your prices are low enough, you might make sales there.

You're better off to try the local photo shops. If they sell mats, they're probably buying them from commercial sources whose prices you might be able to beat. If they aren't selling mats, tell them why they should be. Likewise with local artist-supply shops and department stores. You might even try home-improvement centers, gift shops, and galleries.

Once you have lined up your customers, you can start turning out mats on a production basis. A single 32 x 40-inch sheet of mat board will yield eight 8 x 10-inch mats, and you can use much cheaper material (chipboard or card stock) for mounting boards. Of course, you will need to make larger and smaller mats, but remember that you can use leftovers from large mats to make smaller mats. Just determine how many mats you can turn out in an hour and how much you must make as an hourly rate. If the figures are compatible, you're in business.

You can make moldings and sell them through various outlets. Pick several attractive moldings that you can make at a good pace and low cost with readily available materials, and frame several small items you can carry with you as samples. Then visit local lumberyards, home-improvement centers, department stores, artist-supply stores, and frame shops with your samples and an order book.

If you can work in your garage or basement turning out molding at a rate of 100 feet an hour, at a cost of 25 cents a foot, then sell it for 50 cents a foot, your gross income will be $25 an hour. Of course, you must spend time selling and seeing to other related chores, but you will still end up with a tidy profit.

Ah, but you have to persuade others to buy your product, right? Show your potential customers an attractive molding they can buy for 50 cents a foot and resell for $1 a foot, and they won't be potential much longer. That's a 100 percent markup for the retailer.

Still skeptical? Well, when was the last time you saw top-quality frame molding at a local outlet for a buck a foot? But you're probably wondering if you can, in fact, produce frame molding at a rate of 100 feet an hour and at a cost of only 25 cents a foot. Let me remind you that I buy pine 1 x 4 at 25 cents a foot that I rip into 1 x 2, which I then turn into a basic, rustic box molding at a cost of 12.5 cents a foot. And I am able to turn this molding out at a rate of 200 feet an hour. So 100 feet an hour at a cost of 25 cents a foot was a deliberately conservative example.

Visit art galleries and get the names of local artists. Then show the artists how they can save money buying mats and moldings from you. Chances are, you will find some artists who consider matting and framing a nuisance and an intrusion on their creativity. They might gladly turn over all such work to you.

When you have saturated all the local markets, take your show on the road. Combine business with pleasure by taking a few days to see sights and visit potential customers outside your immediate vicinity.

When your framing income matches or exceeds the income from your full-time job, that might be the time to take the plunge and make framing your profession. If you begin cautiously and proceed gradually, you should be able to avoid the hazards associated with operating a small business. With some planning, effort, and a little luck, you should be able to turn this interesting hobby into an enjoyable career.

SOURCE DIRECTORY

Following is a list of companies whose products are mentioned in this book, as well as mail-order sources of picture frames, frame moldings, mounting and matting materials and tools, framing tools, hardware, hand tools, and power tools. Be sure to write or phone the mail-order companies for copies of their catalogs. And, by all means, visit the World Wide Web sites listed for more information, product news, and ideas.

Adjustable Clamp Company
417 North Ashland Avenue
Chicago, IL 60622-6397
TEL: (312) 666-0640
FAX: (312) 666-2723
Manufactures America's largest selection of clamps, clamp fixtures, and accessories, as well as vises, miter boxes, and miter saws.

Adorama
42 West 18th Street
New York, NY 10011
TEL: (212) 741-0052   orders and information
(212) 741-0466   customer relations
(800) 223-2500   orders
FAX: (212) 463-7223
E-mail: goadorama@aol.com
A major mail-order supplier of photographic equipment and materials, including mounting and matting products.

AFE Picture Frame Company
18 Commerce Road, Unit N
Fairfield, NJ 07004
TEL: (800) 878-4814
FAX: (201) 575-1559
Offers custom hand-cut, beveled, single or double mats, up to 40 x 60 inches, available in any Crescent mat color or material.

Alto's EZ Mat
607 West 3rd Avenue
Ellensburg, WA 98926
TEL: (509) 962-9212
(800) 225-2497
FAX: (509) 962-3127
E-mail: altosmat@eburg.com
Web site: http://www.altosezmat.com
Makes top-quality mat cutters, mat-cutting guides, circle cutters, and oval templates. Also publishes Cut-by-Cut, a bimonthly newsletter, chock-full of advanced mat-cutting designs and mat-cutting tips.

American Frame Corporation
Arrowhead Park
400 Tomahawk Drive
Maumee, OH 43537-1695
TEL: (419) 893-5595
(800) 537-0944
FAX: (800) 893-3898
A mail-order supplier of metal-section and wood-section frame kits, frame hardware, foam backing board, mat board, and Plexiglas.

American Mat & Frame Company, Inc.
195-E San Pedro Avenue
Morgan Hill, CA 95037
TEL: (408) 778-1150
(800) 537-0984
FAX: (408) 779-6026
A wholesale source of hand-cut, beveled, rectangular, and oval photo mats; picture frames; and easel backs.

Black & Decker U.S., Inc.
701 East Joppa Road
Towson, MD 21286-5559
TEL: (410) 583-3900
Manufactures the WORKMATE Work Center and Vise, cordless and electric power tools, bench tools, and accessories.

Coda, Inc.
30 Industrial Avenue
Mahwah, NJ 07430-2207
TEL: (201) 825-7400
FAX: (201) 825-8133
Manufactures table-top mounting and laminating equipment designed for use with pressure-sensitive adhesives, overlaminates, and adhesive-coated mount boards. Also makes a wide range of precut and precoated mount boards made of various materials and available in standard and custom sizes up to 48 x 96 inches.

Contemporary Photo Graphics
510C Sagamore Parkway
West Lafayette, IN 47906
TEL: (800) 728-3222
FAX: (317) 463-4443
Provides oval and rectangular mats made of Crescent standard or rag board. Grooved, inlaid, and other specialty mats available.

Royal Cook, Artist
Reflections in Wood
1999 Ash Court
North Bend, OR 97459
TEL: (541) 756-9733
(888) 805-8685
Produces hand-carved, finely detailed nature, wildlife, animal, bird, western, and American Indian works suitable for shadow-box and deep-relief framing. Price list available.

Crescent Cardboard Company
100 West Willow Road
Wheeling, IL 60090
TEL: (847) 537-3400
(800) 323-1055
FAX: (847) 537-7153
Web site: http://www.crescent=cardboard.com
Manufactures an extensive line of mat boards, poster boards, mounting and backing boards, self-adhesive mounting boards, and precut mats, including standard and acid-free products.

Custom Matte Corporation
1975 Waldorf, Northwest
Grand Rapids, MI 49504
TEL: (616) 791-0011
(800) 777-2841
FAX: (616) 791-0522
Provides precut Crescent mats in standard and custom sizes.

Delta International Machinery Corporation
246 Alpha Drive
Pittsburgh, PA 15238
TEL: (412) 963-2400
FAX: (412) 963-2489
Manufactures a complete line of stationary and job-site power tools and accessories for the do-it-yourselfer and professional, including table saws, radial-arm saws, miter saws, planers, grinders, and belt-and-disc sanders.

Diamond Machining Technology, Inc.
85 Hayes Memorial Drive
Marlborough, MA 01752-1892
TEL: (508) 481-5944
FAX: (508) 485-3924
Web site: http://www.dmtsharp.com/~dmtsharp
Makes a complete line of diamond hones, sharpeners, and sharpening accessories, as well as tools for easing the sharp edges of glass.

Dixie Matting & Graphics
915 County Road 55
Clanton, AL 35045
TEL: (205) 755-7558
(800) 245-8064
FAX: (205) 755-9905
Offers custom, hand-cut Crescent mats with oval or rectangular openings.

Doran Enterprises, Inc.
2779 South 34th Street
Milwaukee, WI 53215
TEL: (414) 645-0109
FAX: (414) 645-1744
Supplies Premier brand mounting adhesives, rollers, and cutters.

Dremel
4915 21st Street
Racine, WI 53406-9989
TEL: (414) 554-1390
      (800) 437-3635
FAX: (414) 554-7654
Web site: http://www.dremel.com
Manufactures the popular Dremel line of precision power tools, some of interest to framers, such as the Contour Sander Kit, disc/belt sander, and Versatip Multipurpose tool for woodburning, cutting and fusing rope, and hot-cutting plastics and polystyrene.

The Easier the Better International
2215-R Market Street, Suite 158
San Francisco, CA 94114
TEL: (415) 474-0132
FAX: (415) 661-3081
Manufactures the unique, patented Photo-in-a-Well—a precut, self-aligning, double mat that allows photographs to be snapped in place without adhesives or tapes.

Elite Picture Frames
9775 Marconi Drive, Suite D
Otay Mesa, CA 92173
TEL: (800) 854-6606
A mail-order supplier of traditional and unusual rectangular and oval ready-made frames, as well as metal and wood sectionals. Also offers stretched canvas and canvas clips.

Elkat, Inc.
P.O. Box 32
Posen, IL 60469
TEL: (800) 677-3808
Makes custom mats to customers' specifications with rectangular, square, oval, or multiple openings. All types and colors of Crescent board available.

Eubank Frame, Inc.
2330 Scenic Drive
P.O. Box 425
Salisbury, MD 21801-9579
TEL: (410) 546-3331
Manufactures the Uni-Frame for inexpensively displaying posters and artwork without traditional frames.

Exposures
1 Memory Lane
P.O. Box 3615
Oshkosh, WI 54903-3615
TEL: (800) 222-4947   orders
      (800) 572-5750   customer service
FAX: (414) 231-6942
A mail-order source of frames for pictures and collectibles, archival materials, and storage and display products.

Frame Fit Company
7353 Milnor Street
P.O. Box 8926
Philadelphia, PA 19135
TEL: (215) 332-0683
      (800) 523-3693
FAX: (800) 344-7010
A mail-order supplier with a good assortment of custom-made wood and metal frames and moldings.

Frame Wealth, Inc.
RD #2, Box 261-7
Otego, NY 13825
TEL: (800) 524-8582
FAX: (607) 432-8830
A mail-order source of frames, frame moldings, liners, display hardware, and some framing supplies and tools.

Gemini Moulding, Inc.
524 South Hicks Road
Palatine, IL 60067
TEL: (708) 359-2005
　　　(800) 323-3575
FAX: (800) 238-3575
Offers custom-cut Crescent single, double, and triple mats with single or multiple openings. Oval, circular, cathedral, and other specialty mats available. Also stocks Crescent Composite mats.

Graphik Dimensions, Ltd.
2103 Brentwood Street
P.O. Box 10002
High Point, NC 27261-3002
TEL: (800) 221-0262　orders
　　　(800) 332-8884　customer service
FAX: (910) 887-3773
A mail-order source of a large selection of standard-size and custom-cut metal and wood frames and kits, including frames for canvas, all at good prices. Also offers matting and glazing tools, mounting boards, and precut mats.

Harbor Freight Tools
3491 Mission Oaks Boulevard
P.O. Box 6010
Camarillo, CA 93011-6010
TEL: (805) 388-2000
　　　(800) 423-2567　orders
　　　(800) 444-3353　customer service
FAX: (800) 905-5220
A mail-order source of a large line of hand tools, power tools, accessories, supplies, and hardware at good prices.

Hartville Tool
13163 Market Avenue North
Hartville, OH 44632
TEL: (800) 345-2396　orders
　　　(800) 345-2396　customer service
A mail-order supplier of hand tools, power tools, bits, blades, clamps, vises, benches, and accessories.

Herrschners, Inc.
2800 Hoover Road
Stevens Point, WI 54492-0001
TEL: (800) 441-0838
A mail-order source of cross-stitch kits, yarns, threads, and other needlework tools, supplies, and accessories, as well as mat boards, sectional frame kits, mat cutters, and picture-framing kits.

Image Maker
9420 Eton Avenue
Chatsworth, CA 91311
TEL: (800) 832-2342
FAX: (800) 248-4368
Makes hand-cut Crescent mats with single or double openings in standard sizes or to customers' specifications.

Island Art
P.O. Box 22063
Brentwood Bay, BC V8M 1R5
Canada
TEL: (604) 652-5181
　　　(800) 663-7501
FAX: (604) 652-2711
Offers precut Crescent mats in standard and custom sizes.

Jerry's Artarama
P.O. Box 58638
Raleigh, NC 27658-8638
TEL: (919) 878-6782
　　　(800) 827-8478
E-mail: U ARTIST@aol.com
Web site: http://www.jerryscatalog.com
A mail-order source of a large line of artists' and framers' supplies, including moldings, frames, precut mats, mat board, foamboard, and mat-cutting systems.

Jesada Tools
310 Mears Boulevard
Oldsmar, FL 34677
TEL: (813) 891-6160
　　　(800) 531-5559
FAX: (813) 891-6259
E-mail: jesada@packet.net
Web site: http://www.jesada.com/catalog/
Manufactures a large line of top-quality router bits, bit sets, circular-saw blades, dado heads, and saw-blade stabilizers. Also offers jigs and fixtures, abrasives, and other products of interest to woodworkers and picture framers.

Kaibab Artistic
106 East 13200 South
Draper, UT 84020
TEL: (800) 972-8913
　　　(801) 553-0231
Specializes in Crescent mats, intricately and decoratively computer enhanced, with a variety of opening configurations.

Klingspor Corporation
P.O. Box 3737
Hickory, NC 28603-3737
TEL: (704) 326-9663
　　　(800) 228-0000
FAX: (800) 872-2005
A mail-order supplier of power tools, router bits, circular-saw blades, plate (biscuit) joiner blades, and dado heads, as well as a complete line of sanding supplies, tools, and accessories.

Lee Valley Tools, Ltd.
12 East River Street
Ogdensburg, NY 13669
TEL: (800) 871-8158　orders
　　　(800) 267-8735　customer service
FAX: (800) 513-7885
A mail-order source of woodworking and picture-framing tools, including clamps, vises, brushes, and contour-sanding grips.

Lee Valley Tools, Ltd. (Canada)
1080 Morrison Drive
Ottawa, Ontario K2H 8K7
Canada
See Lee Valley Tools, Ltd., (above) for phone and fax numbers, as well as products offered.

Leichtung Workshops
4944 Commerce Parkway
Cleveland, OH 44128
TEL: (216) 831-2555
　　　(800) 321-6840
A mail-order supplier of miter boxes, mat cutters, and other tools and materials for picture framing and woodworking.

Light Impressions
439 Monroe
P.O. Box 940
Rochester, NY 14603-0940
TEL: (716) 442-7318　international
　　　(716) 271-8960　technical assistance
　　　(800) 828-6216　U.S. and Canada
FAX: (800) 828-5539
A major mail-order supplier of mounting, matting, and framing materials and tools, as well as a large line of archival storage and display products.

Logan Graphic Products
1100 Brown Street
Wauconda, IL 60084
TEL: (847) 526-5515
　　　(800) 331-6232
FAX: (847) 526-5155
Offers mat-cutting equipment and a large selection of precut Crescent mats with rectangular, oval, domed, and other opening configurations.

Mat Source
516 Commercial Street
Glendale, CA 91203
TEL: (818) 956-6117
FAX: (818) 956-0837
Specializes in hand-cut mats, made of Crescent mat board to customers' specifications.

Don McMichael, Artist
McMichael Studios
703 Mallard Lane
North Bend, OR 97459
TEL: (541) 756-2927
FAX: (541) 756-7933
E-mail: beluga@mail.coos.or.us
Produces exquisite signed and numbered limited-edition prints, miniatures, and posters of whales—some of the finest whale art sold in the international marketplace. All lithographs produced from original oil paintings and printed on pH-neutral, museum-quality papers. Send for current list.

Meisel Hardware Specialists
P.O. Box 70
Mound, MN 55364-0070
TEL: (800) 441-9870   orders
(612) 471-8550   customer service
(612) 479-2138   technical assistance
FAX: (612) 471-8579
A mail-order source of hardware, fasteners, hardwoods, adhesives, and sanding and finishing products.

Meisel Visual Imaging
9645 Webb Chapel Road
Dallas, TX 75220
TEL: (214) 358-8230
(800) 527-5186
FAX: (214) 358-8211
A mail-order source of complete photo-lab services, including retouching, mounting, laminating, and UV protection.

Mid America Frame, Inc.
900 North Country Road Y
Plattsburg, MO 64477
TEL: (800) 634-1911
(816) 539-3706
Offers double and single Crescent mats with rectangular, oval, and multiple openings, as well as four styles of easel backs.

Midwest Products Company, Inc.
400 South Indiana Street
P.O. Box 564
Hobart, IN 46342
TEL: (219) 942-1134
(800) 348-3497
FAX: (219) 947-2347
Manufactures Micro-Cut strips and sheets of walnut, mahogany, and cherry, ideal for inlaid and laminated frame moldings, available by the bundle.

MLCS, Ltd.
P.O. Box 4053
Rydal, PA 19046
TEL: (800) 533-9298
FAX: (215) 938-5070
E-mail: MLCSltd@aol.com
Manufactures the heavy-duty Can-Do Clamp and the Merle Adjustable Corner Clamp.

Christian "Dutch" Mostert, Artist
663 Mallard Lane
North Bend, OR 97459
TEL: (541) 756-3765
Produces superb signed and numbered limited-edition prints, mostly of maritime-related subjects, East Coast, West Coast, and tropical scenes. Many include vintage marine and automotive details. All lithographs produced from finely detailed watercolors and printed on pH-neutral, museum-quality stock. Write for current list.

Nielsen & Bainbridge
Head Offices
40 Eisenhower Drive
Paramus, NJ 07653
TEL: (201) 845-6100
   (201) 368-9191   for nearest dealer
   (800) 927-8227   product information
   (800) 537-9311   C&H technical service
FAX: (201) 342-6084
E-mail: nielsen_bainbridge@esselte.com
Manufactures Nielsen aluminum moldings, Nurre Caxton wood moldings, Bainbridge mat boards, and Artcare Archival System precut mats and frames, as well as C&H PRO Series and Art-Mate mat cutters and squares, board and glass cutter, Oval-Master oval and circle cutter, Thumbnail frame-joining system, accessories, and supplies.

Onyx Mat Board, Inc.
32-45 Hunters Point Avenue
Long Island City, NY 11101
TEL: (718) 392-8888
   (800) 777-6287
FAX: (718) 729-0025
Offers precut Gallery Mats in standard sizes cut from regular, black-core, and marble-finish boards; Spectrum Mats in a variety of face papers with red, blue, and gray cores; and the silk-faced Elan Series with gold filet. Standard precut sizes from 5 x 7 to 16 x 20 inches and custom sizes available.

The Pierce Company of Minneapolis
9801 Nicollet Avenue
Minneapolis, MN 55420
TEL: (612) 884-1991
   (800) 338-9801
FAX: (612) 884-2015
Offers photographic, art, and framing accessories and supplies, as well as the full line of Crescent mat boards and precut mats in photographic sizes.

Preston's
Main Street Wharf
Greensport, NY 11944-0798
TEL: (800) 836-1165
A mail-order source of prints, posters, and three-dimensional works with a nautical theme.

Prime Arts Ltd., Inc.
8911 Rossah Road
Cincinnati, OH 45236
TEL: (513) 793-0313
   (800) 543-4251
FAX: (513) 793-2318
Provides hand-cut and die-cut mats in a large line of collage, embossed, French-style, and other specialty patterns.

Product Market International, Inc.
P.O. Box 297
Ellicott City, MD 21041-0297
TEL: (410) 750-3299
FAX: (410) 750-3272
Markets Avery Myers precision cutters.

Quill Corporation
100 Schelter Road
Lincolnshire, IL 60069-3621
TEL: (800) 789-1331   orders
   (800) 789-8965   customer service
   (800) 789-6640   CD-ROM catalog
FAX: (800) 789-8955
Web site: http://www.quillcorp.com
A major mail-order supplier of office furnishings and supplies, drafting supplies, paper cutters, scissors, adhesive tapes, certificate frames, and kraft paper.

Redi-Cut Mat Company, Inc.
122 Hamilton Drive
Novato, CA 94949
TEL: (415) 883-2511
FAX: (415) 883-9047
Specializes in bevel and die-cut mats for photographs in all standard sizes.

Ryobi America Corporation
5201 Pearman Dairy Road
P.O. Box 1207
Anderson, SC 29622-1207
TEL: (800) 525-2579
Manufactures a large selection of top-quality cordless and portable electric power tools and accessories, including drills, sanders, biscuit joiners, and routers.

Ryobi Canada, Inc.
P.O. Box 910
Cambridge, ON N1R 6K2
Canada
TEL: (800) 265-6778
See Ryobi America Corporation (above) for products offered.

Sears Power & Hand Tools
2740 West 79th Street
Chicago, IL 60652
TEL: (800) 377-7414 orders/customer service
  (800) 473-7247 repair service
  (800) 366-7278 replacement parts
  (800) 827-6655 maintenance agreements
Offers a large selection of portable and stationary power tools, hand tools, miter boxes, clamps, accessories, fixtures, attachments, blades, and bits at good prices.

Jim Snook, Cartoonist
Snook's Nook in Rocky Point
27226 Rocky Point Road
Klamath Falls, OR 97601-8534
TEL: (541) 356-2353
  (800) 232-0210
Produces humorous calendars, posters, and framable cartoons for anglers, hunters, campers, car enthusiasts, cat lovers, dog lovers, horse lovers, rodeo fans, RV travelers, and others.

Stanley Tools
Division of the Stanley Works
600 Myrtle Street
New Britain, CT 06050
TEL: (203) 225-5111
Web site: http://www.stanleyworks.com
Manufactures top-quality hand tools for woodworkers, including hammers, punches, nail sets, saws, utility knives, hobby knives, pliers, screwdrivers, levels, squares, and steel tape rules.

Sunshine
P.O. Box 8318
Northridge, CA 91327
TEL: (818) 343-5855
Features precut and custom-cut Crescent single and double mats with rectangular, circular, and oval openings. Also offers offset corners, 3-D reverse bevels, and scalloped ovals and circles.

Taylor-Made Mats
1342 Clough Pike
Batavia, OH 45103
TEL: (513) 427-0042
Offers a full line of Crescent standard and specialty mats, as well as a large assortment of specialty and decorative mats, including stenciled designs, name blocks, and wallpaper overlays, using customers' wallpaper.

Tiki Enterprises
587 A Bat Street
Victoria, BC V8T 1P5
Canada
TEL: (604) 383-0441
FAX: (604) 380-1622
Offers the Ready Mat line of precut mats in the most popular Crescent colors, with rectangular or oval openings in standard sizes from 5 x 7 to 16 x 20 inches.

Tool Crib of the North
P.O. Box 14040
Grand Forks, ND 58208-4040
TEL: (800) 358-3096
FAX: (800) 343-4205
A mail-order supplier of portable and stationary power tools, bits, blades, jigs, guides, accessories, clamps, and miter boxes.

Trend-Lines
135 American Legion Highway
Revere, MA 02151
TEL: (617) 853-0225   technical assistance
      (800) 767-9999   orders
FAX: (617) 853-0226
A mail-order supplier offering a good selection of portable and stationary power tools, hand tools, miter boxes, miter cutters, mat cutters and guides, blades, bits, and accessories.

TRIMTRAMP, Ltd.
151 Carlingview Drive
Unit #11
Toronto, ON M9W 5S4
Canada
TEL: (416) 798-3160
      (800) 387-8746
FAX: (416) 798-3162
Manufactures miter tables that convert portable circular saws into three-fence, bench-type saws for cutting frame and construction moldings. Also offers extension stands for power miter saws.

Universal Moulding and Frames
90 Milburn Road, Unit 5
Hamilton, ON L8E 3L9
Canada
TEL: (905) 578-0161
FAX: (905) 578-9884
Manufactures the Matte-Frame, a frameless, freestanding mount for photographs from 3 1/2 x 5 to 8 x 10 inches. Also offers Decorative Rub-On Accents for decorating mat corners. Precut mats with Rub-On Accents also available.

University Products, Inc.
517 Main Street
P.O. Box 101
Holyoke, MA 01041-0101
TEL: (413) 532-3372
      (800) 628-1912   orders
      (800) 762-1165   customer service
FAX: (800) 532-9281
A mail-order supplier of mounting, matting, framing, display, and storage materials and tools. Offers a large selection of materials for conservation, restoration, and preservation of photographs and artworks.

Vancouver Pro Pack Trading, Inc.
2891 Simpson Road
Richmond, BC V6X 2R2
Canada
TEL: (604) 276-2883
FAX: (604) 276-2802
Offers a line of ready-made photograph and fine-art frames, as well as precut double mats made with Crescent mat board.

Vaughan & Bushnell Company
11414 Maple Avenue
P.O. Box 390
Hebron, IL 60034-0390
TEL: (815) 648-2446
FAX: (815) 648-4300
E-mail: vaughanmfg@aol.com
Web site: http://www.hammernet.com
Manufactures top-quality straight-claw, curved-claw, and tack hammers, as well as other striking tools, including the author's favorite picture-framing hammer: the 10-ounce No. 9 Little Pro.

Vibrant Photo and Electronics, Inc.
6660 Kennedy Road, Unit 14
Mississauga, ON L5T 2M9
Canada
TEL: (905) 564-6224
　　　(800) 561-6510
Provides a large line of precut rag mats in twenty-four of the most popular Crescent colors, with rectangular or oval openings, in standard sizes from 4 x 6 to 11 x 14 inches. Single and double mats, precut top mats, and custom cutting available.

Bob Victor's Mid-America Chops
1100 Southeast Rice Road
Topeka, KS 66607-2373
TEL: (913) 234-3219
　　　(800) 255-0535
FAX: (913) 234-3312
Offers Design Plus Mats, a line of die-cut double mats made of Crescent boards for photographers. Rectangular, oval, and multiple openings available from wallet size to 8 x 10 inches and outside dimensions from 8 x 10 to 16 x 20 inches.

Warren Tool Group, Inc.
10610 Freedom Street
P.O. Box 286
Garretsville, OH 44231
TEL: (216) 527-5681
　　　(800) 543-3224
FAX: (800) 543-3225
Manufactures a large line of clamps, clamp fixtures, vises, grinder brushes, wire wheels, flap-sanding wheels, and abrasive discs.

West Coast Picture Corporation
P.O. Box 13706
Portland, OR 97213
TEL: (503) 282-7295
　　　(800) 547-3787
FAX: (503) 282-7297
Manufactures ready-made wood frames and bevel-cut mats made of Crescent mat board, as well as collage and panel combinations.

Wild Wings
P.O. Box 451
Lake City, MN 55041-0451
TEL: (800) 445-4833
FAX: (612) 345-2981
A mail-order source of fine-art prints with wildlife and western motifs.

Wolfcraft
1222 West Ardmore Avenue
P.O. Box 687
Itasca, IL 60143
TEL: (630) 773-4777
FAX: (630) 773-4805
Web site: http://www.wolfcraft.com
Manufactures a variety of products of interest to picture framers, including Quick-Jaw clamps, folding workbenches, the Hook Driver, and kits for converting palm sanders into corner/detail sanders and angle grinders into plate (biscuit) joiners.

Woodcraft Supply Corp.
210 Wood County Industrial Pkwy.
P.O. Box 1686
Parkersburg, WV 26102
TEL: (800) 225-1153　orders
　　　(800) 535-4482　customer service
　　　(800) 535-4486　technical assistance
FAX: (304) 428-8271
A nationwide retail and mail-order source of miter saws, miter trimmers, mat-cutter systems, clamps, vises, books, framing accessories, fasteners, hardware, adhesives, and finishing products.

The Woodworker's Store
4365 Willow Drive
Medina, MN 55340-9701
TEL: (800) 279-4441
FAX: (612) 478-8395
A mail-order source of a large selection of hardware, fasteners, hardwoods, Micro-Cut woods, veneers, inlays, moldings, adhesives, and finishing materials.

Woodworker's Supply of New Hampshire
One Woodworker's Way
Seabrook, NH 03874
TEL: (603) 474-9663
        (800) 645-9292
FAX: (800) 853-9663
A regional and mail-order source of a huge selection of portable and stationary power tools, hand tools, miter boxes, miter cutters, clamps, accessories, fixtures, attachments, blades, bits, picture-frame moldings, mat cutters and guides, abrasives, adhesives, hardware, fasteners, finishing products, and shop supplies.

Woodworker's Supply of New Mexico
5604 Alameda Place Northeast
Albuquerque, NM 87113
TEL: (505) 821-0500
See Woodworker's Supply of New Hampshire for toll-free and fax numbers, as well as products offered.

Woodworker's Supply of North Carolina
1125 Jay Lane
Graham, NC 27253
TEL: (910) 578-3001
See Woodworker's Supply of New Hampshire for toll-free and fax numbers, as well as products offered.

Woodworker's Supply of Wyoming
1108 North Glenn Road
Casper, WY 82601
TEL: (307) 237-5354
See Woodworker's Supply of New Hampshire for toll-free and fax numbers, as well as products offered.

XYLO, Inc.
2000 Louisville Road
P.O. Box 8062
Savannah, GA 31412
TEL: (912) 233-1263
        (800) 627-5040
FAX: (912) 233-3646
Manufactures the largest selection of poplar and other wood frame moldings available, including more than 200 profiles and over 50 custom finishes.

INDEX